Punnele in Back —

RETHINKING THE POLITICS
OF LABOUR IN CANADA

EDITED BY
STEPHANIE ROSS
AND LARRY SAVAGE

Fernwood Publishing • Halifax & Winnipeg

Editing: Mary Beth Tucker
Cover design: John van der Woude
Printed and bound in Canada

Published in Canada by Fernwood Publishing
32 Oceanvista Lane, Black Point, Nova Scotia, B0J 1B0
and 748 Broadway Avenue, Winnipeg, Manitoba, R3G 0X3
www.fernwoodpublishing.ca

Fernwood Publishing Company Limited gratefully acknowledges the financial support of the
Government of Canada through the Canada Book Fund and the Canada Council for the Arts,
the Nova Scotia Department of Communities, Culture and Heritage,
the Manitoba Department of Culture, Heritage and Tourism under
the Manitoba Publishers Marketing Assistance Program and the Province of Manitoba,
through the Book Publishing Tax Credit, for our publishing program.

Library and Archives Canada Cataloguing in Publication

Rethinking the politics of labour in Canada / Stephanie Ross and
Larry Savage.

(Labour in Canada)
Includes bibliographical references.
ISBN 978-1-55266-478-0

1. Labor unions--Political activity--Canada. 2. Labor movement--
Political aspects--Canada. 3. Labor movement--Canada--History.
I. Ross, Stephanie, 1970- II. Savage, Larry, 1977-

HD8106.5.R48 2012   322'.20971   C2011-908404-X

CONTENTS

LABOUR IN CANADA SERIES

This volume is part of the Labour in Canada Series, which focuses on assessing how global and national political economic changes have affected Canada's labour movement and labour force as well as how working people have responded. The series offers a unique Canadian perspective to parallel international debates on work and labour in the United States, Great Britain and Western Europe.

Authors seek to understand the impact of governments and markets on working people. They examine the role of governments in shaping economic restructuring and the loss of unionized jobs, as well as how governments have promoted the growth of low-wage work yesterday and today. They also analyze the impacts of economic globalization on work and labour movements, and how recent economic trends have affected women, minorities and immigrants.

Contributors then provide insight on how unions have responded to global labour market deregulation and globalization. They present accessible new research on how Canadian unions function in both the private and public sectors, how they organize and how their political strategies work. The books document recent success stories (and failures) of union renewal, and explore the new opportunities emerging as the labour movement attempts to rebuild the economy on sound environmental principles.

Over the past thirty years, the union movement has increasingly been put on the defensive as its traditional tactics of economic and political engagement have proven unable to protect wages, maintain membership and advance progressive agendas. Yet there has been far too little discussion of how the terrain of Canadian politics has shifted and how this has, in turn, affected the Canadian labour movement. There has also been far too little acknowledgment of how working people have attempted to develop new strategies to regain political and economic influence. This series aims to fill these major gaps in public debate.

The volumes are resources that can help unions successfully confront new strategic dilemmas. They also serve to promote discussion and support labour education programs within unions and postsecondary education programs. It is our hope that the series informs debate on the policies and institutions that Canadians need to improve jobs, create better workplaces and build a more egalitarian society.

Series editors
John Peters and Reuben Roth

Labour in Canada series editorial committee:
Marjorie Griffin Cohen, Julie Guard,
Grace-Edward Galabuzi, Joel Harden, Wayne Lewchuk,
Stephanie Ross, Larry Savage, Mercedes Steedman and Erin Weir

RETHINKING THE POLITICS OF LABOUR IN CANADA: AN INTRODUCTION

Stephanie Ross and Larry Savage

Workers in Canada and around the world are under concerted attack. From the first crises of the Keynesian era in the early 1970s to the Great Recession of the late 2000s, employers and governments everywhere have worked tirelessly to remove the economic, political, legal and social bases of working-class power established in the aftermath of the Second World War. While no national working class in the advanced capitalist world could be said to have taken power in the sense meant by socialist revolutionaries, there is no doubt that workers had, for a time, established a real capacity to demand and win greater economic, political and social justice for the less powerful. Like its global counterparts, the Canadian labour movement played a key role in the expansion of political rights to those without wealth, the creation of the welfare state, the social wage, redistributive public policies and the promotion of social justice and equality for both working-class people and members of other oppressed groups. Though these advances may have seemed like irrevocable contributions to human progress, they have proven anything but. Since the mid-1970s, Canadian labour's political influence and capacity to defend, let alone extend, these gains has been seriously undermined by the strategies of both capitalist interests and the neoliberal state. The suffering caused (and yet to be caused) by this unravelling of the labour movement's twentieth-century achievements cannot be underestimated. Understanding how and why workers were able to exert this collective power, how they lost it and how they might re-establish it are the central concerns of this book.

The concerted attack on labour has not gone unchallenged. In Canada, the national Day of Protest against Wage Controls in 1976, the Solidarity Movement in British Columbia in the 1980s and the Ontario Days of Action in the 1990s demonstrated Canadian workers' willingness and capacity to resist neoliberal reforms and policies in both collective and politicized ways, even if these struggles achieved few of their stated goals in any permanent way. These past and present struggles, though laden with challenges, contradictions and limits, cannot help but be inspiring: they remind us that people still can and will mobilize against the seemingly overwhelming forces of economic and political power. They also signal that workers are searching for a new kind of politics, even if its exact form remains unclear.

However, in the wake of these mass displays of working-class solidarity, top-down demobilizations and a retreat to familiar party-union relationships and electoral strategies have also been common. And why not, since the victories of the immediate post-war era were to no small extent attributable to the capacity of working-class parties to attract significant votes, whether to form a strong opposition or even to take the reins of government. Prior to the 1970s, labour parties the world over implemented significant elements of the labour movement's economic and political agenda. However, over the last thirty years in Canada, traditional electoral strategies have proven extremely limited, if not counterproductive. When in power, parties linked to the labour movement have increasingly abandoned the agenda of economic and social equality that brought them to power, opting instead to lower the expectations of their own working-class constituencies in an effort to make peace with capital and govern in the interests of "all the people." When out of power, labour parties and their adherents have counselled against too militant protest or too radical demands and subjected workers to the tyranny of waiting until the next election, a limiting political logic which not only diminishes the labour movement's capacities between election campaigns but also narrows the scope of what properly constitutes labour politics itself. In some ways, this narrow electoralist mentality has driven a wedge between party activists and labour and social movement activists, thus weakening the link between the parliamentary and extra-parliamentary strategies which made previous gains possible.

The limits of the labour movement's traditional electoral political efforts have spawned calls to take up a variety of new strategies and tactics, including non-partisan mass protests, issue-based union-community coalitions and direct actions that place immediate pressure on the source of harm. Union participation in the demonstrations against the proposed Free Trade Agreement of the Americas in Quebec City in 2001 and the G20 meetings in Toronto in 2010 demonstrated labour's willingness to take up such strategies. However, protest on its own, without concern for controlling or influencing the state's levers of power, which is central to consolidating gains won through protest, has also proven difficult to sustain. With neoliberal governments generally unmoved by social movement demands, whether delivered in the form of polite petitions or mass protests, street politics seems to have hit up against some important limits. Seemingly faced with dead ends in every strategic direction, an assessment of the politics, prospects and possibilities for the Canadian labour movement is urgently required.

The question of new and effective political strategies and tactics is all the more urgent for the labour movement as it braces for a new round of neoliberal austerity measures from all levels of government. As in previous eras, new political identities and strategic repertoires are often forged in moments of heightened struggle and conflict as workers and their organizations struggle to cope with new circumstances. In the early twenty-first century, one of the most pressing questions facing the Canadian labour movement is whether the fight to prevent government cuts to public sector jobs and services will unify working-class people, providing them with a renewed sense of purpose and collective interest, or divide them, setting those who have been able to negotiate strong collective agreements for themselves against those who have not. This battle raises much larger issues that renewed labour politics must confront: who is it that the labour movement speaks for politically? Whose interests will labour prioritize? How does labour make those commitments real rather than rhetorical?

Working-class people and their organizations must confront these issues in a hostile political and ideological climate in which, rightly or wrongly, unions are seen as defenders of sectional rather than the general interest. The negative effects of the Great Recession of the late 2000s and the longer-term decline in working-class wages and living standards have made it much more difficult for unionized workers in general, and public sector workers in particular, to defend their collective agreements and their rights to dignified and secure work. This fragmentation of working-class identity and community and the public's chilly response to public sector workers' claims was highlighted in the late 2000s by the backlash against a series of high-profile public sector strikes. As Tom Walkom has argued, the political right has mastered the art of mobilizing "reverse class resentment" based on the real feelings and experiences of insecurity of many working-class people. In his own words:

> Today, class resentments have been turned on their head. The focus of anger is not the silk-hatted capitalist but his unionized workers, with their job protection guarantees, their pension plans and their good wages.... Increasingly, in the world of media and popular culture, it is not the rich who are blamed for their excesses but the poor — the undeserving welfare recipient, the shiftless single mother, the employment insurance cheat. Resentment has become a potent tool of the right.... The left's resentments were predicated on the notion that if some are privileged, all should be. For all of its problems (and resentment is a difficult force to control), it was at least optimistic. At its best, it encouraged people, through their governments, to improve the lot of those who were hurting. The new resentment is based on the presumption that if I don't have something, neither should you. Its aim is not to improve anyone's lot but to cut down to a common level of misery those uppity enough to think they deserve better. (Walkom 2010)

With more jobs cuts, privatizations and legislative curbs on workers' rights to bargain and strike on the horizon, it remains an open question whether the labour movement has the capacity to understand the appeal of the right-wing message to other workers, to turn that resentment towards its proper targets and to unify with the broader community against the neoliberal right.

The chapters that follow, and the critical assessments they contain, take stock of the politics of labour in Canada, and establish a framework for thinking about labour's past, present and future strategic direction. In doing so, the contributors have adopted an expansive understanding of the working class, the labour movement and, by extension, the kinds of organizations and strategies to be included in a discussion of labour politics. As Craig Heron (1996) reminds us, the labour movement has always encompassed a wide range of people and organizations produced by working-class communities for their own collective self-defence, and its influence stretched far beyond official membership lists. As such, "working class" also had a broad meaning, encompassing all those whose survival depended on their capacity to labour for others, whether they actually engaged in waged work or not. However, particularly since the Second World War, both the working class and the labour movement have come to be understood much more narrowly. Working class meant waged — and especially white, male industrial — workers, and the labour movement meant state-certified workplace-based unions and their political parties. Labour politics came to be understood as unions' (and their members') engagement in elections via political parties. However, this understanding of the movement, its constituency and its political expression is historically specific and, as Rosemary Warskett and Donald Swartz argue in the first chapter of this volume, premised on a false separation of the economic and the political typical in capitalist societies. Contrary to this tendency, this book brings together subject matter traditionally discussed as labour politics with an analysis of newer (or rediscovered) forms of working-class organization and social movement-influenced approaches to politics increasingly important in the Canadian labour movement. In other words, while unions and political parties remain important, so too are the new organizational forms and strategies that have emerged alongside, and sometimes in opposition to, these longstanding approaches. In this manner, this book seeks to take stock of these new forms of labour politics, understand their emergence and assess their impact, while acknowledging that the way forward remains unclear.

CONTEXTUALIZING LABOUR AND WORKING-CLASS POLITICS IN CANADA

The first section of this book explores the various political perspectives at play in the Canadian labour movement, seeking to put these political-ideological orientations into their historical, political-economic, social and cultural context. Rosemary Warskett and Donald Swartz explore the narrow and legalistic form of labour solidarity entrenched and institutionalized in the wake of the Second World War, and argue that the seeds of labour's current political impasse are to be found in that era. Stephanie Ross explores the conceptual categories of business unionism and social unionism commonly used to classify different approaches to workers' interests, identities and strategies. Ross points to their much more complex concrete expressions, and argues for a more careful assessment of different forms of workers' political activity, particularly since so many strategic recommendations for the movement's revival emphasize the centrality of social unionism to renewal. These chapters share a common concern with the factors that shape the expression of labour and working-class politics, and in particular, the relationship between collective identity, organization and political strategy.

While workers' common dependence on their capacity to sell their labour power provides them with a powerful shared experience of structural inequality, it would be unwise to take for granted some essential working-class identity that springs automatically from their location in the relations of production. While those relations provide the basis for working-class communities and organizations, there is a wide range of variation in how workers experience and understand class. The boundaries of working-class communities and the allegiances they invoke have always been shaped by occupation, region and nation, gender, "race" and ethnicity, sexual orientation and the relative economic success of different segments of the working class. While materially grounded, the construction of workers' collective identities and shared interests has always itself been a political project, the subject of contestation whose outcomes are open and indeterminate.

As such, these chapters do not assert some essential or romanticized working-class identity against which concrete expressions are measured and found wanting. Rather, they explore the processes by which class identities and allegiances are given particular political expression at given moments in time, and explore the effects of these expressions on the labour movement's (in)capacity to mobilize, represent and attract the allegiance of a demographically diverse working class. They also explore the implications of defining the working class in particular ways, of including or excluding groups of workers and of defining certain kinds of interests and priorities as the (il)legitimate subject of the labour movement's attention. In that sense, labour politics is a central part of the historically contingent process of class formation.

Understanding labour politics as part of the process of class formation requires us to pay attention to the factors which, as Therborn (1983) puts it, form, re-form and de-form working-class consciousness and hence politics, factors which are both external and internal to the labour movement itself. In the current moment, the corporate media is a key force of enculturation, with its normalization and universalization of middle classness, framing of the working class — and especially the working poor and racialized and sexual minorities — as victims of their own poor choices, and casting of workers' organizations as collective attempts to gain unfair advantage or compensate for a lack of individual ability or initiative. These powerful messages have detached many workers from identification with the labour movement. However, the right-wing demonization of working-class people and their unions can only explain part of the hostility that the labour movement faces today. Workers' own organizations play a central role in defining and reproducing working-class identities and consciousness. Insofar as many workers fail to see themselves reflected in the labour movement's messages, priorities and organizations, this is not merely a right-wing fabrication. Rather, it reflects real inequalities amongst working-class people that have been allowed to grow, and to which unions have paid insufficient attention. Instead, unions have left much of the task of addressing broader societal and economic inequalities to their political allies in the electoral arena, with decidedly mixed results.

THE CHALLENGE OF ELECTORAL POLITICS

The rise and fall of the post-war social democratic project has unquestionably coloured the labour movement's relationship to electoral politics, its engagement with particular political parties, voting strategies and the nature of the electoral system itself. These relationships are the subject of the second section of the book. While elections have always been a central preoccupation of labour politics, the sudden and unexpected rise of the federal New Democratic Party (NDP) to official opposition status in the Canadian House of Commons after the May 2, 2011, federal election requires us to take a fresh look at organized labour's relationship to parties and elections. The fact that the federal NDP has never been closer to achieving power has caused much excitement in labour circles, but given the record of social democratic parties in government, it is unlikely an NDP victory will deliver the redistributive policies sought by the movement. Bryan Evans provides a critical assessment of labour's longstanding relationship with the NDP and makes the case that organized labour's own "culture of defensiveness" has helped to maintain its enduring links with the NDP, despite the party's diminishing interest in the policies historically associated with social democracy. Peter Graefe provides an analysis of labour politics in Québec, arguing that the distinct trajectory of Québec unions caused the movement to adopt political strategies which diverged from those of the Canadian labour movement as a whole. Graefe's discussion reminds us that the politics of labour in Canada has always been fragmented. We falsely homogenize and dehistoricize labour politics by assuming that coalescing around social democracy, and specifically the NDP, represents a permanent political expression of the labour movement. Instead, there has always been debate within unions, both in English Canada and in Québec, about how to best represent workers' interests electorally.

That said, all the electoral strategies pursued by labour have had to confront the fact that capital has managed to set the broad framework for what constitutes acceptable politics and policy in Canada. Part of the challenge of working-class electoral politics rests with the very nature of the capitalist state, and its role in reproducing effective conditions for capitalist economic and social relations. Even when parties sympathetic to labour are elected, they have found it extremely difficult, if not impossible, to implement their agendas. This limitation on labour parties' ability to use the state apparatus to implement workers' agendas is longstanding (and certainly not specific to Canada), but capital's ability to discipline "disobedient" governments has grown dramatically since the mid-1970s. The increased dominance of neoliberal political discourse has prompted some unions and labour parties, to varying extents, to internalize neoliberal imperatives, accepting them as the new status quo or as part of the basic framework for economic, political and social decision-making. In short, the labour movement and its political allies sometimes chase short-term goals to gain power or wield more influence, rather than to imagine ways of using that power or influence to transform society.

Larry Savage picks up on this last point by exploring the labour movement's contemporary engagement with strategic voting campaigns. He argues that this approach has been a failure for labour, as both an instrumental tactic designed to block the election of right-wing parties and a practice which ultimately undermines labour's capacity to develop a political alternative to neoliberalism. Dennis Pilon assesses labour's approach to electoral reform, making the case that shifting union support for voting system reform has reflected broader strategic considerations about how best to secure progressive public policy changes for unions and the working class in particular historical moments. Savage and Pilon both demonstrate that short-term tactical calculations can sometimes lead to the collapse of broader strategic options for the labour movement and stunt the movement's ability to create new political options for itself.

THE PROSPECTS OF EXTRA-PARLIAMENTARY ACTIVISM

The weakness of social democratic labour parties in the electoral sphere has in many ways contributed to the varied and expanding terrain of labour politics outside of, or parallel to, traditional electoral politics. These strategies have also emerged as a result of discontent with the limits of the "responsible" workplace-based unionism and its related strategies and tactics that were institutionalized in the post-war era. Union practices of the 1950s and 1960s were found wanting both in terms of the kinds of workers they represented and the methods they adopted to defend those workers' interests. The dominant pop cultural image of the hard-hatted industrial white male union member stems from this era, but so too did the demographic transformation of the working class as women and various minorities populated the burgeoning public and private service sector. Beginning with the feminist movement of the 1960s and 1970s, a range of groups fought for inclusion in union structures and decision-making processes, challenged prevailing and narrow definitions of union issues, and pressed for the adoption of strategies and tactics used by the social movements of oppressed communities. In their struggle for inclusion, women, Aboriginal peoples, queer workers and racialized workers injected new life into labour politics through the expansion of the union agenda to include issues outside the workplace and the greater use of community-based coalition strategies.

Many unions in Canada recognized the dramatic changes to both the working class in general and their membership make-up in particular, and have made efforts to broaden their appeal. As Amanda Coles and Charlotte Yates discuss in their chapter, unions responded to feminist pressure inside and outside their ranks by developing educational initiatives on gender inequality, creating women-controlled union structures (like caucuses and committees) and adopting gender equity issues in collective bargaining and legislative priorities. In their exploration of the relationship between organized labour and Aboriginal politics, Suzanne Mills and Tyler McCreary also detail union initiatives to ensure Aboriginal voices are heard in their decision-making structures and to support solidarity-building between white workers and Aboriginal communities. However, both of these chapters also point out that despite important strides in recent decades, unions still have a long way to go on the equity front. Unions' commitments to social justice and equality for women, Aboriginal peoples and other minority groups remain limited by unions' economistic understandings of workers' interests and sectionalist definitions of their constituencies, particularly when economic times get tough.

In many ways, the post-war labour relations framework, and unions' acceptance of it, continues to restrict the labour movement's agenda, membership and strategic options. As a result, a host of new organizations have emerged to mobilize and represent segments of the non-unionized working class in Canada. As Simon Black explains, the rise (and return) of community unionism since the late 1960s is in part a response to the growing numbers of unemployed and poor workers displaced by deindustrialization and technological change and therefore separated from a workplace on which to base their activism. Anti-poverty organizations, union-community coalitions and workers' centres have also arisen because unions have lacked the capacity, interest and/or strategic foresight to represent sections of the working class that fall through the cracks of traditional models of union representation: poor workers; immigrant and migrant workers; and workers in sectors dominated by part-time or contingent work arrangements. Unions have not confronted the very particular model of working-class representation entrenched in the post-war era, which may have worked for a sub-set of the working class but has real limits in the "new economy." As Kendra Coulter demonstrates in her exploration of labour's engagement with the anti-poverty movement, the diversity which exists amongst "poor workers" has generated at least three organizational trajectories: the organization of low-wage workers into unions; the establishment of poor workers' organizations; and the development of multi-organizational anti-poverty campaigns. The same could be said of the working class more generally, forcing us to think about how the labour movement could usefully engage in some creative organizational innovation in order to better address this diversity.

Simon Black, Kendra Coulter and Aziz Choudry and Mark Thomas all explore concrete examples of community unionism in Canada, detailing the way that poor people, whether employed in low-wage work, unemployed or on social assistance, as well migrant and immigrant workers, have created new organizational forms to exert collective power. Some community unions have focused on workplace issues through workers' centres. Other community unions have attended to the inequalities working-class people face in the rest of their lives, such as lack of decent, affordable housing, unscrupulous landlords, eviction, denial of social welfare benefits and deportation. All community unions, however, share a tendency towards extra-parliamentary and direct action-based strategies, using mass mobilizations of their membership to target and pressure economic and political power holders, not least because they are not subject to the "boundaries of constraint" that the law places on unions. Dennis Soron adds another dimension to this discussion with his exploration of labour's participation in coalition-building on the issue of the environment. In a very sober assessment of the obstacles that both labour and environmental activists face in sustaining alliances that go beyond a single environmental issue or campaign, an insight which applies to a full range of union-community coalitions, Soron argues that social unionism, as a general union commitment, is not enough, given the real material conflicts to sort out between different ways of defining and acting on workers' interests.

All this raises a broader question of the relationship between different kinds of strategies and tactics, and in particular the relationship between direct action and street protest on the one hand, and more institutional electoral and workplace-based strategies on the other. Aziz Choudry and Mark Thomas tackle this question in their juxtaposition of the United Food and Commercial Workers' (UFCW) judicial strategy to protect and expand rights for migrant workers with the work of the Immigrant Workers Centre (IWC) in Montreal. The two case studies offer readers an opportunity to consider both the potential and limits inherent in top-down and bottom-up approaches to labour politics. In some ways, whether implicitly or explicitly, new working-class organizations are often conceived as alternatives to unions which have managed to escape the limits of institutionalization. Undoubtedly, the law has worked to contain both workers' militancy and radicalism, and has atrophied unions' mobilizational capacities by removing the need for a wide layer of members to participate in the collective defence of gains. However, permanent mass mobilization is also difficult to sustain, and other ways of entrenching gains are needed. While the emergence of new organizations based on direct action highlight the limits of the law, they do not resolve this challenge.

Ironically, given the pressing need for greater organizational and strategic innovation, defending existing models of union representation against attacks by right-wing governments has been and continues to be a main thrust of labour politics in Canada. In his exploration of the labour movement's engagement with the Canadian Charter of Rights and Freedoms, Charles Smith considers the labour movement's pursuit of legal strategies as a method of advancing its strategic interests. Smith points out that unions retreat to the judicial sphere when they are unable to press their demands effectively in either the economic or political spheres. However, he argues that labour's judicial-based strategies have produced mixed results for labour, and that, ultimately, in granting small protections to unions, courts have simultaneously reinforced legal constraints on workers' ability to organize, associate and challenge the inequalities inherent in the employment relationship. This and discussions elsewhere in the book call on unions to consider more carefully what in the post-war model of labour relations is worth defending, what needs to be transcended and what never really worked to create power for workers in the first place. In this sense, the law both enables as well as constrains, and the labour movement must think more carefully about how to intervene in this dynamic.

WHERE DO WE GO FROM HERE?

From the global economic forces precipitating an international race to the bottom, to capital's ability to tame governments willing to reject neoliberal imperatives, to the disorganization of unions and division and resentment within the working class, workers seeking to transform society face huge obstacles. This book aims to clarify some of these obstacles and explores the various routes open to the labour movement in its efforts to rethink political strategies. This will not be an easy task. Although the times increasingly call for more radical and militant political strategies, working-class politics is not inherently so. A renewed sense of political vision and strategic direction will not come automatically from mere lived experience, but must be fought for and consciously constructed in the debates workers' organizations are now having about how to best confront the challenges of neoliberalism. Critical education inside and outside of unions is crucial to shaping class consciousness, political and organizational capacities and a sense of what is possible and necessary. We hope this book makes a contribution to this process.

Part I

CONTEXTUALIZING LABOUR
AND WORKING-CLASS POLITICS

1. CANADIAN LABOUR
AND THE CRISIS OF SOLIDARITY

Donald Swartz and Rosemary Warskett

In 2009, members of United Steelworkers (USW) Local 6500 in Sudbury and Local 6200 in Port Colborne, Ontario, began a strike that was to last nearly a year against mining giant Vale Inco. Despite successful lengthy strikes in the past, this one ended with a very significant loss: future hires will be excluded from the more secure defined benefit pension plan, and their defined contribution pension plan will bear all the risks of the financial markets.

The Vale Inco workers' loss occurred in the wake of the global financial crisis that erupted during the fall of 2008 and showed just how risky financial markets could be (Albo et al. 2010). This crisis quickly developed into a deep recession, and labour markets were profoundly affected. The weakness of Canada's pension regime was revealed as companies defaulted on pension payments or moved to defined contribution rather than defined benefit plans, in order to avoid making up the shortfall caused by collapsing stock markets. Suddenly, the emperor appeared to have no clothes. The financial crisis called into question three decades of policies promoting liberalized financial markets and ever-expanding free trade as the best of all possible worlds. Many heralded the demise of neoliberalism and the rise of a renewed Keynesianism reminiscent of the developments following the crisis in the 1930s.

The Canadian Labour Congress (CLC) responded by calling for substantial reforms to Employment Insurance and the public pension system, but it lacked the capacity to mobilize the labour movement to back these demands. Indeed, the Vale Inco strike was ignored by most of the labour movement, and few unions provided the required level of strike support and solidarity. The failure of the labour movement, and the left generally, to meaningfully intervene gave capital and the state time to find their footing. Governments instead spent trillions of dollars bailing out banks and other financial institutions in a desperate bid to avoid a collapse of the financial system. Any talk of a new Keynesianism quickly disappeared. Neoliberalism was to be saved at the expense of the working class. Whether in Canada, Wisconsin or Greece, the existing wages, benefits and even rights of workers, rather than the systemic limits of capitalism, are cast as the problem.

The rollbacks imposed on Vale Inco workers have become commonplace and, together with the ease with which governments have imposed the costs of rescuing the financial sector onto workers, reflect the extent of the labour movement's defeat over the past two decades. How did the labour movement get into its current state? What are the prospects for reversing its decline and building an effective movement? In addressing these questions, we examine the culture of solidarity that the labour movement developed during and after the Second World War, which continues to structure union struggles. While this solidarity allowed workers to make important gains into the 1970s, it nonetheless was limited by a narrow and male-dominated conception of the working class, the interests to be defended and the kinds of collective action needed. In the context of a neoliberal capitalist world order from the 1990s on, these limits have become debilitating, existing solidarities have been eroded, and new forms of solidarity will be needed to refound effective labour politics.

THEORIZING THE POLITICS OF THE LABOUR MOVEMENT

In capitalist society, the social relations of production create a structural antagonism between those who buy and those who sell labour power. While the employment contract as a purchase of labour time gives the buyer the right to determine what the seller is to do and how, exercising that right involves the use of power. In turn, workers have historically recognized that the will and ability to act collectively is necessary to defend and advance their interests against those of their employers. Resistance to management's power and control is the basic impetus to associate with others and form unions.

Understanding the formation of unions as a means for individual workers to defend themselves against exploitation and management control is just a starting point for the analysis of labour movement solidarity. The consciousness and actions of unionized workers cannot be derived simply from the basic capitalist relations of production. Lenin did just this when he argued in *What Is to Be Done* that unions by themselves can only develop union consciousness; that is "the conviction that it is necessary to combine in unions, fight the employers, and strive to compel the government to pass necessary labour legislation, etc." (quoted in Hyman 1971: 13).

This approach is both overly reductionist and ahistorical. As Richard Hyman (1971: 41) points out, Lenin's classic statement rests on a rigid and highly problematic dichotomy between union and revolutionary consciousness that masks "a continuum along which escalation is in certain circumstances possible." Workers, after all, are not only wage labourers; they enter the workplace as complex human beings with a range of economic, social, political and cultural interests. The antagonism inherent in the social relations of production takes place under varying circumstances and at different moments of crisis or non-crisis of the capitalist political economy, such that the conflict between labour and capital is variously constructed. Thus, at certain historical moments, unions have made demands that went beyond narrow economic concerns. As Bryan Palmer (1983:

297) has shown, the Canadian labour movement of the 1880s fought "explicitly within the realms of culture, striving to link inequality and exploitation in the political economy to the oppression of everyday life." More recently, unions have raised demands challenging gendered, racialized and other inequalities (Yates and Coles, this volume; Choudry and Thomas, this volume; Mills and McCreary, this volume). Workers' struggles clearly vary historically, giving rise to distinct forms of what Fantasia (1988: 19) has called "cultures of solidarity."

Extending Fantasia's approach, we conceive of solidarity as a multifaceted and complex concept. It is both a material and symbolic manifestation of labour's collective power. Building solidarity is about the construction of collective power, the ends to which that power is put and the means used to achieve them. Through solidarity struggles, new visions of what is possible emerge and develop (Fantasia 1988: 233). Anyone involved in strike action knows that once workers get on the picket line, their views of the workplace, of management and of the issues take on a different hue. Ideas emerge, are discussed and analyzed. More politicized workers engage in informal street education as workers walk the line. A strike is one of the few times that most union members attend a meeting and experience the solidarity created by standing firm together against management's demands. In certain places and moments, the whole community becomes involved, the strike becomes a topic of political discussion and the range of solidarity is broadened. In this sense, cultures of solidarity "are neither ideas of solidarity in the abstract nor bureaucratic trade union activity, but cultural formations that arise in conflict, creating and sustaining solidarity in opposition to the dominant structure" (Fanastia 1988: 19).

Solidarity is evoked symbolically in moments of conflict and at major labour movement meetings, usually through singing "Solidarity Forever." By standing up and singing together, the labour group defines who is with them and who is against them, as well as the aims of workers' solidarity (Warskett 1992: 109–10). In other words, when the labour movement invokes solidarity, it embodies the concept of collective power and the benefits that could be gained by its use. It reminds workers that, as individuals, they can achieve very little; the possibility of realizing common demands rests on collective mobilization and struggle.

Defining the meaning of solidarity lies at the very basis of labour movement politics. Clearly, the more inclusive the notion of solidarity, the greater will be the capacity for struggle. Indeed, the construction of solidarity does not have to be limited to those who are currently union members. It can extend to the unorganized, the unemployed, those doing unpaid domestic and other kinds of labour, the injured, disabled and ill and the retired. The scope of the labour movement's solidarity is linked to how broad or narrow are the things being fought for and against, whether limited to employers and the current terms and conditions of employment or taking on systemic economic or political problems. In other words, solidarity can be directed at narrowly constructed immediate demands or broadly constructed social, political and cultural transformations, with the potential to reach beyond union members and into their communities.

While broader, more inclusive conceptions of labour solidarity can and do emerge, the efforts of unions and workers to sustain and deepen them face several fundamental challenges. Here we focus on the principal challenges of sectionalism, economism, the effects of the separation of the political sphere from the economic and the dynamism of capitalism itself.

Sectionalism is the tendency to limit the culture of solidarity to a specific group of workers. Historically, the division of labour into specific trades limited solidarity across craft lines. Even when craft unions did form cross-union labour centrals, it was to the exclusion of non-craft workers. With the rise of industrial capitalism, individual workers were brought together first and foremost by sharing an employer and a workplace, and this common experience gave workers the impetus to unionize. However, the uneven development that characterizes capitalism ensures that the immediate issues vary across workplaces and make broader identifications with other workplaces more difficult. There are also multiple differences among workers beyond the workplace, from skill and ethnicity to gender and race, all of which can give rise to sectional forms of solidarity. The challenge of economism is related to that of sectionalism. Whatever their differences, workers are all sellers of labour power and therefore have a common interest in its price. Their economic needs are typically immediate and most subject to negotiation with their specific employer. Given that workers can most easily unite around economic advance, there is a strong tendency for unions to prioritize economic over other demands.

The labour movement's economistic tendency is reinforced by a third obstacle to building solidarity: the separation, within liberal democratic capitalism, of the economic from the political sphere. As Ellen Wood (1988: 150) has noted, "Capitalist Hegemony… rests to a significant extent on a formal separation of the 'political' and 'economic' spheres, which makes possible the maximum development of purely juridical and political freedom and equality without fundamentally endangering economic exploitation." In contrast to the inequality of the economic sphere, the political sphere appears to consist of equal citizens who democratically elect governments that in turn construct a liberal democratic state guaranteeing formal individual equality and civil liberties.

This separation has several consequences for the labour movement. First, workers tend to see themselves as facing two different types of problems — economic and political — requiring different solutions. Second, politics appears to be external to the union and can even be seen as an inappropriate intrusion that threatens solidarity. Third, "politics" tends to be reduced to questions of government and electoral activity. Other forms of politics, whether in the workplace or through community organizing and mobilization, are placed within the questionable arena of extra-parliamentary activity and at worst fall within the realm of the illegal. All other aspects of workers' lives as full social and cultural beings disappear from view. In general, the state attempts to ensure the perpetuation of the capitalist system, and as such tries to guarantee that labour-capital conflict does not profoundly disrupt the accumulation process (Panitch 1977). However, the separation of the economic and political spheres profoundly obscures the state's class character. The law is seen as impartial or blind, and the state as a neutral arbiter of disputes. Any shortcomings of the law are not seen as systemic, but as capable of being redressed by changing the government of the day.

Finally, challenges stem from the very dynamism of capitalism itself. In contrast to mainstream economics' otherworldly models, capitalism is never in equilibrium. Technologies, labour processes, sectoral and spatial distributions of production and workers, and cultural formations are constantly changing, exposing existing solidarities to powerful centrifugal pressures that can and do undermine it (Berman 1983). The labour movement, and the working class as a whole, is forced to fight not only to maintain existing solidarities but also to fashion new ones fitted to these continuously changing circumstances.

ORIGINS OF THE CONTEMPORARY LABOUR MOVEMENT: 1940–1965

How has the Canadian labour movement addressed these obstacles to building a broad and inclusive culture of solidarity? While the roots of the Canadian labour movement go back to the 1800s, the central elements of the "modern" labour movement's character took shape in the 1940s. In 1935, inspired by the creation of the Congress of Industrial Organizations (CIO) in the United States and the promise to move beyond the exclusive craft-based organizing model, Canadian workers established affiliates of the new industrial unions. Much of the initial national and local leadership was provided by communists and socialists, many of whom were veterans of failed organizing efforts earlier in the decade (Abella 1973; Palmer 1983). After a halting start, the CIO unions began to grow rapidly: between 1940 and 1944 alone, union membership doubled, reaching 24.3 percent of the labour force, and tens of thousands of workers engaged in often bitter struggles for union recognition (Canada, Department of Labour 1975: 28–9). In 1943, one-third of unionized workers were engaged in strikes (MacDowell 1978: 176).

This wave of militancy rested on a new sense of class solidarity within significant sections of the working class, symbolized by the decision of the United Mine Workers to provide organizers for the new CIO unions. Unionization now went beyond skilled craft workers to encompass all male blue-collar (Abella 1973) and to some extent female (Sugiman 1994a and 1994b) workers, although seldom equally, partly because women were ghettoized into a limited range of "less skilled" and hence lower paid manufacturing jobs.

At the workplace, some of the ethnic divisions that had undermined earlier struggles, particularly those between Anglo-Irish, Eastern European and French workers, were increasingly transcended (Palmer 1983). The substantial support for the CIO unions within the Trades and Labour Congress and the 1940 merger of the new CIO unions with the older All-Canadian Congress of Labour to form the Canadian Congress of Labour (CCL) attested to its breadth (Abella 1973). Communist Party members and other radicals played a key role in strengthening these developments, successfully pushing the CCL to adopt a coordinated campaign for a common industrial minimum wage and the Workers' Educational Association (WEA) to undertake educational activities aimed at fostering independent critical thinking in a wide range of areas (Taylor 1999). A general politicization within the working class was also underway, reflected in the democratic socialist Co-operative Commonwealth Federation's (CCF) dramatic rise in popularity, the election of a CCF and a Communist Party candidate in the 1943 federal by-elections, the elevation of the CCF to official opposition in Ontario that same year, and the election of a majority CCF government in Saskatchewan in 1944. Older, narrow understandings of solidarity had not disappeared, nor had this new solidarity congealed into a definite form; its boundaries and content were both varied and fluid.

While the prospect of CCF electoral victories had dissipated by 1945, industrial militancy did not. Permanent legislation supporting workers' rights to unionize and bargain collectively was squarely on the political agenda. In his famous 1946 ruling establishing mandatory union recognition and the automatic dues check-off that brought an end to the Windsor Ford strike, Justice Rand cogently expressed the need to forge a political "compromise" with the labour movement. Taking his cue from PC 1003 (the temporary wartime legislation recognizing union rights), Rand (1958: 1251) added: "This is machinery devised to adjust, toward an increasing harmony, the interests of capital, labour and the public in the production of goods and services which our philosophy accepts as part of the good life." In the wake of Rand's ruling, permanent legislation protecting workers' union rights was virtually inevitable. In 1948, the federal government passed the Industrial Relations and Disputes Investigation Act, which was followed by similar legislation in most provinces.

This was a signal achievement for Canadian workers: union recognition reduced the arbitrariness of managerial authority, made workers' lives more secure and paved the way to negotiate real improvements in wages and benefits (Panitch and Swartz 2003: 13–15). Still, the legislation did not extend to federal and provincial government workers. Those whom it did cover found their ability to use their newly gained rights enmeshed in an extensive web of legal restrictions. Union recognition was limited to situations where a majority of workers in a state-defined bargaining unit supported it. Strikes during the term of a collective agreement were prohibited, and wide-ranging restrictions on picketing, sympathy strikes and secondary boycotts were imposed, tasking the union — namely, its leaders — with the responsibility of ensuring their members acted in accordance with the law.

The legislation presented unions with a whole new set of obstacles to expansive solidarity. By linking union recognition to state-defined bargaining units at specific workplaces, it channelled unions towards workplace bargaining and away from broadly based struggles, a constraint reinforced by the restrictions on sympathy strikes and secondary boycotts. The certification approach to recognition and the requirement to resolve workplace disputes through the grievance procedure rather than collective action also "directed the efforts of union leaders away from mobilizing and organizing and towards the juridical arena of the labour boards," making knowledge of the law crucial and "foster[ing] a legalistic practice and consciousness" (Panitch and Swartz 2003: 20). The recognition process, based on majority vote, exclusive bargaining agency and the Rand Formula, also ensured that unions would have at least some reluctant, even unwilling, members in their midst.

The labour movement's responses to these challenges cannot be separated from the Cold War context in which they arose. Nowhere was this war waged more fiercely than in the labour movement. Reformist union leaders, many associated with the CCF and supported by the state, launched a vicious crusade against communist and other radical leaders. While these efforts were less successful than those in the U.S., many of the Canadian labour movement's most skilled and dedicated organizers were marginalized (Abella 1973; Palmer 1983: 245–52). Too often, their replacements had a limited commitment to democratic practices, and were chosen for their loyalty to the CCF rather than their organizing and mobilizing abilities.

By the early 1950s, the labour movement had consolidated itself around a particular conception of solidarity that pivoted around the apparent separation of the economic from the political. Solidarity did not extend to those seeking to challenge capital's supremacy in the workplace or society. The unions' overriding concern was with workers' economic interests as sellers of labour power and they sought to organize them and to bargain for such improvements in wages, benefits and working conditions in a way that was consistent with their employer's profitability. A corollary of this conception of solidarity was that the broader social, cultural and political issues affecting workers as parents, spouses or citizens were placed beyond the boundaries of union collective life as irrelevant and/or sources of division that threatened solidarity. Union membership was limited to those employed in workplaces where the union was the certified bargaining agent even though this was not a legal requirement. Unions included blue-collar and white-collar workers, although the latter, especially those working in the public sector, were not seen as workers in quite the same way as those in the private sector (Warskett 1992).

Union members' collective mobilization was more or less limited to supporting collective bargaining located in individual bargaining units. While the legal framework and employer resistance promoted this localism, so did the union leadership's desire to avoid establishing structures that provided broader platforms for the remaining radical voices isolated in individual locals (Heron 1996; Swartz 1992). The unions' internal life was centred on bargaining and enforcing collective agreements, with narrow, practical training programs replacing the broader critical education once provided by the WEA. Still, politics mattered. Unions recognized that collective bargaining had limits and that government policies affected the actual and potential well-being of their members. Politics, however, took place in the parliamentary arena, encompassing lobbying (often in support of sectional interests) and elections. Most union leaders in English

Canada looked to the CCF (which transformed into the NDP in 1961) as the political arm of the labour movement.

In the post-war context of growing nationally oriented economies, this understanding of solidarity enabled unions to negotiate real improvements in wages and benefits that were to no small degree generalized across the working class. Real wages grew by an annual average of 4.2 percent during the 1950s and 3.7 percent in the 1960s (Panitch and Swartz 2003: 243). Even so, its limits were apparent. Union density remained around its 1948 level of 30 percent for the next two decades (Panitch and Swartz 2003: 245). This partly reflected the extent to which unorganized workers received many of the gains won by the unions, but also the shortcomings in organizing strategy, especially in the female-dominated service sector, which remained virtually union-free.

THE SIXTIES REVIVAL: 1965–1993

This impasse was broken by the wave of industrial militancy that was part of the broader generational shift of the 1960s. In 1966, a new record was established for the number of strikes and workers involved. Significantly, one-third of these were wildcat strikes conducted in defiance of the law and also, frequently, union leaders themselves (Jamieson 1973: 94–99). The changes were particularly far-reaching in Québec, where the emergence of a relatively radicalized working class and intelligentsia finally questioned the limits of the political settlement developed elsewhere in 1940s Canada and demanded and won collective bargaining rights for the public sector in 1965 (McRoberts and Postgate 1980). The developments in Québec reverberated across Canada, not least because federal workers there were part of this politicization. In 1967, the federal government introduced the Public Service Staff Relations Act granting collective bargaining rights to its workers, and this was followed by most provincial governments. In the vast majority of cases, however, crucial issues such as job classifications, pensions, staffing and technological change were partly or wholly excluded from bargaining. In several provinces, those directly employed by the government or in particular sectors, such as hospitals, were denied the right to strike.

Nonetheless, the labour movement welcomed the new legislation. Union density began to climb again, reaching a peak of 40 percent of the paid labour force in 1983 (Panitch and Swartz 2003: 245). More importantly, the character of union membership began to change and was reflected in the emergence of a "left caucus" by the end of the 1970s and later, the election of Bob White and Jean Claude Parrot as president and vice-president of the CLC and Judy Darcy as president of the Canadian Union of Public Employees (CUPE). The emergence of the Canadian Union of Postal Workers (CUPW), in particular, injected a new radicalism into the labour movement, as did the growing presence of women resulting from public sector organizing breakthroughs. Many of these women were influenced by and active participants in the broader feminist renewal. They raised issues such as women's reproductive rights, equal pay, sexual harassment and daycare, fought with considerable success to have them taken up at the bargaining table and in the political arena and even pushed unions to incorporate feminist organizing principles into their own internal practices (Briskin and Yanz 1983; Maroney 1983; White 1993; Warskett 2001). Many sections of the labour movement broadened their understanding of solidarity to encompass previously excluded issues and extended their collective mobilization of members into the extra-parliamentary arena, often in conjunction with social justice organizations.

For the most part, however, the labour movement's understanding of solidarity remained unchanged, as was evident in the failed attempt to organize the private service sector — and bank workers in particular — in the 1970s. Initially, the independent and feminist Service, Office and Retail Workers of Canada (SORWOC) had some success in organizing predominantly female bank workers in BC. Following a Canada Labour Relations Board decision clarifying that the banks could be organized on a branch-by-branch basis — the labour movement's normal approach — the CLC also entered the field, creating the Bank Workers Organizing Committee (BWOC) at its 1978 convention. However, the banks took full advantage of the law and turned the certification process into a long drawn-out affair, draining campaign resources and pulling organizers away from bank workers and into the courts, while exploiting its multi-branch structure to undermine union majorities. Where that failed, and recognizing that the few certified units had little bargaining power, the banks delayed and/or refused to bargain. By the mid-1980s, two-thirds of the small number of branches that had unionized were decertified (Warskett 1988, 2001 and 2007). More recent efforts to organize other large companies with multiple locations (like Canadian Tire, Walmart, McDonald's and Starbucks) have suffered the same fate.

The labour movement's embrace of the legal framework governing labour relations is not the only explanation for this failure. SORWOC's experience showed that no single union could mount a campaign on the necessary scale, and a service sector breakthrough would require a collaborative effort by several unions, even though only one at most — and none if a new union was created — would see their membership increase. Union solidarity, in other words, would need to have a strong class consciousness in which organizing workers took precedence over increasing the membership of one's own union. Unfortunately, the labour movement's dominant sectionalist solidarity precluded such collaboration. While the vast majority of CLC affiliates had supported the creation of a fund to "organize the unorganized" in 1972, its use was unspecified. When it appeared that it would be used to organize bank workers into a new union, affiliates' enthusiasm waned and their response to the CLC's request for organizers to bolster the BWOC campaign was limited.

Private service sector employers' implacable resistance to unionization of their workforce reflected not only capital's normal opposition to unions but also a recognition that the broader economic context had changed dramatically since the late 1970s. Caught between growing international competition and wage militancy, profits were being squeezed and growth rates had declined. The labour rights and social reforms once seen as necessary to reviving capitalism in the wake of the Great Depression were now viewed as obstacles to capital accumulation. Workers had to be accommodated to the "new reality." The federal government had already imposed a temporary restriction on all workers' bargaining rights with its 1975 wage controls program, representing a more general trend of governments' greater reliance on coercive measures to subordinate workers to the new exigencies of profitability (Panitch and Swartz 2003: 87). A wave of back-to-work legislation grew steadily through the 1980s, temporarily depriving particular groups of public sector workers of their right to strike, but in several instances, federal and provincial governments suspended the right to bargain and/or strike for all their workers, and introduced permanent restrictions on the union rights of public and/or private sector workers. Cutbacks in and contracting out of public services undermined existing wage levels and job security, and labour standards were lowered in the private sector.

The labour movement was hardly willing to roll over and play dead. Bowing to pressure from their more militant members, the CLC took the unprecedented step of calling the first national General Strike (Day of Protest) in Canadian history on October 14, 1976, in opposition to wage controls. Led by autoworkers, most unions adopted "no concessions" policies and vowed to strike in defence of existing gains. Governments' increasing resort to back-to-work legislation through the 1980s itself attests to the public sector unions' willingness to struggle. Up until 1987, the annual number of strikes remained (with one exception) above those registered in the mid-1960s (Panitch and Swartz 2003: 244).

However, resistance should not be confused with success. The Day of Protest was the end rather than the beginning of the CLC's mobilization and the wage controls program was left to run its course. The impressive struggle in BC in 1983, where a broad range of popular organizations joined the unions in a Solidarity Coalition to oppose the Social Credit government's package of repressive legislative measures, ranging from numerous restrictions on union rights to lower educational standards and the dismantling of civil rights protection, was abruptly ended by the infamous "deal in Kelowna" between BC Federation of Labour president Jack Munro and BC premier Bill Bennett (Palmer 1987). While some of the most repressive measures were withdrawn, many remained in place, and new restrictions were introduced during the government's term and again after its re-election in 1986. The number of strikes across Canada fell steadily from 1981 onwards, and real wages stagnated over the 1980s, pointing to the declining strength of the labour movement.

The labour movement's central problem in this period was that the solidarity it had fashioned remained inadequate given the magnitude of the challenges confronting it. The labour movement had been built to bargain, and its solidarity was constructed around negotiating and enforcing collective agreements. Broader political education and mobilization had little place within this world, and years of neglect had debilitating effects on union members' consciousness. The labour relations system overdeveloped unions' technical and legal capacities and consciousness at the expense of the mobilizing capacities needed in the 1970s and

1980s. As CUPW President Jean Claude Parrot (1983: 60) put it: "You meet with lawyers, you meet with government representatives, and if you don't go back to the source, the membership, you are going to become a technical, legal guy."

Union leadership was also a problem. Some simply lacked the will to fight, but a commitment to the legal labour relations framework and to the law more generally guided most union leaders' actions, such as CLC President Dennis McDermott's attack on CUPW in 1978 for refusing to obey back-to-work legislation. The separation of the economic from the political clearly marked the labour movement's understanding of solidarity. Law was part of the political, and the labour leadership's strategy for dealing with it was through supporting the NDP. Both union and party leadership feared that, given the unions' party ties, struggling in the streets would undermine the NDP's electoral prospects. However well founded this fear, the question of whether an NDP government would solve the unions' problems was a different matter. The unions' hopes in this respect were dashed in July 1993, when the Ontario NDP government imposed its Social Contract (Walkom 1994; Panitch and Swartz 2003). The effects of the Social Contract reverberated across the country, thus representing a dramatic turning point in the political strategy of Canadian labour in general.

THE CONSOLIDATION OF NEOLIBERALISM AND THE CRISES OF SOLIDARITY: 1993–2011

All eyes across the country were on Ontario when the NDP was elected in 1990 on a platform promising substantial reforms. While the NDP had formed a number of provincial governments in the western provinces, the party's victory in Ontario — Canada's largest and most industrialized province — was seen as strategically important to advancing the goals of the labour movement. Immediately upon its election, however, the NDP government was confronted by the deepest recession since the Second World War as a cyclical slump was powerfully reinforced by the consolidation of a neoliberal global economic order. In the face of global competition, corporations were extensively restructuring their operations, shifting some production toward low-wage countries and rationalizing those which remained through "lean" production methods, outsourcing and temporary and part-time work. Governments that had opened the way for this through the adoption of free trade and other similar agreements were called upon to facilitate this shift by reducing corporate tax levels, restructuring their operations so as to create new opportunities for private accumulation and embracing fiscal restraint so as to ensure that the same pressures facing private sector workers were brought to bear on those in the public sector.

The NDP initially turned to mild Keynesian spending measures to contain the slump, but capital's unrelenting opposition soon converted them to the new fiscal orthodoxy, which saw "out of control" government spending as the problem and cuts to public sector workers' wages as the solution. When the public sector unions refused to acquiesce voluntarily, the government legislated wage cuts, using the term "Social Contract" to portray its coercive measure as consensual.

The Social Contract undermined the unions' confidence in their basic political strategy, producing uncertainty and confusion. It was not merely that the NDP had failed to deliver unions' desired reforms: it joined Liberal and Conservative governments in attacking basic union rights. Notably, the public sector unions refused to endorse the Social Contract and had the public support of the Canadian Auto Workers (CAW) and USW, key private sector unions with close ties to the NDP, although, in private, the public sector unions were pressed to acquiesce for the good of the party (Walkom 1994: 135, 140).

As Ontario's unions struggled to find their way, they were confronted with the election of Mike Harris's Conservative government. Its "Common Sense Revolution" included a 21 percent cut to welfare rates; a repeal of all the NDP's labour legislation reforms (adding new restrictions in the process); the laying off of some thirteen thousand provincial employees; and giving the provincial government wide-ranging powers to restructure municipalities and the health sector. Working in conjunction with a wide range of social justice groups, links with many of whom had been formed during the struggle against the Canada-U.S. Free Trade Agreement in the late 1980s, the Ontario Federation of Labour unveiled an imaginative plan for a series of one-day strikes in different cities that came to be known as the "Days of Action" (Gindin 1997; Munro 1997). After a promising beginning, including a march of over 200,000 people in Toronto on October 26, 1996, the plan came apart. Major strategic differences existed among the unions: while the CAW and some public sector unions wanted to continue the protests, the bulk of the private sector unions, led by the Steelworkers, wanted to return to electoral politics and channel the opposition into rebuilding support for the NDP. But unions also faced real difficulties in mobilizing their members, who were increasingly fearful for their own jobs, around issues that did not affect their immediate economic interests. In the end, the legislation remained unchanged, and the local union-community coalitions created in the cities where protests had taken place disappeared (Munro 1997).

The unions were incapable of finding a new solidarity that transcended one framed by the existing separation of the economic from the political. Indeed, existing solidarity was weakened. Capital's relentless restructuring was eroding union membership and bargaining power, especially of the old CIO unions in their traditional areas of strength. Organizing continued, and many of those added were women, racialized workers and students. But there were no major sectoral breakthroughs, as the preoccupation with adding members to each union's own ranks precluded the kind of cooperative efforts needed to organize any of the large multi-branch companies. At the same time, labour market transformations, like the spread of part-time and various forms of low-paid precarious work, created more barriers to union expansion (Clark and Warskett 2010: 252). Consequently, new organizing failed to keep pace with labour market growth, with the result that overall union density fell significantly, to just below 30 percent by 2009 (HRSDC 2010).

New tensions within the labour movement were also created in the scramble for members. Since the 1980s, several union mergers had led some private sector unions to see themselves as general unions and to organize in several sectors beyond their traditional jurisdictions. Public sector unions also branched out, not least because privatization shifted some of their members to the private service sector. Inevitably, jurisdictional conflicts, encroachments and raiding resulted, exacerbating divisions within the labour movement. Moreover, the spread of precarious work tended to aggravate inequalities within the working class, creating new divisions between organized and unorganized workers, and established workers and new hires.

Politically, at the institutional level, many unions clung to the NDP. The main innovation, led by the CAW, was to adopt strategic voting, identifying the Conservatives as the main threat to working people and urging their members to vote for the party in their riding most likely to defeat them (Savage, this volume). There was certain logic to this insofar as it acknowledged that the NDP was not qualitatively different from the Liberals, although it weakened those in the party who were interested in changing this. However, strategic voting underlined the CAW's increasing defensiveness in the face of developments in the auto industry and its concern to protect its members' sectional interests. While job loss due to incessant restructuring was an ongoing concern, the union's weakening position within the industry in the 1990s and 2000s was due to its inability to organize the growing numbers working for the new, highly profitable transplants like Toyota and Honda. In this context, the CAW opted to join the "Big Three" automakers in seeking state subsidies to preserve their members' jobs, reinforcing the discourse of competitiveness and further demobilizing their members.

Various structural changes being wrought by the consolidation of neoliberalism were also "dis-organizing" the working class as a whole. As Sam Gindin (2004: 8–9) argues, "by structuring options that reinforced individualized responses, [neoliberalism is] individualizing working class consciousness, [has] undermined its organizational formation, and — to a remarkable degree — successfully narrowed the range of socially legitimate options." For instance, while real wages have been stagnant or in decline, this has not prevented increases in working-class consumption. The spread of part-time work, home work and multiple job-holding has allowed households to increase income by providing more hours of labour, and cheap credit has enabled workers to cope with cuts to Employment Insurance, health care and the growing cost of education. All of these changes have promoted individual rather than collective responses to workers' ever more pressing needs.

As a result, comparatively better-off workers whose wages, pensions and benefit plans are now under attack "face increasing isolation in their struggles, and increasing pressures not to risk their jobs. Unemployment is always an issue, but now this is augmented by the fear that losing 'a good job' condemns workers — even after regaining employment — to join the new majority of those with insecure, poor quality, relatively low-paying jobs" (Gindin 2004: 11). The potential for difference being turned into resentment inherent in this situation has been heightened by the state's increased reliance on regressive forms of taxation (like sales taxes) and movement away from universal social programs. It is not just that lower-income workers may view the hard won benefits of better-paid workers as unwarranted privileges. Better-paid workers can also come to resent their less well-off counterparts, the most exploited among them, for undermining existing standards and those on welfare for the drain they put on their hard-earned incomes. An early sign of these internal working-class divisions was the support among Ontario workers for the Harris Conservatives in 1995, especially their cuts to welfare rates (Hale 1997), and was clearly evident in the working-class vote for Rob Ford in the 2010 Toronto mayoral election (Grant 2010; Saberi and Kipfer 2010).

CONCLUSION

The narrow solidarity the Canadian labour movement fashioned in the wake of the Second World War enabled workers to make real gains in the three decades that followed. However, as capital and the state were increasingly convinced that those gains had to be reversed if the accumulation of capital was to revive, their turn from Keynesianism to neoliberalism after 1980 entailed undermining the strength of the labour movement. The labour movement was totally unprepared for this attack, and its existing culture of solidarity was incapable of effectively mobilizing against it. Indeed, as the defeats piled up, labour and working-class solidarity has, if anything, eroded. While the labour movement is far from dead, a sober assessment cannot escape the conclusion that it is mired in a profound crisis. How might its trajectory be reversed?

Here we can offer a few observations. Any revival of the labour movement rests on the construction of a qualitatively different culture of solidarity with a capacity for collective struggle that can challenge the far-reaching changes in the organization of production, the labour market, the role of finance and the individualist culture of the current global capitalist order. The various ideas for renewal currently circulating in and around the labour movement such as putting more resources into organizing, strengthening labour councils, re-establishing jurisdictional boundaries between unions, adopting better policies at conventions or even electing more militant leaders, however welcome, do not begin to address the sectionalism, economism and separation of the economic from the political that mark the labour movement's existing solidarity and indeed working-class culture in general. Sam Gindin (2004: 2) best summed up the kinds of changes required when he wrote: "We are, in a sense, 'starting over'."

A qualitatively different culture of solidarity would need to be premised on an understanding of the ultimate incompatibility of capitalism with the needs and aspirations of the working class. It would also entail far-reaching changes in the basic structures and practices of the labour movement, encompassing the relation between industrial and political activities; the kind of demands raised in bargaining; the role, selection and skills of paid staff; the relations between leaders and members; the nature of union educational activities; who can be a member and the relation between those who are union members and those who are not (Panitch and Swartz 2003; Gindin 2004). Some glimmers of rethinking such issues exist: CUPW's inclusion of voluntary recognition for rural and suburban postal workers in the 2003 round of negotiations with Canada Post is an example of a more inclusive and non-sectionalist approach to bargaining demands. Some local unions also provide support for the efforts of workers' action centres to organize non-union workers around labour standards. However rare such instances are, their existence suggests their possibility is not merely a fanciful wish. Whatever the prospects for such a transformation of the labour movement, it will assuredly not result from efforts to change individual unions. A necessary condition for changes on the scale required is the emergence of a constituency based in several unions prepared to take up the challenge of remaking the labour movement's culture of solidarity as a whole.

2. BUSINESS UNIONISM AND SOCIAL UNIONISM IN THEORY AND PRACTICE

Stephanie Ross

Debates about the labour movement's proper political direction often cast business unionism and social unionism as mutually exclusive union strategies, with social unionism, understood as engagement with social justice struggles beyond the workplace, generally preferred as the route to revitalized union power. Undoubtedly, the critique of narrow forms of unionism is crucial to labour movement revitalization if unions are to reclaim their capacity to speak and act meaningfully on behalf of a far greater proportion of working-class people than is now the case. Such capacity for articulating and fighting for more universal interests is all the more important given the rising "reverse class resentment" which characterizes public debates over unions' proper role and actions, particularly when they engage in militant actions (Walkom 2010). Social unionism, as both commitment and strategy, points in such a direction.

Because business unionism and social unionism are such important organizing concepts in both academic analyses and activist political mobilization, we need to think carefully about whether they are useful tools for organizing our thinking and making claims about labour movement strategy. I argue that the counter-position of business unionism and social unionism is often based on simplistic understandings of these modes of union action. In particular, strategies and tactics are often mistaken for a philosophical approach to unionism, casting collective bargaining as an inherently narrow expression of union members' interests and an inevitably bureaucratizing mode of action. Similarly, social unionism is often interpreted — by both proponents and critics — as action outside of the workplace separate from, and sometimes in competition with, workplace-based action. Such assumptions lead to several problematic results: an undervaluing of workplace-based power and action; an overestimation of the ease of making gains for workers in the political and social spheres; and a lack of attention to the important relationship between struggles inside and outside the workplace. These assumptions undermine our ability to understand what it will take to sustain labour's more effective engagement in economic and social justice struggles.

In this chapter, I unpack the "ideal types" of business unionism and social unionism and explore their more complex and contradictory expressions. Because union thinking and strategic action are worked out in the course of contingent historical struggles, both within workers' organizations and in relation to employers, the state and other workers, the concrete patterns of unions' claims and practices mix these two modes of action. Thus, understanding the strengths, limits and implications of union practices requires some careful and nuanced analysis.

UNDERSTANDING UNION PRACTICES

Union practices can be analyzed according to three major elements: collective action frame, strategic repertoire and internal organizational practices (Ross 2007 and 2008; Hrynyshyn and Ross 2011). First, unions develop and adopt "collective action frames" that provide a sense of meaning and purpose to their activity: they define workers' interests and identities, the nature and causes of their problems and the solutions necessary to solve them. Collective action frames also provide motivations for why people should involve themselves in union activity (Goffman 1974; Snow and Benford 1988; Benford and Snow 2000). In other words, collective action frames imply a particular "culture of solidarity," a sense of "who is with us and who is against us" which workers develop in the course of struggling to exert their collective power in particular circumstances (Fantasia 1988; Swartz and Warskett, this volume). Second, out of a wide range of possibilities, unions adopt a particular strategic and tactical repertoire for acting on those claims and pursuing common interests (Tilly 1978; Tarrow 1998). Finally, union frames and strategic repertoires are defined, shaped and implemented via a variety of internal organizational practices and power relations within union structures which define who decides what and who does what. These internal structures and relationships involve the roles, relative importance of and division of labour between elected leaders, appointed staff and member activists and general membership in both decision-making and implementation.

As many observers of unions have pointed out, historically recognizable patterns have emerged that link together particular collective action frames, strategic/tactical repertoires and internal organizational practices (Kumar and Murray 2006: 82–6). Some identities, grievances and solutions tend to lend themselves more to some strategies and organizational practices than others. Business unionism and social unionism represent two such patterns in union thinking and action. However, despite such trends, the three elements are not rigidly attached; rather, there has always been much room for variation and contingency in the way unions organize, express and act on workers' interests. As U.S. economist and labour historian Robert Hoxie (1914: 203, 211) put it in the influential article in which he coined the term business unionism, "trade unionism… [is] not a simple, consistent entity, but a complex of the utmost diversity, both structurally and functionally." Union types "do not in practice represent exactly and exclusively the ideals and activities of any particular union organization or group. That is to say, no union organization functions strictly and consistently according to type." Moreover, there is no reason to believe that collective action frames are themselves always internally consistent. Instead, because unions' roles are themselves multiple and often contradictory, so too are the ways that unions frame and act on their goals and purposes. That said, let us now explore the complex of ideas and practices that has become known as business unionism.

"MORE, MORE, MORE, NOW": BUSINESS UNIONISM AND WORKERS' ECONOMIC INTERESTS

The phrase "business unionism" emerged in the early twentieth century to describe a form of unionism most associated with the craft unionism of Samuel Gompers, the erstwhile socialist cigarmaker, president of his New York City craft union local and the first president of the American Federation of Labor (AFL), from 1886 to 1924. For Gompers, workers' economic interests were not just important, they were the central concern of unionism. Economic and social revolution, promoted by socialists and radicals, was irrelevant if not dangerous to workers' interests. Rather, "proper" union action was to make gradual improvements to workers' lot within the existing political economic system (Gompers 1919; Reed 1966).

The collective action frame emanating from Gompers' approach to unionism and influencing many sections of the North American union movement contains the following elements. First, union members' identities and interests are defined by their craft, occupation or job rather than their membership in or allegiance to the working class as a whole. Often rooted in deeply felt craft or occupational pride, such unions adopt an exclusive rather than inclusive scope of organization based on both identity and strategic considerations. Although industry-wide forms of worker consciousness and organization have emerged alongside craft unionism since Gompers' time, this has not displaced a tendency to define the "community of interest" as well short of the entire working class. Such attachments can be understood as the result of the capitalist division of labour which fragments workers' material experience of work and encourages identification with their immediate co-workers (Swartz and Warskett, this volume), the certification practices of government-appointed labour boards (Warskett 1988) and workers' own creation of intense "place-bound loyalties" in their struggles to defend their work practices against the relentless reorganization of employers (Harvey 1998: 64). Business unionists accept these sectionalist attachments and the interests linked to them as natural and emphasize defending the particular rather than universal interest, especially when those two conflict.

Second, business unionists define workers' interests as primarily economic or materialistic. The union's role is to protect the immediate economic interests of union members, "delivering the goods" in the form of higher wages, better working conditions and job security. Gompers famously expressed this view when he asserted that the American worker's desire was for "more, more, more, now," not workers' control over industry or social revolution. For him, "the trade unions pure and simple are the natural organizations of the wageworkers to secure their present material and practical improvement," not "to imagine a new society constructed from rainbow materials" (Gompers quoted in Moody 1988: 56; Gompers 1919: 20). In other words, the horizon of union action is straight-forward and short-term: to produce constant and immediate improvements in the material conditions of union members' lives. This pragmatic orientation is often referred to as "pure and simple" or "bread and butter" unionism.

Third, business unionism diagnoses the source of workers' problems as rest-ing not with capitalism as such, but rather the behaviour of particularly greedy employers and the unfair distribution of surplus or profit created through the work process. Although the interests of capitalists and workers are in fundamental opposition in this view, as the pie to be shared is only so big and workers seek a bigger slice of it at the expense of employers, business unionists remain con-servative with respect to the capitalist economic framework in that they do not seek to change the system which generates this unfair distribution (Reed 1966: 13–4, 16–20). As Hoxie (1914: 212) pointed out, business unionism "accepts as inevitable, if not as just, the existing capitalistic organization and the wage system as well as existing property rights and the binding force of contract." On that assumption, then, the solution for workers is to negotiate or otherwise extract a more "fair" distribution of that surplus from their employers, reducing rather than eliminating the source of economic inequality. From Gompers' perspec-tive, to pursue a more radical course of social transformation would merely invite state repression of the labour movement and serve to marginalize it from "respectable" society (Jacoby 1991: 193).

Business unionism's typical strategic repertoire reflects these purposes and motivations. As workers' interests are economic, so too are unions' main strate-gies for defending those interests. Collective bargaining is the business unionist's primary focus, as it is assumed to be the method by which workers can exert the most power over their employers to extract gains. Defence of the collective agreement becomes the union's primary task. Collective bargaining is reinforced by other strategies which increase workers' bargaining power. The techniques of job control unionism, such as controlling the types and supply of necessary labour needed by employers by requiring apprenticeships, limiting who can perform bargaining unit work through the union shop, defining job territories or regulating rates of productivity (that is, negotiating the wage-effort bargain) allow the union to "sell" their members' labour at the highest possible price (Kealey 1976). Expanding the scope and rate of unionization also increases bargaining power as it works to take wages (and working conditions) out of competition and subject all employers to the same contractual obligations to their employ-ees. Unionization also spreads a particular kind of industrial legality: voluntary agreements between unions and employers, achieved through a stable collective bargaining relationship, established and extended on a workplace-by-workplace basis and backed up by union strength, internal solidarity and militancy, are the basis of workplace reform, not legislation (Heron 1996; Fudge and Tucker 2004). If public policy changes are to be pursued, this is generally confined to pragmatic struggles to increase union bargaining power (through legislated union shop or fair wage requirements, for instance) or accrue benefits to the industry in which the union is located (such as subsidies to employers to support expansion and job creation), thereby promoting job growth or security (Hoxie 1914; Reed 1966).

Because collective bargaining is considered central to carrying out business unionism's vision of union purpose, other strategic avenues are by extension de-emphasized or even rejected. For business unionists, anything interfering with workplace unity amongst union members or preventing them from acting in solidarity to defend collective bargaining rights and outcomes is to be avoided. Despite Gompers' eventual acceptance that workers had to be engaged in some forms of political or electoral activity, particularly to achieve legislation that would either defend or increase unions' bargaining power, he remained skeptical of state-backed reforms, which could be taken away by fickle legislators chasing the labour vote, and extremely leery of politics' potentially divisive implications for unions as collective bargaining organizations (Babcock 1974: 57–8). As such, business unionism has long been identified with a non-partisan political stance, as partisan allegiances create divisions amongst union members. Instead, political activity should be confined to pragmatic calculations, in which choices between existing political parties are made on the basis of punishing enemies and rewarding friends. Gompers' pragmatism meant he would "appeal to the devil and his mother-in-law to help labor, if labor could be aided in that way" (Reed 1966: 16). Business unions thus shop for the best political deal for their members and keep their options open by refusing to make permanent affiliations with any particular party.

Historically, such non-partisan orientations have been common amongst Canadian unions. The craft-dominated Trades and Labour Congress of Canada long refused to affiliate permanently to any political party (Horowitz 1968; Brodie and Jenson 1988). Similarly, the formation in 1982 of the Canadian Federation of Labour by building trades unions was in part based on the latter's discontent with the Canadian Labour Congress's (CLC) "close ties" with the New Democratic Party (NDP) and continuing identification with the Gomperism of U.S.-based craft unions (Rose 1983: 89). More recently, Jim Given, the Seafarers' International Union executive vice-president, explained his union's endorsement of the two Conservative Party candidates in the Niagara Region in the 2011 federal election in this way: "We don't look at it in terms of parties…. We're going to support the candidate that is getting things done for our members" (LaFleche 2011). Some versions of contemporary strategic voting by Canadian unions, even those that aim to prevent vote splitting that would see labour's neoliberal "enemies" get elected, are influenced in part by this Gomperist calculus (Walchuk 2010; Savage, this volume).

However, we must acknowledge strategic variation within the range of unions that tend to be labelled business unionist. As Bryan Palmer (1992: 169) points out, despite the strong influence of Gomperism over Canadian craft unions in the 1890s, this "was never some monolithic structural process of incarceration, in which workers were only stifled and moved in the directions that business unionism allowed." For instance, a strategic focus on collective bargaining or workers' economic interests in itself does not preclude militancy, that is, a willingness to take direct and uncompromising action in opposition to management in the pursuit of workers' own goals (Allen 1966; Kelly 1996; Gall 2003). As Greg Kealey (1976) demonstrates in his examination of Canadian craft unions in the 1880s, the practice of collective bargaining was grounded in such militancy, making use of the strike and the boycott to assert craft prerogatives over employers' attempts to introduce new and intensified work processes. Kumar and Murray (2006: 82) concur that business unionism in Canada "has historically tended to be more conflictual than cooperative in the pursuit of its primarily economic objectives." While Hoxie (1914: 213) argued that "in method, business unionism is prevailingly temperate," in part because getting a good deal from employers can often involve maintaining a good working relationship with them, business unionists past and present use the strike and other forms of collective direct action to exert and defend their bargaining power. As Edwards (in Gall 2003: 9) points out, "'militant' does not mean politically left-wing, but refers to the extent to which workers perceive themselves as having interests which are opposed or inconsistent with the interests of management, and act accordingly… even though [they may] accept the right to manage." This defence of sectional interests via militancy is partly what Raymond Williams (1989) was trying to capture in his concept of "militant particularism" (although he emphasized the way that such struggles, though specific to a group of workers, could be made to represent the general struggles of workers against capital).[1] Even though, through the twentieth century, a more cooperative form of business unionism has evolved, emphasizing "responsible unionism," partnership with management and an identification of workers' interests with employers' success, this is not the only form that workplace-focused unionism can take (Moody 1988 and 2007; Wheeler 2002: 19; Nissen 2003).

Business unionism's strategic emphases have implications for unions' internal organizational practices. Hoxie's (1914: 212) original definition referred to business unionism's mirroring of corporate structure and hierarchical decision-making: "In harmony with its business character it tends to emphasize discipline within the organization and is prone to develop strong leadership and to become somewhat autocratic in government." Moody (1988: 56–7) pulls this element of business unionism to the forefront, arguing that it occurs when the union is run like a business, union financial assets and resources (like the security and stability of union staff) are maximized and protected, and the protection of the union organization is prioritized over other goals. Business unionism thus models its internal organizational practices on those of its powerful corporate counterparts, assuming that power flows from expertise and top-down discipline. There is a unity between purpose and organizational form: as John L. Lewis, president of the United Mine Workers of America, put it: "trade unionism is a phenomenon of capitalism quite similar to the corporation. One is essentially a pooling of labor for the purpose of common action in production and sales. The other is a pooling of capital for exactly the same purpose. The economic aims of both are identical — gain" (quoted in Moody 1988: 57). Since top-down control, coordination, efficiency and discipline produces gain for corporate structures, so too is it assumed to produce gain for workers' organizations.

Several of business unionism's core strategies have tended to generate or reinforce top-down internal organizational practices. Job control unionism, for instance, can promote the use of specialized union staff to interpret increasingly complex work rules and detailed collective agreements. Over the course of the twentieth century, collective bargaining involved progressively more complex economic and legal issues, creating a rationale for a more elaborate division of labour of appointed experts who, because they are "more knowledgeable," deploy delegated authority from union members to defend the membership's interests, acting on their behalf and increasingly in their place (Ross and Jenson 1986; Parker and Gruelle 1999; Schenk 2003). In other words, the focus on collective bargaining in general, and job control unionism in particular, tends to generate and reproduce "contract unionism," which focuses inordinately on the interpretation, defence and enforcement of contracts (Clawson 2003; Camfield 2011: 11–14). This work is typically carried out according to a "service model of unionism": while members may decide policy, union leaders and hired staff execute policy, administer agreements and process grievances on their behalf (Fletcher and Hurd 1998: 38; Schenk 2003). It has been widely argued that such an arrangement creates the tendency for members to become passive and reliant on full-time staff to resolve problems rather than engaging directly, whether individually or collectively, in such activity, making it less likely that the capacity for militancy is sustained.

While the bureaucratization of internal union life was well underway in early twentieth-century craft unions, who used nationally appointed "walking delegates" and local business agents to administer and impose common craft standards and national strike funds (Kealey 1976; Palmer 1992), such tendencies were further reinforced and generalized with the legal institutionalization of collective bargaining in the post-war era and the rise of "responsible unionism" (Fudge and Tucker 2004; Smith, this volume). As part of the class compromise which made the legal entrenchment of unions' rights to organize, bargain and strike (under certain conditions) possible, union leaders' place at the table was premised on their provision of "responsible union leadership." Employers and the law demanded union leaders' willingness to moderate union demands, enforce collective agreements and restrain spontaneous outbursts of militancy by their memberships. In exchange for a peaceful, orderly long-term relationship between union and management, union leaders became "managers of discontent," policing the enforcement of the collective agreement and, in particular, disciplining members who refused to adhere to contracts or who sought to act in ways outside the bounds of the legally prescribed process. Mills (1948: 119) described the trade-off entailed in this arrangement: "to insure peaceful plants and profitable enterprises in a stable economy, the leaders of labor will deliver a responsible, which is to say, a well-disciplined, union of contented workers in return for junior partnership in the productive process, security for the union, and higher wages for the workers of industry." For some commentators, these developments were both natural and positive, representing a "maturing" or "sobering" of formerly "youthful" and "rambunctious" union leaders and a more orderly and efficient collective bargaining system (Hoxie 1920; Commons 1921; Lester 1958). For others, so-called responsible unionism represents a neutering of workers' organizations, a subordination of workers' interests to those of employers and an abandonment of the basis of their bargaining power, namely the exercise of disruptive collective action (Moody 1988; Wells 1995a and 1995b). More recently, Moody has adopted the term "bureaucratic corporate unionism" to denote the top-down, responsible partnership unionism being practised by some unions in the US (Moody 2007: 184).

"WHAT WE DESIRE FOR OURSELVES, WE WISH FOR ALL": SOCIAL UNIONISM AND SOCIAL JUSTICE

In contrast to business unionism, social unionism is more expansive in both its collective action frame and strategic repertoire. Social unionism begins with a more expansive understanding of the community of interest it speaks to and for. Social unionists tend to frame issues in terms of general community or working-class interests, and not merely of those segments of the already unionized working class. While unionism may be a means for advancing workers' economic interests in particular workplaces, it is also the base from which broader social change is made in the interests of the working-class majority. As Co-operative Commonwealth Federation (CCF) pioneer J.S. Woodsworth (1948: 30) expressed it, "what we desire for ourselves, we wish for all." Whereas business unionism tends to be sectionalist, social unionism rejects the naturalness of occupational or other differences that divide groups of workers from each other and strives to make connections between the particular and the general interest. As such, particular workers' interests are framed as representing those of others, whether symbolically or materially, and others are exhorted to see their own stake in their battles. This anti-sectionalist ethos is used to mobilize the union's members in support of struggles outside their own workplace as well as to frame their own interests as those with which the wider society should identify.

Second, social unionism tends to define workers' problems and interests as more than economic. Because union members are more than merely wage-earners, but are also citizens with a wide range of other identities, they have experiences, problems and therefore interests that extend beyond the workplace (Kumar and Murray 2006: 82). Class inequality is reflected in the unequal distribution of income and wealth, but also in the concentration of political power in the hands of elites who make public policy and structure the rules of the game. Class inequalities are also reflected in the unequal access to social influence and status, the cultural representation of elite (rather than working-class) lives and values as "normal" and the greater exposure of workers to physical, emotional and economic risk by virtue of their position in these unequal relationships and structures. These problems are experienced beyond the labour-management relationship and have solutions which rest outside collective bargaining. Union members also experience other forms of inequality and discrimination (like racism, sexism and homophobia) that intersect with class and workplace relationships but are not confined to the workplace. In that sense, social unionism is also anti-economistic, in that improvements to workers' wages cannot solve all the problems they face in a class-divided society. The Canadian labour movement's struggles for legislated labour reform, including prohibitions on child labour and fights to expand the social wage, including unemployment insurance, universal public health care, public education, public pensions and universal child care, are expressions of both anti-sectionalism and anti-economism.

However, there is significant variation within the social unionist collective action frame over the roots of these problems, and in particular on the stance that unions should take with respect to capitalism as a system. While social unionism is united by a general commitment to social change beyond the workplace and beyond the unionized working class, there are important ideological differences over the causes of the social injustices being fought, the type of social change being pursued and the particular content of workers' broader interests and identities. Robinson (2000: 114), Kumar and Murray (2006: 28), Camfield (2007: 285) and Shantz (2009) all argue that a social democratic political outlook, which accepts the current capitalist social order and adopts electoralist strategies on behalf of a labour party, is definitional of social unionism. However, while social democratic electoralism has been prominent in the Canadian labour movement, it by no means represents the full diversity of concrete practices and ideological orientations of unions invoking the term "social unionism." Instead, social democratic/reformist unionism, social movement unionism and anti-capitalist forms of unionism can all be appropriately seen as expressions of social unionism, but as variants that should neither be confused with each other nor used interchangeably (Ross 2008). In other words, radicalism — or its absence — is not in itself definitional of social unionism.

Social unionism's strategic repertoire is also more expansive than that of business unionism. Because workers' interests are not solely economic or workplace-based, social unionist strategies and tactics reflect a broader collective action frame. While collective bargaining can be used to address broader social justice concerns, like enhanced job creation through restrictions on overtime, conversion of part-time positions to more stable full-time work and negotiation of social justice funds to transfer employer profits to community initiatives at home and abroad, there are limits to what can be achieved in one workplace. As Dan Clawson (2003: 112) points out, "it would take quite a union to win" the kinds of wage increases required to make housing affordable for particular groups of low-wage workers living in the most expensive U.S. cities, and so political strategies to increase the availability of affordable housing for everyone are needed. As such, the social unionist repertoire also includes more explicitly political strategies such as electoral mobilization on behalf of worker-friendly parties (Pilon et al. 2011; Evans, this volume); non-partisan lobbying and campaigns for worker-friendly legislative reforms; union-community coalitions (Tufts 1998; Black, this volume; Coulter, this volume); building non-union forms of working-class organization (Cranford and Ladd 2003; Choudry and Thomas, this volume); extra-parliamentary mobilizations like demonstrations or political strikes (Munro 1997; Camfield 2006); international solidarity actions (Dreiling and Robinson 1998; Carr 1999); and community volunteerism and charitable fundraising (Manchee 2006). Although some argue that this repertoire has tended to involve greater militancy as a response to the limits of legalistic unionism (Clawson 2003), both "cooperative" and "militant" approaches to social transformation are well represented.

Finally, social unionism is generally assumed to generate internal organizational practices based on the mass participation of union (and community) members in political mobilization and a rejection of the service model of unionism. The logic behind this view is that the effective exertion of union power on broader social justice questions "requires that larger and larger segments of the community be brought into the effort to win basic rights for workers, particularly those most marginalized and vulnerable in the new economy" (Fantasia and Voss 2004: 131). This is both because the forces arrayed against such demands are powerful, and because it is the only way to challenge the increasingly common view that unions are acting in their own narrow interests in such struggles (CLC/ Vector 2003). The emphasis on participation is especially strong in the organizing model of unionism, which is premised on the exertion of collective power via mass membership participation in social movement tactics involving direct action, mass demonstrations and confrontations with economic and political elites (Fletcher and Hurd 1998; Clawson 2003).

As with business unionism, the reality of social unionism's internal organizational practices is more complex than the ideal type would imply. In particular, the frequent counter-position of social unionism and the service model of unionism mistakenly assumes that broader social justice commitments and political strategies are always implemented through participatory democratic organizational practices. In fact, neither the social unionist collective action frame nor strategic repertoire as such requires or results in internal union democracy in the deeper sense. Rather, as many have pointed out in mounting criticisms of the organizing model of unionism, activism in the wider political realm can also be managed by union staff in ways that are consistent with the service model of unionism (Camfield 2007; Gall 2009). The same can be said for practices using the rest of the social unionist repertoire, in which union leaders "encourage member *involvement* without member *control*" and "expect to turn member involvement on and off like a faucet" (Parker and Gruelle 1999: 26, emphasis in original).

THE COMPLEXITY OF CONCRETE UNION PRACTICES

While ideal types can be useful as a lens for comparing the concrete ideas and actions of unions, they have their limits. Although these types allow us to organize reality in a certain way, clarifying what distinguishes union approaches from each other, they can also give us a false sense of clarity if we over-generalize. In particular, while we can observe the tendency for certain collective action frames, strategic repertoires and internal organizational practices to appear together, it is important to pull apart the elements of union action so as to see how more combinations of these three are not only possible but actually practised by Canadian unions. In doing so, we must be careful not to assume that using a particular strategy or tactic represents a whole set of ideological motivations about unionism's proper goals. Similarly, we should not assume that a particular repertoire always has the same effect, regardless of how it is framed. In other words, we must look beyond the tactic used and see whether it is meant to serve narrow or broad interests; to make radical transformations or reforms that remain within the existing system; to be implemented through top-down or participatory means; or to be made via cooperation with political-economic elites or militant opposition.

The counter-position of business unionism and social unionism as ideal types also ignores the fact that, for most unions, these are two related faces of union activity, often in tension with each other but sometimes mutually reinforcing. The more general reality of unionism under capitalism is one of multiple roles. As Flanders (1970: 15) put it, "trade unions have always had two faces, sword of justice and vested interest." For Flanders, all unionism, and not just business unionism, is job-conscious rather than class-conscious, because all unions only represent a segment of the working class. Muste (1948: 332–5) also emphasized unions' "divided soul": they are "armies" but also have the structure of the "democratic town meeting" in which the "generals" are elected and "the declaration of war and… the terms of the peace" are voted on. Unions must both "fight and discuss." As such, unions are always pulled between their status as institution, with a legal responsibility and democratic mandate to represent particular workers, and as movement, with the aspiration to expand the realm of social justice for all who experience exploitation and oppression (Cohen 2006: 149). This basic fact offers both pressure and potential. Whether unions are able, in Williams' (1989: 249) words, to "connect particular struggles to a general struggle" and make real the "claim that the defence and advancement of certain particular interests, properly brought together, are in fact the general interest" is always an open question, and one which workers and their organizations must continually debate and renegotiate, particularly in the face of changing circumstances.

Moreover, contrary to what appears in these two ideal types, strategies based in the workplace and the political and social spheres have often been mutually dependent on each other for success. For instance, many "narrow" collective bargaining aims have laid the foundation for broader working-class victories in the realm of both law and public policy (such as occupational health and safety legislation, paid maternity leave and working-time regulation). In the Canadian context, workplace-based union strategies have often been tied to and broadened by a commitment to social democratic politics, albeit premised on a strategic division of labour between the unions and "their" political party, the NDP (Schenk and Bernard 1992; Kumar and Murray 2006: 82–3). In this sense, militant particularism can be progressive rather than merely narrow or reactionary, if beachhead struggles create a basis for the extension of gains to others (a whipsawing effect[2] by unions) and represent a particular version of a universal interest, rather than creating an island of privilege that no one else can get to. Strikes at Vale Inco in Sudbury and Port Colborne (2009), the City of Windsor (2009), Canada Post (2011) and Air Canada (2011) and the lockout at U.S. Steel in Hamilton (2010–11) can all be understood in this way. While all were local, defensive and militant particularist struggles, they also represented a larger working-class interest in opposing employer demands for two-tier contracts that would degrade wages, benefits and working conditions for future generations of workers.

Unions' relationship to capitalism more generally is also contradictory. As Anderson (1977: 334) argues,

> trade unions are dialectically both an opposition to capitalism and a component of it. For they both resist the given unequal distribution of income within the society by their wage demands, and ratify the principle of an unequal distribution by their existence, which implied as its complementary opposite that of management.

In other words, unions are both functional for capitalist labour markets as a contractor of labour and are rebellious against the prerogatives of private property and unilateral management control. As a result, it is wrong to interpret Mills' characterization of labour leaders' role as "managers of discontent" as merely involving the suppression of rank-and-file activity. Instead, leaders are sometimes required to "whip up the opinion and activity of the rank and file" against the employer, at other times to "sit on it, exploiting it to maintain a continuous organization" (Mills 1948: 9). Even in the context of institutionalized collective bargaining, this tension can be observed, as leaders often wish for a free hand in negotiations, and yet understand the power that an angry and mobilized membership can provide. As Hyman (1971: 37) puts it, union leaders' attempts "to sustain a delicate balance between grievance and satisfaction, between activism and quiescence" create the potential for more participatory, militant or radical action within the collective bargaining process.

In other words, rather than being separate spheres of action that unions must choose between, particularly robust unionism combines strong workplace power — even on economic interests — with a capacity to mobilize on social justice questions. A crucial problem in contemporary strategic thinking, however, is that strategies are mistaken for the collective action frames and internal organizational practices they have been historically connected to. Whereas the business unionist frame and the "service model" of unionism is usefully rejected, the strategic practices of collective bargaining, exercising workplace power and providing services to union members are not (Fletcher and Hurd 1998).

Indeed, one without the other can be dangerous for the labour movement. Most analysts of union renewal have focused on the negative implications of practicing business unionism in the absence of a genuine commitment to social justice. Such a unionism, based only on defensive self-interest, may make opportunistic use of social unionist discourse to mask that self-interest and contributes to the long-term weakening of the social and material basis of business unionism itself while broader public support for unions wanes as the gap between union and non-union grows.

Less adequately explored is the pursuit of social unionism while giving insufficient attention to collective bargaining and workplace power. At its most extreme, workplace-based struggles can be dismissed or de-emphasized because they are considered narrow or sectionalist, creating a disjuncture between those who use the union's resources for outward-oriented struggles and those who want — and need — the union to act on workplace concerns. While unions should not be chained to the imperative to deliver the goods at all costs, an ongoing failure to do so can result in declining internal legitimacy and support, particularly if concrete connections between union members and broader struggles are not continually made and are meaningful. Moreover, social unionism practised in this way isn't necessarily democratic either: a self-selected leadership group can shame the membership into supporting other struggles at their own expense, without their genuine consent. Such an approach does not foster the kind of buy-in that is the basis for making real connections to broader social struggles, and does not contribute to sustainable labour movement renewal. In this sense, a strong capacity for workplace action — and the solidarity this is based on — makes meaningful engagement in broader social justice struggles possible.

CONCLUSION

Ultimately, it is more fruitful to think of both business unionism and social unionism as specific complexes of ideas and practices or, as Camfield (2007: 284) has termed it, "modes of union praxis," whose elements came together in particular historical and institutional contexts but are not inevitably tied to one another. In short, workers' collective power is both economic and political and, rather than having to choose between them, strategies built of these kinds of power can be connected and made to serve broader identities and more radical goals.

Admittedly, the defence of union members' immediate economic interests through a highly bureaucratized system of collective bargaining has become privileged in both labour law and union practice (if not policy), and the exclusive focus on such activity has had negative consequences for the labour movement as a movement for economic and social justice. However, this is the result of historically specific economic and political processes which were not inevitable and did not completely extinguish alternative conceptions of workers' interests, allegiances, strategies and practices of democracy. Recognizing the co-existence of historicized ideal types of both "business unionism" and "social unionism" in the labour movement in general, and specifically within unions themselves, provides the basis for an ongoing rethinking of the movement's collective action frames, strategic and tactical repertoires and internal organizational practices. Such an approach does not just allow us to see the more complex expressions of business unionism and social unionism in the Canadian labour movement, but makes it possible to be more careful in our strategic analysis of the kinds of union practices to be preserved and rejected, and under what ideological, legal and organizational conditions.

Notes

1. For Raymond Williams (1989: 249), "almost all labour struggles begin as particularist," wherein people act to defend their immediate, common interests in their local workplace or community. However, in the process of struggling to defend the local, the way these struggles symbolically represent the general interest becomes more clear. David Harvey (1995) adopted this concept to explore the way that such local struggles become articulated to global or universal ones, but also to highlight the place-bound nature of such militancy and the solidarity it generates. This particularism creates challenges in making connections to workers not part of immediate, tangible solidarities, often requires workers to juggle competing loyalties and sometimes forces a choice to prioritize the particular when it conflicts with the general interest.

2. Whipsawing is a tactic used by unions in industries with multiple employers and bargaining units in an effort to set ever-improving industry-wide levels of compensation and working conditions. The union generally targets the most profitable industry leader and bargains hard for the best possible deal. Once the contract is settled, the union attempts to force other industry employers to reach the same deal under threat of strike. In the neoliberal era, this tactic has been used increasingly by employers with multiple bargaining units, who target the weakest local and attempt to force all other locals to that lower standard.

Part II

THE CHALLENGE OF ELECTORAL POLITICS

3. THE NEW DEMOCRATIC PARTY IN THE ERA OF NEOLIBERALISM

Bryan Evans

On May 2, 2011, the federal New Democratic Party (NDP) made history by capturing nearly 31 percent of the popular vote in Canada's forty-first general election, electing 103 Members of Parliament, and forming the official opposition for the first time in its fifty-year history. The federal NDP wasted no time in attempting to consolidate this realignment of Canadian politics. With the federal Liberals relegated to third place, the NDP leadership moved quickly to propose eliminating the word "socialism" from its constitutionally entrenched statement of principles in an effort to "modernize" the party in its quest to replace the governing Conservatives in the next election. The NDP's newfound electoral success has put the party in the spotlight of Canadian politics in an unprecedented way and thus generated a new wave of interest in the party's policy positions and political practices. It is impossible not to see the NDP's electoral fortunes as an expression, at least in part, of a broad-based refusal to accept the social and economic insecurity that has become the norm under neoliberalism. The question is, however, to what extent is it the NDP's project to confront and challenge neoliberalism?

The answer to this question requires an understanding of social democracy as a political and ideological project. Social democracy is a centre-left ideology that contends capitalism can be retained as a means of social and economic organization, albeit with major reform. The period of post-war capitalism in particular saw the creation of extensive welfare states as the means of achieving this reform (Briggs 2007: 16–17). This classical social democracy entailed significant state involvement in social and economic life; the application of Keynesian demand management and income redistribution policies; labour-business-government collaboration on economic and industrial policies (also known as corporatism); a commitment to a mixed economy where markets are strongly regulated; and a commitment to full employment (Giddens 2003: 35). However, since the 1980s, a "new" social democracy has emerged, sometimes referred to as the "Third Way," that is committed to globalization, expanding economic competition, the role of the market economy and accepting of greater levels of economic inequality than in the immediate post-war period (Latham 2001: 25). While theorists like Giddens (1998) contended that Third Way social democracy was a progressive response to neoliberal capitalism, it was in fact an adaptation of social democracy to the latter's hegemonic position rather than an alternative to it. Neoliberalism can be defined as "the belief that open, competitive, and unregulated markets, liberated from all forms of state interference, represent the optimal mechanism for economic development" (Brenner and Theodore 2002: 2). Since the 1980s, the new social democracy has come to embrace these key principles (Moschonas 2002). Social democracy's continuous adaptation to prevailing political and economic conditions of capitalism, whether Keynesian or neoliberal, suggests that it is neither a vehicle for resistance nor a transformational political project. How then do we explain why a significant component of organized labour continues to align itself, in one form or another, with the NDP — a party that demonstrates increasingly less concern with class-based redistributional issues? In short, social democracy's political role has been to integrate labour into capitalism. Indeed, most contemporary unions themselves offer no substantive critique of capitalism or its neoliberal variant, preferring instead to embrace the amorphous politics of social democracy. As such, organized labour's own reformism has itself transformed, shifting from a broadly Keynesian redistributional approach to a neoliberalized social democracy concerned with assisting capital accumulation (Moschonas 2002: 16, 2).

THE NEW DEMOCRATIC PARTY: THE TRAJECTORY OF "MODERNIZATION"

The demise of the Co-operative Commonwealth Federation (CCF) and the founding of its successor, the NDP, in 1961, represented a specific reorientation of Canadian social democracy that not only left the political and ideological legacies of the Great Depression era behind, but also established a more central role for labour unions in the party. The intent of the CCF elders and Canadian Labour Congress leaders who built the NDP was to broaden social democracy's electoral appeal by presenting a more moderate and therefore "modern" face. These leaders believed it strategically important to leave the Great Depression behind as "ordinary" Canadians appeared to be entering an era of perpetual prosperity and broad-based consumption. This was an explicit adaptation to and acceptance of the mixed market economy, regulated capitalism, the declassed politics resulting from the conditions of the Cold War and a newly expanded working-class consumerism (Morton 1977; Avakumovic 1978).

The New Democratic Party program explicitly stated its support for a mixed economy managed through various advisory, planning and investment agencies. It declared itself "the party of full employment" and proposed to achieve this goal through a "guaranteed employment act to ensure everyone a job as a 'social right'" (Whitehorn 1992: 53). In addition, public planning and investment agencies were proposed to promote steady economic growth and full employment without inflation. Taxation policy would divert funds from private to public investment, redistribute the national income on a fairer basis and help to regulate the pace of economic activity. Corporate taxes would be increased, while lower-income groups were promised tax relief (Avakumovic 1978: 194). It was with respect to public ownership that the NDP's program differed markedly from the CCF's *Regina Manifesto*. Gone was the detailed list of industries to be nationalized and instead a general principle to expand public ownership where necessary was stated (Avakumovic 1978: 193).

The Keynesian framework began unravelling in the 1970s under the stress of "economic stagnation, inflation and a looming fiscal crisis of the state" (Carroll 2005: 12). This was a crisis for social democracy not only because its *raison d'être* — the redistributive welfare state — was increasingly unsustainable, but also its theoretical guide — Keynesianism — did not apply to the emerging new economic reality (Kitschelt 1994: 3; Upchurch et al. 2009). Former federal NDP research director Jim Laxer criticized the party for being "locked in the 1950s and 1960s" through its adherence to "a Keynesian formula long after it had ceased to be a useful guide to analysis and policy" (Laxer 1984: 2, 5). For Laxer, the problem was that the NDP did not understand how fundamental the changes in the Canadian economy through the 1970s and 1980s had been. The NDP's fidelity to Keynesianism, and more specifically a focus on consumption rather than production, meant that the party "often appeared to be the last defenders of an economic system that is in decline — demanding that it live up to its former greatness" (Laxer 1984: 2). With its Keynesian compass increasingly unreliable and lacking an alternative understanding of the capitalist political economy, the party would drift. Rather than challenge the ascendance of neoliberalism, it would instead seek a détente.

In the early 1980s, the nation-state-centred political compromises of the mid-twentieth century gave way to a qualitatively different capitalism. Specifically, the period of Keynesian compromise running from 1945 to the mid-1970s was characterized by strong rates of economic growth, increasing real purchasing power for workers and the expansion of welfare state provision (Dumenil and Levy 2005: 9). Moreover, the state provided the public policy framework to ensure economic stability and mitigate the worst effects of market failure (Shields and Evans 1998: 14–16). Through the 1970s, this model unravelled while growth rates fell, exposure to international competition intensified, and unemployment and inflation rose simultaneously. Indeed, the average annual growth rate fell from 4.8 percent in the 1950s and 1960s to 3.2 percent in the 1970s and 1980s. Consequently, the state entered into a fiscal crisis as revenues declined and demand for social programs grew (Skidelsky 2009: 116, 126).

Historically, social democracy has always engaged in a reconsideration of program and strategy in the face of electoral defeats (Gamble and Wright 1999: 2). However, each successive adaptation has entailed an explicit rejection of a class-based politics, a firmer embrace of the prevailing system of power and an acceptance of the inequality that accompanies it (Przeworksi 1985; Panitch and Leys 1997; Moschonas 2002). This process has been intensified by social democracy's engagement with neoliberalism, which quickly became the dominant policy response to these changed economic circumstances. Since the 1980s, social democratic parties everywhere have acknowledged "the necessity of adapting to international markets and the austerity policies capital has demanded, arguing mainly their own superior technical capacity to develop and administer the neoliberal policies that will match market imperatives" (Piven 1992: 18). Consequently, post-war social democratic commitments to affording workers with greater social, economic and workplace rights were displaced by a much greater interest in competitiveness and capital accumulation (Motta and Bailey 2007; Schulman 2009).

Through the 1990s, both the federal and provincial levels of the NDP incrementally abandoned long-standing commitments to public ownership, redistributive social policies and the right of workers to organize and be covered by a range of social protections (Glyn 2001; Carroll and Ratner 2005). This marks a discernable second refoundation of the party's ideological orientation. Here the foundations were strengthened for a social democracy that did more than consolidate the explicitly "liberal" and post-class political orientation that had shaped the origins of the NDP. Along with their social democratic counterparts in advanced capitalist countries, New Democrats "began to incorporate neoliberal policies into their programs and rule as neoliberals in power" (Albo 2009: 119).

THE NDP IN GOVERNMENT: THE PROVINCIAL EXPERIENCE

What a party does with government and the resources it can command is revealing. In Canada, there has been over thirty years of experience with social democratic governments at the provincial level that allows us to see the evolution of the party's orientation through the transition from Keynesian to neoliberal capitalism. In the 1970s, the NDP ran governments in three western provinces, and these followed rather classic social democratic approaches such as a broadening of the welfare state, passing labour-friendly laws and using the state as an instrument for economic development. The NDP has also achieved electoral success in Ontario and Nova Scotia. However, the experience with five NDP governments elected since 1990 strongly suggests that the historic ideological and policy interest in working-class concerns in general, and those of organized labour in particular, have diminished to such an extent that the NDP in government is little more than an expression of pragmatic public management. Long-serving NDP governments have not taken advantage of consecutive legislative majorities to enact anti-strike breaker legislation, and all have been obsessed with balanced budget fiscal orthodoxy at the expense of more redistributional measures (Pilon et al. 2011: 27). In the following, brief overviews of the NDP in power are presented.

Saskatchewan

With the provincial general election of 1944, Saskatchewan became the first province to elect the CCF to government. A number of pioneering reforms were initiated, including North America's first government-financed hospitalization program, a program that created the foundations for more comprehensive medicare; two weeks' paid vacation; a maximum forty-four-hour work week; collective bargaining for public servants; the highest minimum wage in Canada; and the creation of new Crown corporations to assist with the province's economic development (Avakumovic 1978: 174–75). The CCF remained in power until its defeat in 1964. Subsequent NDP governments through the 1970s continued a policy of employing the state for development purposes. Premier Allan Blakeney led the province from 1971 to 1982. During those years the role of the government expanded. Higher taxation on resources, joint ventures involving both government and business, as well as a significant role for Crown corporations served to increase resource royalties received by the government (Warnock 2004: 366; Blakeney 2008).

Defeated in 1982, the NDP led by Roy Romanow returned to government in 1991. Rather than using the powers of the provincial government to promote social and economic development, the Romanow years would be characterized by fiscal conservatism and support for privatization. Elimination of the $5.2 billion provincial debt and returning the province's public finances to balance stood at the centre of the platform. Once in government, the first budget signalled this would certainly be a form of social democracy different from that of the 1970s. Rather than roll back the privatizations and regressive tax policies of the previous Progressive Conservative (PC) government, the NDP continued the policy of lowering taxes and royalties on the resource sector. As a consequence, government revenues were insufficient to support both a balanced budget and new investments in social programs. Hospital closures ensued, the education budget was reduced, and social assistance rates were capped at their 1982 levels. There was also little interest in improving protection for workers. Romanow did not hesitate to legislate striking nurses back to work in 1999, and what had been one of the highest minimum wage rates in the country was allowed to fall to one of the lowest (Warnock 2004: 369–70, 373).

The ascent of a much more market-oriented approach to economic policy was clear. The policy shift was significant as a regime of tax incentives and deregulation intended to "make the province and its policies more attractive to investors" was put in place (Phillips 1998: 46). The economic development minister was unequivocal in stating the objective was to ensure business was "treated a little easier" than it had been by previous NDP governments (*Globe and Mail* November 4, 1992; Yeates 2001: 60). The privatization agenda continued and remaining government equity in the Potash Corporation of Saskatchewan, Sask Oil and several other Crown corporations was sold and foreign ownership rules established by the previous PC government were removed (Warnock 2004: 371). Resource royalties were lowered from 27 to 17 percent. The resulting loss of revenue ensured the government did not possess the fiscal capacity to improve or expand public services (Weir 2004: 4–5, 10).

Lorne Calvert replaced Romanow as party leader and premier in 2001, but this did not mark a change in direction. In an effort to stop the right-wing Saskatchewan Party from winning power, Calvert "implemented the entire

Saskatchewan Party pro-business economic program" (Conway 2009). The NDP's defeat in 2007 led to another leadership contest, where Dwain Lingenfelter, the vice-president of a Calgary-based oil company, succeeded Calvert. Lingenfelter was the only leadership candidate who did not support introducing anti-scab legislation (Mandryk 2009: B7). The NDP was trounced in the 2011 election campaign that followed. Lingenfelter lost his own seat to the Saskatchewan Party and promptly resigned as leader.

Manitoba

Manitoba was the second province to elect a social democratic government, led by Ed Schreyer from 1969 to 1977. Schreyer's government introduced several important reforms including comprehensive pharmaceutical insurance for seniors, universal not-for-profit nursing home care, a minimum income program targeted to the working poor and an unprecedented "equal pay for equal work" provision in labour law to end gender-based pay discrimination (Bernard 1991: 145). However, as with Blakeney, Schreyer's support for Trudeau's anti-inflation wage controls program engendered a sharp rebuke from labour.

Eight years of NDP government galvanized the Manitoba business community behind the Progressive Conservative Party, led by Sterling Lyon. Lyon was an unrepentant neoconservative and in Canadian terms somewhat ahead of his time. In particular, his government reduced spending on popular social programs and in doing so engendered a political backlash where the PC government was broadly seen to be "hostile to the aspirations of ordinary people" (Chorney and Hansen 1985: 11). For the NDP, the actions of the PC government pushed explicitly class-based issues to the fore in Manitoba. In the ensuing general election of 1981, the NDP, now led by Howard Pawley, modelled their policy agenda on Blakeney's government in neighbouring Saskatchewan. Public ownership was put forward as a means of promoting economic development and to position the provincial government as a "resource entrepreneur" (Netherton 1992: 194). Indeed, upon winning the election and returning to government, the NDP established a new Crown corporation, ManOil, modelled on the Saskatchewan Oil and Gas Corporation, as well as several other resource development corporations mandated to develop the province's north (Wesley 2006: 10). At the same time, the Pawley government was explicit that "it would not seek to strike out on radical paths of either nationalization or of large-scale public spending" (Chorney and Hansen 1985: 12). In addition, the Pawley government implemented significant reforms in labour law, including new regulations preventing the use of strikebreakers, establishing a legal right for striking workers to be reinstated at the conclusion of a strike, pay equity legislation, legislated rights to paternity leave and improved mass layoff notification (Panitch and Swartz 2003: 115).

In 1986, the NDP was narrowly re-elected. Ongoing provincial government deficits and debt became a political issue and the Pawley government turned to a program of public expenditure restraint (Netherton 1992: 198). The NDP's defeat in 1988 marked a historic watershed where the last modestly Keynesian social democratic government in Canada came to an end (Netherton 2001: 222).

As in the case of Saskatchewan, a rather different NDP would be constructed over the next decade.

Under the leadership of Gary Doer, the party returned to government in 1999 and soon made a clear break with the policies of previous NDP governments (*Winnipeg Free Press* November 16, 1997; December 16, 1998). Despite three consecutive election victories, the Manitoba NDP did not challenge the interests of capital. In this respect, one left-wing critic observed, "even within the limits of a social democratic framework, the Doer government is hamstrung by its choice to accept the neoliberal economic regime it inherited from the far-right Tory government" it had replaced (Gonick 2003: 5). The political strategy entailed an economic policy largely consistent with the interests of capital and avoided forcing those interests to mobilize against the government (Gonick 2007: 12).

Through a policy of tax reduction, the Doer government reduced revenues by $800 million, thus squeezing the fiscal capacity of the province and, in turn, undermining support for public services. Into its third consecutive majority, the NDP continued a freeze on social assistance rates initiated by the former PC government in 1995. The result was an effective 35 percent reduction in income support for the poorest Manitobans (MacKinnon and Black 2008: 1). Balanced budget legislation, another legacy of the former PC government, was retained. This legislation prohibited running a deficit and further required that any increase in taxation must be approved in a plebiscite. Labour law changes made under the PCs were largely left intact when Manitoba's business community mobilized against a mere suggestion that the NDP would review them (Gonick 2003: 5; and 2007: 12).

In 2009, Doer was appointed by Conservative Prime Minister Stephen Harper as Canada's ambassador to the United States, and in the subsequent leadership race finance minister Greg Selinger became leader. As a minister, Selinger cultivated a centrist approach entailing tax cuts but approving new spending in health and education (*Toronto Star* October 18, 2009). During the leadership contest, Selinger refused to support introducing anti-scab legislation despite the convention support he had from prominent union leaders (*Winnipeg Free Press* October 17, 2009). Critics argue that Selinger's leadership signals the continuation of neoliberal policies and that, for the left, working for change from within the NDP is a losing battle (Webb 2009).

British Columbia

The 1972 provincial election in BC saw the electoral coalition that had kept Social Credit in power since 1952 fracture, resulting in an NDP majority government, led by Dave Barrett, based on 39.5 percent of the popular vote (Howlett and Brownsey 1992: 279). The British Columbia Petroleum Corporation was established as a government monopoly but with a limited responsibility for the marketing of natural gas and oil. As such, it was a tepid intervention compared to those of the Blakeney government in Saskatchewan. The Insurance Corporation of British Columbia was created, bringing auto insurance into public ownership. In other areas of fiscal and economic policy, the Mineral Royalties Act was introduced, allocating a larger share of mining companies' windfall profits for government purposes and imposing regulations to better manage the extraction of natural resources. In terms of redistributive social policy, the NDP established an income security program for the disabled and seniors; a pharmacare program providing a subsidy for prescription drugs; significantly improved social assistance rates; and increased support for public housing (Sigurdson 1997: 322). Bargaining rights were extended to British Columbia's government workers for the first time and a new Labour Code was adopted (Howlett and Brownsey 1992: 280; Sigurdson 1997: 323). While BC unions were largely pleased with the government, by 1975 tensions grew as the government intervened in several strikes by passing back-to-work legislation (Howlett and Brownsey 1992: 280; Sigurdson 1997: 324). The 1975 election saw the Liberal and Conservative vote collapse and re-coalesce around Social Credit to defeat the NDP.

In 1991, Mike Harcourt led the BC NDP in a victorious election. From the outset, the tenor of the NDP government was one of "appeasing the business sector, avoiding radical departures from the status quo and, above all, appearing moderate" (Cohen 1994: 151). The strategy of moderation, intended to broaden the electoral base beyond its traditional allies in the labour movement, included recruiting candidates who did not possess the standard NDP candidate résumé steeped in labour or social movement struggles. Candidates with "business and management experience were enticed to join the party, attracted both by the prospect of holding office and by the opportunity to work with Harcourt, himself an ideologically moderate and business-friendly NDPer" (Sigurdson 1997: 325–6). From a policy perspective, the party platform was explicitly pro-market, but this was tempered by the inclusion of commitments to increase the minimum wage, set higher corporate taxes, improve severance and layoff legislation, and increase spending on health and education. But even such modest proposals were qualified by an overarching commitment that public expenditures would be constrained by the central objective of balancing the budget (Sigurdson 1997: 327).

Harcourt did deliver on a number of commitments to the party's traditional base. The new Labour Code provided an anti-scab provision; another provision allowing for secondary boycotts; mandatory first contract arbitration; and public sector workers, both in the core public service and in health care, won substantial wage increases, job security and a role in decision-making, thus making a substantive contribution to a limited form of workplace democracy (Sigurdson 1997: 329). High-income and corporate taxes were increased in the first several years of the government but, as in Ontario, the policy focus was increasingly upon improving BC's competitiveness.

Overall, the policy direction consisted of a very modest redistributional aspect but the priority was the focus on fiscal constraint leading towards a balanced budget. Consequently, even while spending on the key social policy areas of health and education increased in absolute terms, it actually declined in per capita terms (Sigurdson 1997: 329). More positively, the Harcourt government created or strengthened new ministries for Women's Equality and Aboriginal

Affairs to give voice at the centre of government to these important constituencies. But this too can, in part, be understood as an element of the BC NDP's efforts to consolidate political support for its increasingly centrist program as class-based demands for redistribution were simply too expensive in the context of public austerity and, perhaps as important, risked mobilizing capital behind one electoral vehicle.

Harcourt was replaced by Glen Clark as party leader and premier in 1996. Substantively, little distinguished Clark from Harcourt. In this respect, it was observed, "Clark may have talked tough on class, but some of his policies… were hardly radical" (Schmidt 2000: 30). The Clark era began with an income tax cut of 1 percent for all British Columbians, regardless of income, and a general freeze on all other taxes. To protect health and education expenditures, the Clark government reduced spending in other parts of the public sector by eliminating 2,200 public service jobs; dismantling three ministries and two Crown corporations; introducing a public service wage freeze; tightening social assistance eligibility criteria; and reducing overall per capita public expenditures by 2.2 percent (British Columbia, Ministry of Finance 1996).

The enduring theme through the premierships of both Clark and his successor Ujjal Dosanjh (who went on to become a federal Liberal MP) is one of public sector austerity. Deregulation, deficit reduction and tax cuts were the means by which a "positive business climate" would be constructed in British Columbia (British Columbia, Ministry of Finance 1998). Ironically, the Balanced Budget Act was introduced in 2000, ironic in that BC's previous Social Credit government had been the first to introduce such legislation in Canada and, upon returning to government in 1991, the NDP repealed it (Phillips 1997: 686).

The 2001 provincial election left the NDP with only two seats. Carole James became leader and continued her predecessors' relationship-building with business. James thus earned accolades from the BC section of the Canadian Federation of Independent Business for "go[ing] out on a limb to court business interests… promis[ing] they would be looked after under an NDP administration" (Annis 2009), and refusing to roll back tax cuts implemented by the right-wing Campbell government (Smith 2010).

Ontario

In 1990, then New Democrat Bob Rae led the party to a historic victory and became Ontario's first NDP premier. Within a year of the election, Ontario's budget deficit had grown to $9.7 billion (Ontario, Ministry of Finance 1991: 3). A government that had initially embarked upon a broadly Keynesian approach to combating the recession turned to a policy of fiscal restraint. But even in its first year, as emphasized in the Speech from the Throne, competitiveness concerns contributed to an interest in labour-business partnerships (Ontario, Legislative Assembly 1990, Nov. 20). Such partnerships would serve to support adjustment to globalization by "promoting human capital development through increased emphasis on training, and orchestrating partnership between business, labour and government to pursue competitiveness" (McBride 1995: 75). Whereas the corporatism of social democratic Keynesianism was designed to negotiate tradeoffs between full employment and inflation through an expansion of the range of public goods and services, neo-corporatism became a mechanism for aligning labour to the interests of business.

Unable to withstand the pressures created by the economic slump, the NDP shifted toward public sector austerity. The ensuing Social Contract Act (1993) was unprecedented both in the abrogation of collective bargaining rights and in the spending cuts sought. Despite its "mixture of post-Keynesian rhetoric and proposals designed to elicit union consent," the NDP government was single-mindedly focused on public expenditure cuts (McBride 1995: 78).

In response to the Social Contract Act, the Ontario Federation of Labour (OFL) convention passed a resolution calling on its affiliated unions to break their ties to the party. A bloc of public sector unions and the Canadian Auto Workers (CAW) did move to disaffiliate. However, another bloc, composed of private sector unions with longstanding formal ties to the party, ignored the resolution and instead called for organized labour's continued support of the NDP.

These divisions over labour's political strategy in the 1995 provincial election contributed to the Rae government's crushing defeat. The election of the right-wing and anti-union Harris Progressive Conservatives forced organized labour to rethink its exclusive reliance on electoralism as their political strategy. This opened the door to an unprecedented embrace of extra-parliamentary activism within the ranks of organized labour. The Days of Action, a series of local general strikes, allied labour with a wide range of social justice movements in an extra-parliamentary resistance to the Harris government's aggressive attacks on social programs and workers' rights (Reshef and Rastin 2003: 133–52). Under the weight of internal divisions over political strategy, the OFL eventually abandoned these extra-parliamentary tactics and renewed its relationship with the NDP. However, the CAW, several of the teachers' unions, the Ontario Public Service Employees Union, the Ontario Nurses' Association and the building trades refused to return to the NDP fold and instead opted to form the Ontario Election Network (OEN) as a vehicle supporting strategic voting in the 1999 election (Pilon et al. 2011: 25; Savage, this volume). Effectively, the OEN marked the re-emergence of a Liberal-Labour alliance that was sustained through subsequent provincial elections in 2003, 2007 and 2011. Ontario's labour movement continues to be deeply divided over its approach to electoral politics.

Nova Scotia

In the 2009 provincial election, Nova Scotia's NDP made history by forming government for the first time. As Larry Savage has noted, "while most provincial sections of the NDP are lambasted by left-wing critics for selling out social democratic principles *after* forming government, the Nova Scotia NDP seemed to jettison its social democratic policy prescriptions *prior* to forming government" (Savage 2010: 20). The party's election platform was a sparse two-page document consisting of several modest commitments. These included the creation of 2,200 jobs; a 50 percent rebate on the provincial sales tax on new homes; a commitment to reduce emergency room wait-times; removal of the 8 percent harmonized sales tax (HST) on electricity consumption; rural roads upgrades; and an expansion of seniors' homecare. All of this would fit within a program of public expenditure constraint. Shortly after assuming government, an NDP audit of public finances predictably found these to be in worse shape than previously thought. Politically this served to dampen the expectations of the NDP's base of social movement and union activists by presenting a "cupboards are bare" excuse not to pursue more substantive reforms (Haiven 2009: 6). Not a word in the platform dealt with traditional social democratic concerns of equality and redistribution (Steele 2009; Fodor 2009: 7). The platform's modesty compelled the mainstream media to characterize the Nova Scotia NDP not as a party seeking serious reforms but rather one "focused on tweaking government" (*Chronicle Herald* May 16, 2009).

The government's fiscal policy focused on deficit busting and austerity. The regressive HST was increased by 2 percentage points and provincial income tax rates were cut for those earning between $93,000 and $150,000. But perhaps the most revealing initiative was the de-indexing of the public service defined benefit pension plan and the introduction of a five-year public sector wage control program that constrained increases to 1.25 percent (*Globe and Mail* April 7, 2010). If the pension fund is not fully funded at the end of that time frame, indexing by any measure would be eliminated. In short, it took an NDP government to declare war on public sector pensions. Through his actions, Premier Darrell Dexter expressed his view that the party "not be shackled by the past" and should "embrace a wider set of values" (Foot 2009).

THE FEDERAL NDP: PLAYING CENTRE

Although never having held the reins of government, the federal NDP reflects trends similar to those of its provincial counterparts. The "make the rich pay" rhetoric typical of the 1970s, replete with nods to public ownership and class-based policy prescriptions, has been replaced by an ideology that sees viable social programs as dependent on a well-functioning market economy (Ivison 2010). Jack Layton won the federal NDP leadership in 2003 "by promising to be practical," which he did with alacrity. The result was that the "ideological uncertainty of the NDP [was] heightened" under his leadership (Walkom 2011). According to James Laxer, under Layton's leadership, the party "moved a long way from any real critical stance about the present economic system and a formal commitment to changing it…. People say right now 'what does the NDP stand for?' It is hard to distinguish between them and the Liberals" (quoted in Ivison 2010).

The 2011 election platform was hardly a clarion call for fundamental change. Key proposals called for the hiring of more medical professionals; reducing the cost of prescription drugs; cutting taxes on small business; tax incentives for small- and medium-sized firms to hire more workers; raising the corporate tax rate to 19.5 percent (but ensuring it would not be higher than the lowest U.S. corporate tax rate); capping credit card rates; and strengthening public pensions

(NDP 2011). A host of other commitments dealing with climate change, public transit and housing strategies served to distinguish the NDP substantively from the Harper Conservatives but, while sensible, had little to do with redistribution of resources and real power. Indeed the platform confirmed the NDP's turn to fiscal conservatism in rejecting deficit financing, a staple of Keynesian economics. One analyst said of the NDP's platform: "Like centrist political parties around the world, they have increasingly abandoned addressing social inequality… for an embrace of markets and small business…. The NDP platform is so utterly conventional… it can hardly raise much in the way of political concerns" (Albo 2011). Notwithstanding the modest increase in public spending suggested, the 2011 platform expressed continuity with the neoliberal policy framework that has been at the core of the Canadian state since the Chrétien and Martin Liberal governments in the 1990s.

One of the more revealing episodes in the 2011 election was Layton's retreat from a comment he made suggesting that the Bank of Canada should keep interest rates low. When confronted with the charge that an NDP government would undermine the autonomy of the central bank, Layton said: "we would not have the government interfering with monetary policy because the arms-length relationship has worked well for Canada" (Payton 2011). If any institution embodies the interests of capital it is the central bank. To declare its strategic policy role as strictly off-limits to political contestation is to accede a great deal of power to the ruling class. Of course, the NDP was sensitive to any attack on its credibility as an economic manager and the relinquishing of any suggestion that monetary policy be subjected to some more broad-based political accountability or community interest was a consistent response. And more so, Layton repeat-edly referred to the "prudent" fiscal records of NDP governments in the western provinces discussed above to prove the NDP's suitability to govern (Geddes 2011).

THE UNION-PARTY NEXUS: UNDERSTANDING THE ENDURING ATTACHMENT

The foregoing profiles the neoliberal shift apparent in every provincial NDP government elected since 1990 and suggests that organized labour, and by ex-tension the working class, have gained little from the NDP in government save perhaps being spared a more aggressive right-wing assault. In provinces where the NDP faces a single right-wing competitor, organized labour fears the right-wing party more than the NDP's fair-weather friendship. In Ontario, where the NDP has traditionally been the third party, organized labour is split, with some supporting the NDP and another coalition of unions providing de facto support to the Liberals as the only party capable of thwarting a Conservative return to government (Savage, this volume).

Despite these variations in party-union relations, the dominant configuration is that of an enduring union-party linkage. The NDP was intended from the outset to "integrate labour and the party more fully" (Archer and Whitehorn 1993: 1). The NDP's diminishing interest in the redistributive policies most associated with social democracy as well as its willingness in government to legislate striking workers back to work and override collective bargaining rights has created tensions between the party and its union allies. But interestingly, no enduring rupture has occurred. Why this is the case is an important question given that the NDP, whether in government or not, is increasingly less programmatically committed to a redistribution of economic and political resources to the working class generally and trade unions specifically. Explaining the enduring fidelity of a significant part of the union movement to the NDP is therefore an important task. The most obvious explanation can be found in the deeply rooted and structured relationship between organized labour and the party.

The relationship, no matter how strained at times, was forged in a long process where both union and party leaders learned how to work together. For unions, the NDP provides a vehicle through which they can actually or potentially influence public policy in favour of workers and their unions (Pilon et al. 2011: 32–4). There is no other party in the country where unions are allocated seats in its decision-making structures. The various structures of the NDP, such as the convention, federal/provincial council, the party executive committee and even meetings of the parliamentary caucus in some cases, allow for organized labour's representation. The key enabling mechanism is the ability for unions to directly affiliate to the party and thus gain an entitlement to such representation (Jansen and Young 2009: 669).

Some have contended that changes in federal election financing law in 2004 and 2006, which limited and then prohibited both money and in-kind contributions from unions to the NDP, would have presented both the NDP and affiliated unions an opportune moment to terminate their long-standing relationship (Jansen and Young 2009: 657; Pilon et al. 2011: 22). But this did not happen. Instead the organizational ties between the unions and the party remained largely intact. Labour representation in key structures was retained (Jansen and Young 2009: 669). The dramatic loss of union resources directed towards the party did not seemingly affect organized labour's influence within the federal party. This is perhaps not surprising, as earlier changes to election financing laws in British Columbia in the 1960s, Québec in 1977 and Manitoba in 2000 also did not result in any fundamental changes in the relationship of organized labour to either the NDP or the Parti Québecois (PQ) (Pilon et al. 2011: 22). While the relationship between labour and the NDP has not undergone any significant lasting transformations, the content of the wider social democratic project has witnessed important change.

CONCLUSION

The content of the social democratic project — both the political objective and the means of its achievement — has obviously been transformed. The politics of the centre-left now express little more than a more moderate and pragmatic management of neoliberalism. Just as social democracy in the post-war decades offered a more redistributive policy and practice in managing capitalism, it now offers a program assisting in the adjustment of workers to the requirements of a global, hyper-competitive market economy. It is for now a party of "progressive competitiveness" (Albo 1994) whose central political objective is to assist workers in adapting to neoliberalism through a policy of skills development, training and knowledge. The politics of class compromise long ago gave way to the politics of class co-optation best captured by the discourse of partnership. Competition between nations and regions requires such. Canada's NDP offers no opposition or alternative to this perspective.

The political practice of NDP provincial governments through the 1990s to the present demonstrates the success of neoliberalism in disorganizing the working class's unions and political parties (Albo 2009: 121). It is now virtually impossible to discern what sets an NDP government apart from those led by traditional parties of business. Notwithstanding historic and contemporary support for the Bloc Québecois, PQ and Liberals within sections of the labour movement, key Canadian unions remain politically engaged with "their" party. However, this can be understood as both a product of the pervasiveness of what now passes for social democratic ideology within the labour movement and a recognition that the NDP offers organized labour a place within the party's decision-making apparatus. Even so, whether in government or opposition, exactly what influence labour has on the political strategy of the party is unclear. Perhaps the culture of defensiveness has become so deeply entrenched within the official labour movement it is not possible to even consider alternatives.

4. QUÉBEC LABOUR: DAYS OF GLORY OR THE SAME OLD STORY?

Peter Graefe

The Québec labour movement is often presented in an uncritically positive light elsewhere in Canada. Given Québec's relatively high level of union density and its labour movement's mobilizations in symbolic work stoppages against anti-union state actions, there is appeal for both the bean counter concerned with organizational maintenance and the romantic embracing big shows of protest. More substantively, labour's political action in Québec has played an important role in advancing social and labour rights for Canada as a whole, whether in extending collective bargaining rights to public sector employees in the 1960s or in introducing anti-scab legislation and universal child care in the 1970s and 1990s.

The strategies used by the Québec labour movement, both electorally and in policy discussions, differ from those employed by the Canadian labour movement, whether federally or in the provinces. Despite their perceived success, these strategies remain largely untried in the other provinces. In a situation where labour outside Québec is casting around for new political strategies, the existence of an alternative tradition of political participation is worth studying. Québec's national character and class dynamics are distinct from those in the surrounding Canadian and American societies and provided a unique series of political possibilities for Québec labour. However, there is enough commonality in terms of the legislative framework around unions, the bureaucratic structures of policy-making and electoral and legislative institutions to draw more lessons than has been the case.

These lessons from the Québec experience are more complicated than either the bean counter or the romantic might think, for strategies that worked in the past no longer provide the same leverage on political outcomes. Specifically, the Québec labour movement faces the twin challenges of articulating a new vision of economic and social development for Québec that could guide political strategizing, and of engaging politics where the character of the national question has taken on a different form with fewer tangible pay-offs. There have been days of glory, but increasingly Québec's experience looks like the same old story experienced by the broader Canadian labour movement.

Following a brief overview of the Québec labour movement's political trajectory over the past century, this chapter concentrates on labour movement strategy since the early 1990s. This timeframe allows us to gauge how the Québec labour movement has positioned itself in politics as the first radical thrust of neoliberal restructuring gave way to a longer process of recrafting Québec's social and economic institutions within a broader neoliberal framework. It also allows for an analysis of how the labour movement's last coherent political strategy, based on progressive competitiveness and partnerships, played out across the 1990s and has since lapsed into forms of *ad hoc* political engagement. Indeed, this brings Québec closer to the other provinces on the labour and politics front than it has been in some time. As in other provinces, there is much to decry in the lack of overall political vision, but also some hope for renewal.

THE DISTINCT POLITICAL TRAJECTORY OF QUÉBEC UNIONS

It is easy to forget how central language is to politics, particularly if you speak English in Canada or the United States. But if you belong to a community that speaks a different language from the majority, you are placed in a unique situation. First, you are at a disadvantage when you participate in the realm of the majority, because you have to interact in a second language and presumably a different culture, and thus you bear all the costs of translation. Second, the language and culture of the majority may not fit perfectly with how your own group sees and understands the world, raising the question of whether it makes more sense to do more of your politics within the space of your minority so that your unique ways of seeing are not swamped by the majority. These abstract propositions, which find some resonance in the historical experience of the Québec labour movement, are central to explaining the development of Québec labour's distinct political flavour.

In addition to linguistic differences, we observe a variety of factors that make the Québec labour movement unique. First, the labour movement in Québec consists of multiple labour federations with the legitimacy and power to speak in the name of affiliated unions when engaging the state and the public. Québec labour federations hold distinct political traditions and are engaged in complex relations of both cooperation and competition with one another. In terms of partisan politics, none of the federations in Québec has had a formal relationship with a political party in the way that unions in other provinces have affiliated with the NDP (Evans, this volume). Nationalism provides a unique political environment, enabling a different set of claims and perhaps legitimating more collectivist claims in the name of the national interest. Finally, as will be discussed more fully below, the institutionalization of state-society relationships in the past thirty years has created a series of partnership institutions that allow Québec labour to influence policy independent of the party in power on a more ongoing basis than in most other provinces. Before turning to contemporary labour politics in Québec, a brief historical overview is in order.

From the very earliest attempts at organization, engagement with unionists from the United States and Canada has been paired with demands for some autonomy to deal with issues of language and culture. The Catholic Church exploited this demand for autonomy in the 1920s with the creation of a Catholic labour federation, the Confédération des travailleurs catholiques du Canada (CTCC). Tied to a conception of essential harmony between the interests of labour and employers and of the Church as the primary locus of societal organization, the CTCC was skeptical of political participation and especially partisan politics (Rouillard 2008).

This confessional and non-partisan position contrasted with competing labour federations linked to American- and Canadian-based unions with stronger traditions of social democratic political activity. However, this parallel tradition never led to the creation of a provincial labour party. While the industrial unions linked with the Canadian Congress of Labour came to support the Co-operative Commonwealth Federation in federal elections, this party enjoyed no electoral traction in Québec and indeed little appreciation for the province's political vocabulary (Savage 2008a: 154–6).

Through the post-war years of Premier Maurice Duplessis (1944–1959), a staunch defender of free enterprise and fierce opponent of union rights and the welfare state, the necessity of labour's political participation became clearer for several reasons. These included concerns about the formal recognition of unions and the legitimacy of strikes arising from such conflicts as the Asbestos strike of 1949 and the Murdochville copper strike in 1956 (Rouillard 2008). But they also included broader concerns about the need for economic planning to counter unemployment and further development of the welfare state to catch up with neighbouring jurisdictions. During these years, the unions were largely social democratic in outlook. While supportive of maintaining Québec's autonomy within Canada, they were also wary of strong shows of nationalism, especially since the leading nationalist organizations were seen as conservative and close to Duplessis (Rouillard 2008). Over this period, the Catholic unions remained non-partisan, but became more militant in negotiations and strikes, as well as more political in the sense of making policy demands and doing member education. The CTCC shed its confessional character to become the Confédération des syndicats nationaux (CSN) in 1960. The unions associated with the international unions likewise strengthened their participation in partisan politics, particularly following the merger of the craft and industrial unions into the Fédération des travailleurs et travailleuses du Québec (FTQ) in 1957, parallel to the formation of the AFL-CIO in the United States and the Canadian Labour Congress in Canada in 1955 and 1956 (McRoberts 1988: 102–5).

While the FTQ had been involved in the launch of the NDP in Québec in 1960–61, its enthusiasm and investment quickly dissipated for two reasons. First, the NDP lacked roots in Québec, and did poorly in federal elections throughout the 1960s, never electing a member (Oliver and Taylor 1991). Second, the rapid rise of nationalism in the 1960s complicated the political situation, as the left divided over the issue of Québec's relationship to Canada. This delayed and ultimately prevented the formation of a provincial NDP party for electoral purposes on the one hand, while alienating the unions from active participation in the federal NDP on the other. The FTQ ultimately followed a number of key labour leaders and organizers, as well as a large share of its membership, into support for the sovereignist Parti Québécois (PQ) (Piotte 2001; Rouillard 2011). This support was never formalized with linkages that would create accountability between the party and the FTQ, but rather took the form of regularly endorsing the PQ in provincial election campaigns, and having high-level union officials sit, in an individual capacity, on PQ executive bodies so as to bring the union perspective into the party.

The other major labour federation, the CSN, remained a step further removed from electoral politics as a result of its pre-history as a Catholic federation. Partly as a result of not endorsing political parties, let alone creating a labour party, it invested more heavily in community politics. In the late 1960s, the CSN developed the idea of creating a "second front" outside of collective bargaining, which consisted of trying to provide some unified direction to community and social movement political action. The idea that this might ultimately create a worker's party nevertheless remained undeveloped outside of Montreal, where the attempt to mount a municipal party, the Front d'action politique, was undermined by state repression during the 1970 October Crisis. The CSN's community focus was coupled with a vigorous critique of the state as a locale of exploitation, and a tendency to not engage the state except in an oppositional logic. Its membership, meanwhile, flocked to the Parti Québécois, even as the CSN leadership condemned it as a bourgeois party. Caught between a leadership interested in a workers' party to the left of the PQ, and a membership already at home with the PQ, the CSN had every reason to maintain its traditional political neutrality (Güntzel 2000: 379; Rouillard 2011).

Through the 1960s and 1970s, the Québec unions entertained an evolving relationship with the new nationalism coming out of the post-1960 Quiet Revolution.[1] While hesitant about the conservative cast of earlier French Canadian nationalisms, there was much in the post-1960 state building for unions to embrace, be it improvements in the social wage or the extension of collective bargaining rights to public employees. These openings brought them to concentrate their demands on the Québec state, and to support the extension of Québec's space of constitutional autonomy (Rouillard 2008). The unions also got entangled in the radicalism of the Quiet Revolution, with the major federations releasing manifestos in the early 1970s containing strong and open critiques of capitalism in Québec and calling for changes of a socialist nature. Here the national question and class came together, as Anglophone control of the commanding heights of the economy meant that economic democratization would be both socialist and nationalist. As such, the radicalization of political perspectives should not be dismissed as a fad or the result of the unions' capture by a cadre of radicals, but as reflecting a deeper questioning of relations of domination. However, the speed with which the FTQ moved from its manifesto into support for the PQ, and the limited grassroots support in the CSN and the Centrale de l'enseignement du Québec (CEQ, the teachers' federation) for moving towards socialism, should prevent us from romanticizing this period. While radicalism ebbed through the 1970s, nationalism grew stronger. The federations were divided on supporting Québec sovereignty in the 1980 referendum, with the FTQ strongly in support, the CSN supporting sovereignty but refusing to campaign and the CEQ refusing to intervene. By 1990, they were all loyal supporters of sovereignty and in the 1995 referendum they supported the Yes side without conditions (Güntzel 2000; Savage 2008b).

OLD HABITS AND NEW STRATEGIES OF ENGAGEMENT

In the early 1990s, Carla Lipsig-Mummé (1991) assessed the Québec labour movement's political and economic strategies and discerned a strategic paralysis of trying the same strategies even if they no longer worked, but also some evidence of strategic innovations. The largest union federation, the FTQ, seemed content to continue its direct involvement in mainstream political activity with open support for, but no formalized ties to, the PQ. In light of the significant gains in labour legislation and the social wage in the PQ's first term in office (1976–1981), this strategy seemed effective. The PQ portrayed itself as favourably disposed to workers and appeared to deliver when in office. In its second mandate (1981–1985), which coincided with the recession of the early 1980s, this strategy became problematic as the government attempted to balance its budget through cutting wages and removing collective bargaining rights for public sector employees. The PQ's concern with maintaining a positive relationship with the FTQ nevertheless pushed it to provide some compensation for these reversals, developing some rudimentary stakeholder participation in economic decision-making.

Whereas the FTQ embraced opportunities to participate in multi-stakeholder forums and consultations, the CSN largely adopted the strategy of the *chaise vide* (empty chair), refusing to participate in such processes consistent with its oppositional stance. While such an outside strategy might have had appeal during the social upheavals in the early 1970s, by the early 1980s it provided little leverage.

Through the 1980s and into the 1990s, the FTQ and the CSN nevertheless revamped their strategies. The FTQ had a head start: from the late 1970s they pushed for social democratic adjustment strategies based on peak-level concertation between business, labour and government. The inspiration here was the corporatism or tripartism practised in certain European countries like Sweden. Through the 1970s, important macroeconomic policy decisions concerning wage settlements, social programs and employment initiatives were decided by negotiations between union federations, employers' federations and the government, rather than by the government alone. While Québec lacked the organization of business and labour interests to allow such a form of corporatism, the FTQ believed that job creation and economic restructuring could be made into positive-sum processes through institutions that allowed social actors to dialogue and pursue concerted action. The FTQ thus pushed the construction of partnership institutions that would enable ongoing participation in policy development. Yet this begged the question of how this would work for labour in the absence of the strong union-party linkages that had made tripartism work in Scandinavia. The CSN arrived at a similar position in its own attempt to think through a development strategy appropriate for an economic context marked by trade and investment liberalization (Graefe 2007).

For both the FTQ and the CSN, their renewed strategies came out of attempts to confront employer pressures around work reorganization and concessions in private sector workplaces facing heavy international competition. Simply opposing such demands risked having plants close or relocate to other jurisdictions. The answer was to negotiate change in order to protect jobs and to ensure the adoption of worker-friendly forms of flexibility. This was packaged as "social partnership," where both unions and employers worked together for competitiveness and job preservation, and where negotiated change provided positive-sum solutions.

At the level of Québec as a whole, a similar argument was made for how partnership and stakeholder representation could serve both economic competitiveness and the interest of workers. This would hold at the level of large-scale macroeconomic and industrial policy and in specific areas such as training and health and safety. While there might be features of this program specific to Québec, the overall vision was one shared with many other labour movements of the period. It was often labelled "progressive competitiveness" as it sought means to ally economic competitiveness with the achievement of labour movement objectives (Albo 1994).

Counter-intuitively, the strategy of concertation made a virtue out of the loose ties between the unions and the political parties. As a senior political advisor for the FTQ explained in a February 2005 interview with the author, his experience with government-business-union partnerships in other provinces was that the government party never trusted the unions because they felt any confidential information would immediately end up in the hands of the NDP. Given the lack of direct union-party relationships in Québec, such experiments could rely on a stronger basis of trust.

The strategy of concertation found fertile ground in the early 1990s because the provincial Liberal government (1985–1994) needed to mobilize a more inclusive sense of the political community given the constitutional battles with the rest of Canada on the one hand and the PQ on the other. As a result, it too was inspired by the idea of social partnerships for competitiveness, and experimented by creating a training and labour force development board run jointly by labour and business representatives. It also launched a cluster-based industrial policy that encouraged firms in a given sector to meet to define shared solutions to common problems such as training, research and development, infrastructure deficits and export promotion.

Meanwhile, in attempting to define an inclusive political economy for an independent Québec, the PQ developed similar themes. The idea of positive-sum compromises between business and labour was golden for the PQ: it always had to struggle between reassuring the business community that Québec sovereignty would not be costly and promising citizens that sovereignty would strengthen social justice and not simply mean changing the colour of the flag. It therefore embraced the idea that participation in a global free trade context could benefit all, provided that appropriate adjustment strategies were instituted. Such policies would fully mobilize all skills and capacities, allowing Québec to compete on the higher end and thereby maintain higher wages and social spending. The PQ likewise touted concertation by social partners in order to identify positive-sum solutions (Parti Québécois 1994). The PQ thereby wrapped its nationalism around progressive competitiveness, creating what could be termed "competitive nationalism" (Graefe 2007).

When the PQ swept to power in 1994, it embraced progressive competitiveness for its economic rationale and especially its portrayal of the nation as a consensual community above the divisions of class. This was dangerous for the labour movement in that "national consensus" would be placed above unions' class demands when the two conflicted. But it also held the possibility that, in seeking to mobilize an inclusive movement in favour of sovereignty, a PQ government would remain open and responsive to labour movement demands.

PARTNERSHIPS: FROM LEVER TO BRAKE

The sense of unions having some pull within the PQ government had some material foundation. The government introduced a payroll tax on large firms to fund workplace-training initiatives and created local economic development boards where labour had a seat. Most notably, while neighbouring Ontario was resolving its budgetary deficit by slashing programs and confronting its public employees, Québec adopted quieter and more consensual arrangements. This difference was symbolized by convening two multi-stakeholder summits in 1996 to find ways of reducing the provincial deficit without raising taxes while also reducing unemployment. In return for agreeing to balanced budgets, the unions leveraged assurances that the government would work on job creation, as well as specific promises of spending on community development and of adopting a family policy including a low-cost universal daycare system.

These strategies nevertheless lost momentum as the decade progressed. Consistent with critiques of progressive competitiveness, employers used the emphasis on consensus to head off policies they opposed, especially in the absence of sustained labour movement mobilization and education. The 1996 summits became a symbol of this critique. The employers' associations after all managed to impose the parameters, such as zero deficit and no tax increases, in advance of the summit. While the unions could point to some wins, including community development and family policy, this came at the cost of accepting a significant downsizing of the public sector as part of the zero deficit pledge, even as employers washed their hands of firm commitments to creating jobs. Similarly, when Labour Code reform came onto the agenda in 2000, including the possibility of changing certification rules to make organizing in the private service sector easier and limiting union avoidance strategies like contracting out, partnerships again became a brake. The government insisted that changes had to account for the competitive pressures of the North American environment, and had to achieve a broad consensus. Employers could therefore use the language of partnership as a veto, refusing to accept changes due to their presumed impact on competitiveness (Charest 2004; Graefe 2007).

While the results of partnership were decidedly mixed and took the lustre off progressive competitiveness, the union leadership held to the strategy. Criticisms of the approach within the labour movement did mount, and left-leaning union activists experimented more seriously with small parties to the left of the PQ such as the Rassemblement pour une alternative politique and the Union des forces progressistes. These parties fused a number of left sectarian parties, but enjoyed an additional lift in harnessing activists from the anti-globalization movement, which peaked in organizing the mass protest against the Summit of the Americas in Québec City in 2001. However, the union leadership's bigger problem was the PQ government's waning interest in such approaches, again pointing to the problem of pursuing a strategy of concertation without the union-party linkages found in the countries inspiring this strategy. In its final mandate (1998–2003), the PQ government continued to promote social consensus but its thinking about development moved away from the idea of social partnerships for competitiveness. Certain reforms, such as those related to regional health boards, indeed rolled back previous gains in stakeholder representation.

To replace partnerships, the PQ looked to European debates about knowledge-based economies, and the idea that one could balance liberalized, market-driven development with smart social investments in social cohesion and human capital. Rather than encouraging concerted action at the heart of economic organization, the idea was to free up private sector entrepreneurial energies while proactively working to create the skills, trust and inclusion that would enable that entrepreneurialism to take more productive forms. The PQ government therefore looked favourably at innovations in child policies and benefits, and poverty reduction strategies precisely because they fit policy thinking about competitiveness in the knowledge-based economy. The union movement applauded these moves as improvements to the social wage. Nevertheless, they came from a strategy of playing to a broader middle-class electorate, rather than of responding to a labour agenda of building a union voice into development decisions (Graefe 2011).

THE NEW MILLENNIUM: STUCK IN THE 1990S?

By the last days of the PQ government, the labour movement was cruising on a strategy with declining political influence and showing little effort to either renew it or rethink the forms of political engagement that could bring it into being. However, one needs to be careful with this critique. As René Charest (2009) has argued, it is too simplistic to adopt *ad hominem* attacks on the Québec unions as bureaucratized organizations, completely co-opted to the status quo, willing to sacrifice their members' interests in order to maintain their privileged status as a social partner. Instead, he suggests we consider how unions are contradictory organizations that have been caught in a capitalist offensive to roll back wages, benefits and other protections in a context where capitalism itself is hegemonic. In such a context, and like other social movements, unions must choose between a strategy of open confrontation, which may wreck the movement, or of trying to conserve resources and capacities for a more propitious time.

The critique here is more modest: it is that the labour federations have not developed an encompassing vision of development that might inform a political strategy beyond reactive responses to individual issues. In addition, they have not reassessed their methods of engaging the political in light of a new conjuncture. Even a strategy of conserving resources requires ongoing capacity building so that those resources can be effectively deployed in new contexts.

The election of Jean Charest's Liberal government in 2003 represented a more radical attempt to change labour's political standing. In an open letter to Québecers in October 2003, Charest publicly decried the "corporatism" of the Québec model as a plum protecting privileged insiders and as an impediment to necessary changes in public policy (Boismenu et al. 2004; Laforest 2007). His government accelerated the introduction of private sector management practices in the public sector, stepped up the use of public-private partnerships for major infrastructure projects and rolled back concertation in local and regional health boards and local economic development councils. In terms of the social wage, the government flirted with winding up the anti-poverty strategy and raising daycare fees in proportion to parental incomes, although there was a successful push-back in both cases.

In the realm of labour relations and labour policy, there were two major challenges in the Charest government's first year. The first was a change in the Labour Code's provisions concerning subcontracting, making it easier to shed union accreditations when contracting out work. The second was a unilateral reorganization of union representation in the health sector, coupled with laws preventing the unionization of certain workers in the family and intermediary health resources sector (Charest 2009: 178). These moves elicited a strong mobilization across the union federations, from blockades of bridges, roads and ports in December 2003 to the mobilization of 100,000 people in the 2004 Montreal May Day parade. Yet when the possibility of a general strike arose in early 2004, the FTQ pulled back due to its reservations of challenging the supremacy of parliamentary power and this momentum was lost.

This withdrawal could easily be presented as a betrayal, but the mobilizations of 2004, extended with the university and college student strike of February-March 2005, helped tame the Charest government's neoliberal zeal. Nevertheless, this did not exclude further anti-labour legislation, such as Bill 43, passed in December 2005, which imposed collective agreements on public sector employees and withdrew their right to strike until 2010. Despite this attack on freedom of association, the response was muted and centred on punishing the Charest Liberals in the 2007 provincial election (Charest 2009).

The use of an electoral strategy of punishing the Liberals, without building the alternative with which to beat them, has not produced tangible gains. The Liberals were re-elected as a minority government in 2007, but the PQ suffered a severe setback as the neoliberal Action démocratique du Québec (ADQ) party surged to become official opposition. The minority Liberal government proved fairly centrist in its politics, shying away from increasing user fees for public services or openly privatizing health care, even as it received reports promoting such changes. Re-elected with a majority in 2008, and faced with the global financial crisis, the Liberals returned to a right-wing platform of public sector austerity to quickly balance the budget. The austerity budget of 2010, including health premiums and user charges, elicited strong public mobilization despite a restrained union response. They were keeping their powder dry for negotiating public sector contracts, hoping to avoid a repetition of the Bill 43 debacle. This did lead to a negotiated contract, albeit in a situation of limited mobilization of the membership, resulting in a financial settlement that failed to reverse declining real wages in the public sector (Mandel 2010).

It is worth noting where push-backs succeeded. Unions were important in forcing the government to follow through with anti-poverty initiatives (Noël 2004) and to preserve the province's universal, low-cost child-care system (Jenson 2009). In the latter case, union success came from marrying workplace action in the form of one-day strikes with a strong mobilization of parents.

These are classic forms of "outsider" politics, of mobilizing the power of protest to shape state policies, whether against worker-unfriendly initiatives or in favour of friendly ones. The unions have also continued to play a central role in institutions of concertation, albeit with mixed results. The unions have maintained their place in labour market training and health and safety (Haddow and Klassen 2005). The replacement of local development and employment boards by councils of local elected officials has reduced union presence at that level, although less institutionalized participation in these continues in some localities (FTQ 2006). But whereas these were once sites for developing positive-sum practices supporting Québec's version of progressive competitiveness, they are now at best supports for maintaining the status quo. Without a shared proactive vision for these spaces of dialogue, concertation becomes a tactical tool for preventing the erosion of previous gains. Just as it prevented the ratcheting up of labour market protections in the later years of the PQ, so it may slow the ratcheting down (Haddow and Klassen 2005).

The relationship with partisan politics therefore remains a stumbling block for the Québec labour movement. The provincial Liberal party has changed significantly since the late 1980s. Given the decline of sovereignist mobilization, there is no need to present itself as including all sectors of society. Additionally, after twenty-five years of neoliberal statecraft, it is less vulnerable to charges of breaking with the institutions and relationships inherited from the Quiet

Revolution, and faces economic actors who have retooled their outlooks and strategies around the neoliberal normal. And unlike the late 1980s, it is faced with a credible right-wing challenger in the steadfastly neoliberal ADQ, and it can draw on the intellectual resources of right-wing think tanks and networks that did not exist twenty years ago.

Turning to the PQ, the unions are faced with the problem that in this morose period for the national project, the project itself is being redefined in ways that are sometimes inconsistent with union aspirations. The close if sometimes strained relationship between labour and the PQ has become increasingly distant. The lesson PQ strategists drew from their 1994–2003 government was that pleasing groups to the left was self-defeating, as they ultimately always ended up demanding more from the government rather than helping it get re-elected (Facal 2003). Linkages to the unions limited the PQ's free hand in crafting policies aimed at the middle class.

After the PQ's defeat in 2003, party leader Bernard Landry allowed the formation of a club within the party called the Syndicalistes et progressistes pour un Québec Libre (SPQLibre). This club assembled some high profile former union leaders, both to create a stronger social democratic voice within the PQ, and to maintain political unity among sovereignists by improving the PQ's credibility as a progressive party ("La création…" 2004).

However, in March 2010, the PQ's national executive decided to expel the SPQLibre from the party, following the latter's open criticism of several policy decisions moving the PQ away from a social democratic vision. The PQ has also upset the labour movement on numerous issues, including making it known that it found public sector salary demands to be too high and demanding budgetary austerity through the financial crisis despite the obvious ramifications for public services and employment.

This falling out with the labour movement is part of a growing conservatism within the sovereignist movement. The progressive nationalism of the 1990s was based on expanding the nationalist tent to include as many constituencies as possible so as to increase the movement's base. The nationalism of more recent years is more interested in activating the sovereignist movement's core by playing on markers of identity and belonging shared by the historic French Canadian community (Lisée 2007). The thrust of measures such as a Québec identity bill has been to partially close a previously very open definition of "the nation." But it is not surprising that a more conservative definition of "who belongs" is tied to a more conservative vision of what social transformations might result from sovereignty (Noël 2007).

This, however, raises a bigger question of how to engage with nationalist politics, one that recently reared its head at the federal level. After the surprise NDP sweep and the collapse of the sovereignist Bloc Québecois (BQ) in the 2011 federal election, the labour movement is suddenly in an odd circumstance. The formation of the BQ in 1990 provided a handy solution to the previous absence of a progressive nationalist party on the federal stage. While the BQ was not formally a social democratic party, it could be relied upon to take stances similar to the NDP, albeit while demanding greater provincial autonomy in social policy. Its leader from 1996 to 2011 was Gilles Duceppe, a former CSN staff representative. When the NDP lost official party status from 1993–1997, the BQ became the consistent voice defending unemployment insurance and collective bargaining rights. The sudden collapse of the BQ is thus alarming on two fronts. First, the FTQ endorsed the BQ and it was clear that the CSN and CSQ were very comfortable giving their own tacit support, yet the party ended up losing party status, removing the channels of influence that the unions had cultivated within federal politics. While the new contingent of NDP MPs included union activists and even the former president of the Public Service Alliance of Canada (Nycole Turmel, who became interim leader after the untimely death of Jack Layton), the relationship between the top union leadership and the federal NDP could best be described as polite but strained. The second cause for alarm is what the BQ's collapse signals for the progressive nationalism of the 1990s, which the BQ continued to incarnate far more than the PQ. The loss of the BQ provides another warning sign that a renewed vision of development, including its engagement with nationalist politics, is long past due in the labour movement.

There are nevertheless signs of hope for renewal on a variety of fronts. Most substantively, there have been party-building experiments involving fringes of the labour movement. The Conseil central de Montréal métropolitain of the CSN had a hand in sustaining Québec solidaire (QS), an amalgamation of left-wing splinter parties, certain elements of the anti-globalization movement and elements of the women's and the community sector (Dufour 2009). This party has had limited success at the polls, but did manage to elect one of its charismatic spokespeople, Amir Khadir, to the National Assembly in 2008. In Montreal, a new civic left-wing party, Projet Montréal (PM), emerged as a viable third party, benefitting from public disgust with the taint of corruption on the municipal scene. This party, which marries ecological and urban quality-of-life issues, drew in part on Montreal-based union networks (Latendresse 2009).

However, union participation has not been central in either QS or PM, and stronger union involvement has tended to follow political success rather than precede it. They remain weak as either vehicles for promoting a particular labour agenda or organizations with accountability to the labour movement. Rather, they have usefully injected some renewed thinking about social democratic, ecological and occasionally socialist alternatives to contemporary neoliberal capitalism, both in terms of public policies and of democratizing the political process.

CONCLUSION

The strengthening of independent left-wing currents in Québec does not automatically create a stronger left. If it fails to build organizations that can effectively compete for state power, force existing organizations to change their programs and strategy or change the terms of social conversations about what is possible, there may not be a lot to praise in it. One possible interpretation of the QS experience is that it has made clear to the PQ that it can ignore the left and only lose a marginal level of electoral support. While it has given the left a clear voice in the National Assembly with Amir Khadir and provided space to articulate a left platform, the net effect, given the current electoral system and the institutional strength of the PQ as a party machine, is to lessen progressive influence over partisan politics. In other words, the concentration of left energies in the electorally weak QS frees the PQ from commitments to the labour movement, even if these commitments increasingly took the form of a gentler neoliberalism. On the other hand, the PQ's influence over the left has eroded the latter's ability to set out an independent agenda to which the PQ must make overtures. As such, the promise of QS is to set some political objectives for moving development in different directions, rather than concentrating energies in the PQ simply to slow the onward creep of neoliberalism.

Absent attempts to rebuild power within the PQ, or to make a headlong investment in building QS, one is left with a status quo that looks increasingly like that in other provinces: one finds a union movement with a weak pull on its members' political loyalties, increasingly informal ties with a party of the centre-left and a largely reactive outsider strategy of lobbying and demonstrating.

That is not to say that Québec labour simply becomes the same as elsewhere. There are institutionalized legacies in terms of relations to the state and to parties that will not simply evaporate. The fact that the PQ never had a formally institutionalized link to the FTQ gives the character of party-union relations a different flavour than labour-NDP linkages elsewhere. The success in obtaining representation within partnership institutions also bequeaths the opportunity for Québec unions to use insider strategies. And while the national question provides less access to the state than was to be had in the 1970s to the 1990s, it does create a different structure of possibilities for political action. To be sure, the lessons of Québec labour in politics remain more historical than current, and tied mostly to questions of walking the tightrope of social partnership and of nationalism.

It is here that the absence of a larger strategic vision becomes a major limitation. Deciding which institutions and relationships from the past are worth protecting and which ones need to be reinvented necessarily relies on a vision of what the labour movement wishes to achieve. However, beyond the need to protect past gains in social policy and industrial relations, and largely reactive calls for industrial policy and adjustment strategies for troubled industries, there is no compelling overarching vision for Québec's contemporary labour movement.

Note

1. The Quiet Revolution is usually dated from the victory of the Liberal Party in the 1960 Québec general election. This marked a period of major change in Québec society, including the rapid development of the state, the recentring of nationalism from an ethnic and cultural "French-Canadian" basis to a more political and territorial "Québec" basis and a greater openness to exploring new ideas and lifestyles (McRoberts 1988).

5. ORGANIZED LABOUR AND THE POLITICS OF STRATEGIC VOTING

Larry Savage

In April 2006, the Canadian Auto Workers (CAW) voted to sever its longstanding relationship with the New Democratic Party (NDP). The split was significant because the CAW had been a key player in the creation and development of the NDP and was an important source of funding for the party. Although the union-party relationship had been unravelling for some time amid a global crisis in social democratic politics, the immediate cause of the breakup centred around the union's strategic voting campaign, which included a high profile endorsement of then Liberal Prime Minister Paul Martin at a CAW convention during the 2006 federal election campaign. While the CAW's decision to promote strategic voting in an effort to block the election of Conservative candidates was a new tactic for the union in the realm of federal politics, the CAW and other unions had been employing this strategy in Ontario provincial elections since 1999.

The increasing popularity of strategic voting among some unions represents a threat to the longstanding political alliance between the labour movement and the NDP and is gradually changing the landscape of party-union relations in Canada. This chapter situates growing union support for strategic voting within the broader context of neoliberal restructuring and argues that, while different union activists promote strategic voting for different reasons, some unions traditionally loyal to the NDP have primarily come to embrace the tactic as a method of shielding themselves from the worst excesses of neoliberal public policy. However, the chapter further argues that union-sponsored strategic voting campaigns in Ontario and at the federal level have not only failed to block the election of Conservative governments, but also undermined the labour movement's ability to act as an independent political force.

Blais, Nadeau, Gidengil and Nevitte define a strategic vote as "a vote for a party (candidate) that is not the preferred one, motivated by the intention to affect the outcome of the election" and explain that "this definition drives home the idea that a strategic vote is based on a combination of preferences and of expectations about the outcome of the election and on the belief that one's vote may be decisive" (Blais et al. 2001: 343). In the case of organized labour, contemporary strategic voting campaigns are employed in order to prevent vote splitting among non-Conservative parties. The strategy has often been misunderstood as a "vote Liberal" strategy (Reshef and Ratsin 2003: 175). However, labour's approach has been more complex. Although strategic voting typically takes the form of voting Liberal in ridings where the Conservatives are competitive and the New Democrats are weak, unions that have adopted strategic voting policies also advocate voting NDP in ridings where the party is competitive. Nevertheless, strategic voting has been both a product and a cause of labour-party friction. While some unions have complained that the NDP's historically poor levels of public support have rendered it a weak vehicle for progressive political change, the NDP has accused these same unions of contributing to the party's poor electoral performance through their continued, unprincipled and short-sighted promotion of strategic voting.

While many on the social democratic left have criticized union strategic voting campaigns for bolstering right-wing parties at the expense of the NDP, Canada's social democratic party does bear some of the responsibility for the emergence of such campaigns. Indeed, the experience of NDP governments in Ontario and other provinces has clearly demonstrated social democracy's inability to present a credible alternative to the new "common sense" of neoliberal restructuring (Evans, this volume). In the words of Greg Albo (2002: 47), "we get neoliberalism even when we elect social democratic governments." Faced with political dead ends in every electoral direction, it is hardly surprising that some unions, lacking both the capacity and the will to think or act politically outside the realm of party politics, have opted for the pragmatic instrumentalism of strategic voting in an attempt to mitigate the damage done to them by neoliberalism.

SOCIAL DEMOCRATIC CRISIS AND NEOLIBERAL ASCENDENCY

Former CAW President Buzz Hargrove has described the traditional social democratic party-union relationship as follows: "the traditional union approach to the NDP, in English Canada at least, had been to view the party as an extension of trade union goals and values into the political arena, and for many years leaders from the shop floor to the union executive offices were NDP party agitators. Political action committees in the CAW and elsewhere were considered branches of the NDP" (Hargrove 2009a: 116). However, the relationship between the labour movement and the NDP has undergone significant change over the course of the last few decades.

Beginning in the mid-1970s, the Keynesian post-war compromise progressively unravelled as the traditional social democratic policy prescriptions of full employment, public ownership and welfare state expansion began to lose favour. Beginning with the Trudeau government's 1975 wage and price controls, federal and provincial governments of every political stripe (including NDP provincial governments) led an assault on union freedoms designed to weaken the collective strength of the labour movement (Panitch and Swartz 2003: 25–44). This new era of neoliberal restructuring was also characterized by employers' more aggressive stance in collective bargaining, massive job losses in manufacturing, an increase in outsourcing and privatization of public services, restrictions on the right to strike, growing use of back-to-work legislation and the introduction of continental free trade.

Initially, organized labour responded to this challenge by maintaining its electoral alliance with the NDP. However, neoliberal globalization, and the new right-wing economic imperatives that accompanied it, forced social democratic parties like the NDP to reassess their own political projects. Ill-equipped to resist the ascendancy of neoliberalism, the NDP shifted to the political centre, particularly in provinces where it formed government, jettisoning key components of the social democratic project of full employment and welfare state expansion (Evans, this volume). In Ontario, the NDP government's decision to address the province's growing debt and deficit by adopting the "Social Contract" — a fiscal austerity program which rolled back wages and suspended collective bargaining rights in the public sector — was met with fierce opposition by public sector unions and had repercussions for union-party relations across the country (Panitch and Swartz 2003: 172–81; Hargrove 2009a: 120). The NDP's significant political and economic shift to the right, which in effect stripped many unions of their traditional political clout in the electoral arena, alienated some segments of the labour movement from the party and led to a re-evaluation of the traditional link between organized labour and NDP.

These party-union divisions have, in turn, led to a significant fragmentation in the electoral approach of unions in English Canada. While some unions — in particular the Communications, Energy & Paperworkers Union of Canada (CEP), the United Steelworkers (USW), the United Food and Commercial Workers Union (UFCW) and the International Association of Machinists and Aerospace Workers — have remained steadfast allies of the NDP, others, most notably the CAW, teachers' unions and building and construction trades unions, have parted company with the party in key regions and entered into strategic alliances with the Liberal Party (and its provincial counterparts) on a case-by-case basis. Admittedly, the latter group of unions (with the exception of the CAW) never did share close ties to the NDP, but their overt and very public support for the Liberals, especially in recent years, has unquestionably called into question the strength of the NDP's contemporary link to the labour movement.

ORGANIZED LABOUR AND STRATEGIC VOTING IN ONTARIO

After the Ontario NDP government's defeat in June 1995, the province's labour movement, momentarily disillusioned with electoral politics, sought to build alliances with progressive community organizations and social movements as part of a broad-based coalition in opposition to the neoliberal policies of the new Conservative government of Mike Harris. Between 1995 and 1998, organized labour and its allies launched a series of rotating general strikes across the province known as the Days of Action. The one- to two-day protests were designed to strengthen links between social movements, cause economic disruption and highlight the damage being done by the Harris government (Reshef and Rastin 2003: 133). The CAW and many of the public sector unions which had resisted the NDP government's Social Contract took a leadership role in organizing the Days of Action and opposed the Ontario Federation of Labour's (OFL) controversial decision to jettison the rotating protests in favour of reconciliation with the NDP in the run-up to the 1999 provincial election.

The OFL's decision to pull the plug on the Days of Action had the effect of pushing unions back into the electoral arena. While most industrial unions and the Canadian Union of Public Employees' (CUPE) Ontario Division decided to give the NDP (now led by Howard Hampton, who had replaced Bob Rae in 1996) a second chance, another group of unions, cognizant of the fact that the party was performing poorly in public opinion polls, came together under the umbrella of the Ontario Election Network (OEN) in an effort to promote strategic voting (Tanguay 2002: 145–64; Reshef and Rastin 2003: 166–82). The Network, made up of teachers' unions, the CAW, the Ontario Public Service Employees' Union (OPSEU), the Ontario Nurses' Association and the building trades unions, took the position that defeating the Harris Conservatives was labour's first electoral priority. The OEN targeted twenty-six key swing ridings, endorsing fourteen Liberals and twelve NDP candidates. In the words of OPSEU President Leah Casselman, "strategic voting means voting NDP in strong NDP ridings, voting Liberal in strong Liberal ridings, and defeating Tories in both" (OPSEU 1999).

However, participation in the OEN was highly divisive within the labour movement, especially among unions traditionally loyal to the NDP. While there was virtual unanimity within the labour movement on the need to defeat the Tories, union activists were sharply divided over strategy. While many longtime NDP activists in the labour movement were prepared to forgive the party for its past sins, others complained that the NDP would simply split the "non-right" vote and allow the Harris Tories to be re-elected (CAW 1998; Reshef and Rastin 2003: 168). There were also divisions within the OEN, with unions like OPSEU deciding to endorse candidates above and beyond the list agreed upon by the organization (OPSEU 1999).

The OEN's effectiveness has been the subject of some debate. Tanguay (2002: 15) has argued that the OEN campaign had a modest effect compared to strategic voting efforts in past electoral contests in Canada and helped to defeat key cabinet ministers in the process. Monahan and Barber have both argued that the OEN's success was limited to the City of Toronto (Barber 1999; Reshef and Rastin 2003: 175). Reshef and Rastin, on balance, considered the campaign a failure. They summarized the factors which hurt the OEN's strategic voting effort as follows:

> The unions did not communicate their strategy and their choices well enough; they often did not endorse the same candidate in a given riding; they only targeted their members and did not inform the general public of the strategy; they waited to release their official list of en-

dorsed candidates until only days before the election; NDP supporters were "touchy" about backing Liberals and could not detach themselves from their long-established partisan allegiance; the non-endorsed candidates refused to give up without a fight, causing the Liberal and NDP candidates to battle each other directly; and finally, many voters (and media reporters) interpreted "strategic voting" to mean "vote Liberal." (Reshef and Rastin 2003: 175)

It should also be noted that the OEN's attempt to mobilize non-Conservative voters around specific candidates in specific ridings prompted a strong counter-mobilization by a well-funded and organizationally sophisticated Conservative Party. Whereas the OEN and its successors relied primarily on a press conference and a comparatively small advertising budget to deliver its message, Conservative candidates were able to mount counter-offensives by rallying the Conservative base on the doorstep. While the Conservative campaign had the organizational wherewithal to identify and motivate its base to head to the polls on election day, strategic voting organizations lacked the capacity, the resources and the voter identification tools needed to compete on the ground. Because strategic voting requires a large number of voters to abandon their sincere preferences in an effort to coalesce around a single candidate, and because there existed divisions among parties, unions and even strategic voting organizations over which candidates were best positioned to defeat the Conservative candidate, identifying and convincing potential supporters to follow through on voting strategically was a very difficult task.

In the end, as a purely instrumental intervention, the Network's electoral strategy ultimately failed when the Conservatives were returned to power with an even larger share of the popular vote than in 1995 and the NDP lost official party status. More importantly, the strategic voting approach demonstrated that the labour movement could not speak with a unified voice, let alone in its own voice, on the question of labour's political vision.

Relations between the NDP and some of the OEN unions went from bad to worse in the aftermath of the 1999 election campaign. Ontario NDP leader Howard Hampton accused the CAW of having handed Harris a second term through its promotion of strategic voting. The party even flirted with the idea of revoking Hargrove's membership, but in the end decided against it (Reshef and Rastin 2003: 178). Contrary to Hampton's assertion that the CAW was partly to blame for his party's poor performance, Hargrove was unwilling to admit that strategic voting was the cause of the NDP's woes, noting that a riding-by-riding analysis demonstrated that in every riding where the party lost, it was by at least 10 percent (CAW 1999). In fact, the party had come a very close second in several ridings, but in general, Hargrove had a point: the Ontario NDP would almost certainly have lost seats, with or without the full backing of the CAW, and it may have lost even more seats without the union's help in those ridings targeted by the OEN. Unrepentant, Hargrove suggested that if just a few thousand more voters had bought into the strategic voting campaign, the Liberals would have defeated the Tories and "we would have had a minority government with our party [the NDP] in control of the agenda" (CAW 1999).

Disillusioned with the NDP at both the provincial and federal levels, the CAW launched an internal task force in late 1999 to reconsider its engagement with electoral politics. Despite the best intentions of some of its framers, who saw the project as a way of laying the foundation for a more radical working-class politics, in May 2002, the *Task Force on Working Class Politics in the 21st Century* unveiled a number of recommendations which, in effect, legitimized the CAW leadership's call for strategic voting and set the stage for a closer relationship to the Liberal Party in subsequent election campaigns (CAW 2002: 16–7).

In the run-up to the 2003 provincial election, under the banner of the newly formed Working Families Coalition[1] (WFC), the CAW joined forces with building trades and teachers' unions to launch a major third-party anti-Conservative advertising blitz (Walchuk 2010: 38). The provincial Conservatives, now under the leadership of Ernie Eves, were defeated in the ensuing election, replaced by Dalton McGuinty's Liberals, who promptly reversed some (but by no means most) of the previous government's anti-union labour law reforms. Despite the Liberal government's tepid approach to serving the interests of organized labour, the WFC redoubled its efforts in the 2007 provincial election, making explicit its desire to see the Liberals re-elected, much to the dismay of unions with traditional ties to the NDP (Savage 2010: 16; Walchuk 2010: 38–41).

It is unclear what impact third-party advertising campaigns like those of the WFC have had on Ontario provincial elections, but the experience of the WFC has underscored that such union interventions have consistently been unable to provide organized labour with an alternate agenda or vision for labour, even when Conservative parties fail to form government. This is because strategic voting is premised on fear: specifically the fear that Conservative governments will repeal hard-won union rights and freedoms. However, proponents of strategic voting within the ranks of labour rarely dwell on how stopping a Conservative victory will tangibly benefit unions in terms of existing public policy. Indeed, the Ontario Liberals, before and after their election victories in 2003 and 2007, remained, like the Conservatives, opposed to anti-scab legislation, collective bargaining rights for agricultural workers and card-based union certification outside of the building and construction trades. In other words, strategic voting is primarily a defensive strategy and not one which builds labour's proactive political influence.

ORGANIZED LABOUR AND STRATEGIC VOTING IN FEDERAL POLITICS

While the roots of contemporary union strategic voting campaigns are to be found in Ontario, the practice has also spilled over into federal politics. When the popularity of Paul Martin's Liberal minority government began to sink in late 2005 amid daily revelations that the government was deeply implicated in a controversial sponsorship scandal, NDP MPs worked with the opposition Conservatives and Bloc Québécois (BQ) to force an election. According to CAW economist Jim Stanford, the NDP's decision to withdraw support for the minority government "was made over the explicit objection of many progressive movements… Aboriginal leaders, urban advocates, the child-care constituency, and labour leaders (not just Buzz Hargrove, but others — including Canadian Labour Congress President Ken Georgetti) all wanted the election later, not sooner" (CAW 2006c). Stanford argued that the Martin minority government, despite its shortcomings, had showed an unprecedented openness to progressive movements and that an election which resulted in a Conservative victory would represent a step backwards for organized labour and its allies.

Less than two weeks into the 2006 federal election campaign, CAW leader Buzz Hargrove dropped a political bombshell by embracing the prime minister at a CAW meeting in December 2005 and presenting him with a CAW jacket. His actions infuriated NDP activists (both inside and outside the union), who, despite their tense relationship with the CAW, had never imagined Hargrove would so boldly endorse a Liberal prime minister. Martin encouraged CAW members to vote strategically, reminding them "the wrong government could put it all at risk… it matters who Canadians choose to lead the country" (CAW 2005a). On Hargrove's recommendation, CAW members overwhelmingly endorsed a strategic voting campaign aimed at "ensuring a Liberal minority with an NDP balance of power, and stopping a Conservative victory" (CAW 2005b). The resolution on strategic voting called on the union to "endorse the sitting NDP Members of Parliament, and individual NDP candidates in potentially winnable ridings" (CAW 2005b). In other ridings, the resolution called on the CAW to "not endorse any specific candidates; rather, individual voters will need to decide what best contributes to electing a Liberal minority with NDP balance of power, and stopping the Conservatives" (CAW 2005b). In effect, the CAW was calling on Canadians to vote Liberal in the vast majority of ridings across Canada.

In late January 2006, the CAW released its list of recommended candidates without much fanfare. The union endorsed forty-three NDP candidates in English Canada who were either incumbents or considered competitive.[2] In other ridings in English Canada, the CAW urged people to vote for the candidate with the best chance of defeating the Conservative candidate. The CAW's Québec section, following its tradition of autonomy, separately endorsed the entire slate of BQ candidates.

Although the CAW resolution (CAW 2005b) called for the union to "endorse the sitting NDP Members of Parliament, and individual NDP candidates in potentially winnable ridings (to be determined following consultation with our local leaders and activists)" and that "in other ridings, the CAW not endorse any specific candidates," Hargrove did not hesitate to personally endorse high profile Liberal candidates with ties to the automotive industry, like Magna executive and former Conservative leadership contestant Belinda Stronach in the riding of Newmarket-Aurora, and Toyota Canada's Assistant General Manager, Greig Mordue, running for the Liberals in Oxford. The CAW's endorsements of NDP candidates, on the other hand, went virtually unnoticed in the mainstream media.

Worried that the CAW's strategic voting campaign was sending union members the wrong message, a group of unions loyal to the federal NDP helped organize a rally in downtown Toronto on January 14, 2006, as a show of support for the party. Speakers took turns denouncing the CAW's strategy, and union activists handed out buttons which read "Buzz Off! I'm voting NDP" (Whitehorn 2006: 116). OPSEU President Leah Casselman, referring to Hargrove's very public endorsement of Prime Minister Paul Martin a month earlier at the CAW Council meeting, told the rally: "The boss does not become the friend of working people just by putting on a union jacket…. The boss is the boss is the boss" (*Toronto Star* January 15, 2006).

Despite the close identification of Hargrove with the push for strategic voting, the CAW was not the only union endorsing the tactic. It was also the preferred strategy of the Public Service Alliance of Canada (PSAC), the largest union representing the federal public service. PSAC regularly endorsed NDP, Liberal and BQ candidates in and around the national capital region, where the bulk of the union's members work and live (CBC News Online 2006). Somewhat ironically, some of the same labour leaders condemning the CAW's strategic voting campaign had long supported strategic voting in provincial politics. Casselman, for example, had been a strong proponent of strategic voting in the 1999 Ontario provincial elections.

Despite the efforts of some unions to prop up Paul Martin's minority Liberal government through strategic voting, both the effects of the sponsorship scandal and a lacklustre election campaign performance proved impossible to counter. The Liberals were replaced by a Conservative minority government, with no one opposition party holding the balance of power. Strategic voting proponents were quick to defend their approach in light of these disappointing results. Hargrove claimed that Decima Research's post-election poll and analysis of the 2006 federal election results demonstrated that the CAW's strategic voting campaign was crucial in preventing a Conservative majority. However, a closer look at the Decima results reveals a different story: that its impact on the campaign was mixed. Decima reported that 65 percent of the electorate was aware of Hargrove's call for strategic voting but in the end it made only 5 percent of voters more likely to cast ballots for Liberal or NDP candidates (Decima 2006: 4, 41). Decima further reported that 17 percent of electors (and only 15 percent of electors in Ontario) voted strategically in the 2006 federal election (Decima 2006: 8). Nationally, the CAW's strategic voting message had no impact on the intended vote of 58 percent of strategic voters. Twenty-two percent of strategic voters reported they were more likely to vote Liberal as a result of the CAW's call for strategic voting, 9 percent were more likely to vote Conservative and 9 percent were more likely to vote NDP (Decima 2006: 41).

In Ontario, strategic voting primarily benefitted the Liberals. Thirty-six percent of strategic voters cast ballots for the Liberals, 30 percent opted for the NDP, and 23 percent voted Conservative (Decima 2006: 49). However, in Québec, awareness of the CAW's strategic voting campaign drove more strategic voters to the Conservatives than to any of the other parties (Decima 2006:

41). There, 45 percent of strategic voters cast ballots for the Conservatives, 19 percent backed the BQ, 13 percent voted NDP, and just 12 percent supported the Liberals (Decima 2006: 48). Nationally, 32 percent of strategic voters cast ballots for the Conservatives, 27 percent supported the NDP, 24 percent backed the Liberals, 7 percent opted for the Green Party and 6 percent supported the BQ (Decima 2006: 21). Overall, the majority of strategic voters (58 percent) wanted a Conservative majority or minority government, while only 34 percent of strategic voters wanted a Liberal majority or minority government (Decima 2006: 17). Despite these findings, both Decima and the CAW argued that a little more strategic voting on the left would have prevented the Tories from winning a minority government. Specifically, the report identified fourteen ridings won by Conservative candidates by less than 5 percent of the vote over Liberal opponents. According to the report, a shift of roughly sixteen thousand NDP votes to the Liberals in these ridings would have resulted in a minority Liberal government (Decima 2006: 45).

In March 2006, the Ontario NDP unceremoniously booted Hargrove from the party for his continued and very public promotion of strategic voting. In response, the National Executive Board of the CAW recommended CAW locals disaffiliate from the NDP, with Hargrove arguing that "the NDP's arrogant decision says that organizations affiliated to the NDP cannot make independent decisions on political strategy. Our union cannot remain under these circumstances" (CAW 2006b). In April 2006, delegates to the CAW Council meeting endorsed the National Executive Board's call to withdraw support for the NDP. Most, although not all, locals took their cue from the resolution and disaffiliated from the party.[3]

In the 2007 Ontario provincial election campaign that soon followed, Hargrove publicly attacked the provincial NDP and endorsed the re-election of Liberal Premier Dalton McGuinty. In the same election, OPSEU endorsed an equal number of Liberals and New Democrats. The USW, CUPE, CEP, UFCW and the Service Employees International Union (SEIU) backed the New Democrats (Savage 2010: 15–6).

Despite Hargrove's retirement in 2008, his union continued to promote strategic voting. According to records filed with Elections Canada, the CAW spent $39,721.28 on a third-party national advertising campaign in support of strategic voting in the October 2008 federal election (Elections Canada 2008). The union targeted forty "slim win" ridings during the campaign where it believed strategic voting would most likely help prevent a Conservative victory (CAW 2008). The CAW directly endorsed nine NDP candidates, ten Liberal candidates, and Green Party leader Elizabeth May. In the remaining twenty slim win ridings, the union urged people to vote for the candidate with the best chance of defeating the Conservative candidate. In virtually every case, that meant voting Liberal. In addition, the CAW endorsed twenty-six "safe" NDP incumbents in English Canada and the CAW's Québec section once again endorsed the entire slate of BQ candidates in Québec.

Despite the union's effort, the Conservatives were re-elected with a strengthened minority government and the opposition parties managed very few slim wins. The Conservatives were victorious in thirty-two of the forty seats identified for strategic voting, the NDP won five contests, and the Liberals carried just three. No Conservative incumbents were defeated and the party lost only one seat it previously held. Overall, in the forty slim win ridings, the Conservatives saw a net increase of ten seats, the NDP saw a net increase of one seat (at the expense of the Liberals), the Liberals saw a net loss of twelve seats and the Greens lost their only seat. All ten of the Liberal candidates directly endorsed by the CAW were defeated by Conservatives in the 2008 federal election.

As in 2006, the CAW indirectly endorsed a number of highly questionable candidates as part of its 2008 campaign. In the BC riding of Fleetwood-Port Kells, the obvious strategic vote candidate, Liberal Brenda Locke, was a former provincial Liberal Member of Legislative Assembly (MLA) whose government had waged war against the province's labour movement. In the Manitoba riding of Winnipeg South, the obvious strategic vote candidate, Liberal John Loewen, was a former Progressive Conservative MLA. These examples shed light on one of the key problems associated with strategic voting, namely the exaggeration of differences between political parties which, for all intents and purposes, are not very different in terms of either ideology or public policy orientations.

Despite mounting evidence that its strategic voting campaigns were ineffective, the CAW continued to promote strategic voting as the key to defeating Stephen Harper's Conservative government. In the 2011 federal election, the CAW targeted fifty priority ridings that it believed would determine the outcome of the election (CAW 2011).[4] In these ridings, the CAW explicitly identified thirty-four Liberals, fifteen New Democrats and Green Party leader Elizabeth May as the union's preferred candidates. The CAW also compiled a separate list of twenty-nine additional NDP incumbent ridings where the union was supporting New Democrat candidates. The union, a strong proponent of gun control, chose not to endorse NDP incumbents who had voted in favour of a Conservative private member's bill to scrap the National Long Gun Registry. The union also declined to endorse the NDP's only Québec MP, Thomas Mulcair, in deference to the CAW's Québec section, which, once again, endorsed the entire slate of BQ candidates.

The union's low-key 2011 federal election strategic voting campaign can only be described as an unmitigated failure. In Québec, the BQ (which, in addition to the CAW's Québec section, enjoyed the support of the Québec Federation of Labour and its key affiliates) was virtually wiped out by the NDP, which captured fifty-nine of seventy-five seats in the province. In English Canada, New Democrats were elected or re-elected in all but one of the twenty-nine NDP incumbent ridings where the CAW endorsed candidates. However, in the CAW's fifty priority ridings, the union's preferred candidates only managed to win ten seats. The Tories won thirty-eight contests, the NDP carried six ridings, the Liberals were victorious in five and Elizabeth May won her BC riding for the Greens. In seven ridings, the CAW's strategically endorsed candidate actually finished in third place, thus undermining the entire logic of the union's campaign. In the BC riding of Esquimalt-Juan De Fuca, for example, the CAW endorsed the Liberal candidate, who finished in third place with just 10 percent of the total votes. The NDP managed to win the former Liberal riding by just a few hundred votes over the Conservatives. In this case, the CAW's strategic voting tactic nearly helped hand the seat to the Conservatives. To be sure, the NDP's unexpected surge in support in the second half of the federal election campaign dramatically changed the dynamic in many ridings across the country, but the CAW made no attempt to revise its strategic priorities in the face of the NDP's growing popularity. In the end, in the fifty priority ridings identified by the CAW, the Tories saw a net increase of twelve seats. The Liberals, on the other hand, witnessed a net decrease of seventeen seats. The CAW's strategic voting campaign had failed, and the Harper Conservatives had achieved their coveted majority.

CONCLUSION

By aligning themselves more closely with the Liberal Party, some unions have taken the gamble that assisting in a Conservative defeat will encourage future Liberal governments (both federally and provincially) to pass pro-labour public policy. However, there is little evidence to suggest that a closer relationship to the Liberal Party has yielded many positive results for the labour movement. While the Liberal Party is arguably more progressive than the Conservative Party or its provincial counterparts, both of these parties are quite strongly committed to neoliberalism and its key public policy components. However, desperate to hold on to its post-war gains and defend itself against the worst excesses of neoliberalism, union support for strategic voting continues to grow. This is true despite the NDP's electoral breakthrough in the 2011 federal election, wherein the party replaced the Liberals as the country's official opposition. In fact, shortly after that election, union activists from across the country ruminated about how strategic voting could now be used effectively by the NDP and the labour movement to convince Liberal voters to abandon their party in favour of the NDP in an effort to stop the Conservatives.

Support for strategic voting has always been, and continues to be, highly contested within the labour movement. Some union activists reject the strategy outright while others defend strategic voting as the only way to prevent the election of right-wing parties bent on dismantling workers' rights and the welfare state. Another group of union activists simply favour strategic voting because it serves their own short-term sectionalist interests. These contradictory motivations exist both between and within unions, thus adding another layer of complexity to union-sponsored strategic voting campaigns. However it is spun, the politics of strategic voting have had a profound impact on the internal politics of the labour movement and have helped change the face of contemporary party-union relationships in Canada. While the specific calculus for strategic voting changes, and will undoubtedly continue to change, with each election, the strategy offers very little to the labour movement over the long term.

This is not to suggest that unions ought to flock back to the NDP en masse and redouble their efforts to build the party. The NDP's electoral success in the 2011 federal election may indeed precipitate such a strategy, but given that there are few signs the party is keen to confront, let alone challenge, neoliberalism (Evans, this volume), unions ought to look beyond the NDP and the ballot box if they are truly interested in building political power for workers.

The labour movement is one of the only political forces in society that has the organizational muscle and resource capacity to organize the plethora of social movement organizations committed to resisting neoliberalism and ultimately building an alternative society. However, pursuing a transformative political strategy requires the labour leadership to think outside the narrow scope of electoral politics. It requires flexible and participatory long-term planning that will not conform to traditional electoral cycles. It requires alliance-building that is open, democratic and sustained. The emergence of a transformative political project for the labour movement would also require unions to devote more resources towards radical labour education and solidaristic political initiatives in support of social movement partners, community groups and other workers' organizations, both unionized and non-unionized. In short, unions would need to transcend their sectional interests in pursuit of a broader working-class agenda.

These prescriptions will require a significant change in the current politics of the Canadian labour movement insofar as they challenge many of the political practices and electoral frames traditionally associated with union political action. Part of the problem, as described by Gindin (2006), is that "the political choices we confront today are not real choices because we don't in fact have the political capacity to implement them and — more distressing — we haven't figured out a way of developing such capacities." This sober assessment of the Canadian labour movement's ability to adopt new ways of thinking and acting politically leads us back the specific issue of strategic voting.

When a union spends time and resources on implementing a strategic voting campaign, there is an expectation that the union will also refrain from criticizing the candidates and parties it seeks to elect. To do otherwise would undermine the logic of strategic voting and defeat the purpose of launching the campaign in the first place. This leads some unions to overlook anti-union platform planks and candidate pronouncements (like support for restrictions on the right to strike and organize, opposition to anti-scab laws and support for back-to-work initiatives) which might otherwise not sit well with the labour movement. If labour is willing to jettison or stay silent on key social and economic demands as part of a shot-gun strategic voting strategy designed to keep a right-wing party from taking or keeping power, how does labour's vision for an alternative society based on principles of social justice and economic equality ever gain a toehold in the minds of union members, let alone in the political arena? Indeed, organized labour incrementally loses the capacity and the imagination to act as a truly transformative movement every time unions embrace the uneasy cross-class alliances that underpin the politics of strategic voting. More importantly, because tactical shifts have an educative effect on the union rank-and-file, and thus help validate ideological shifts over time, union-sponsored strategic voting campaigns — whether motivated by fear, instrumentalism or a combination of both — threaten to compromise the labour movement's ability to press its own political agenda, in its own name, in future years.

Notes

1. The Working Families Coalition, widely considered a union-sponsored Liberal Party front group, was backed by the Ontario English Catholic Teachers Association, the Canadian Auto Workers, the Ontario Secondary School Teachers' Federation, the International Brotherhood of Boilermakers Local 128, the International Brotherhood of Electrical Workers, Millwrights, the International Union of Operating Engineers Local 793, the Ontario Provincial Council of Painters and Allied Trades, the Ontario Pipe Trades Council and Ironworkers Local 721.

2. The one exception was the endorsement of Niagara Falls NDP candidate Wayne Gates, a former CAW local president running in a riding where the NDP traditionally placed third.

3. CAW Local 199 in St. Catharines, Ontario, for example, chose to remain affiliated to the party. In Nova Scotia, many CAW locals remained affiliated after the Nova Scotia NDP passed a resolution in May 2006 that urged "the federal party and provincial and territorial party organizations to amend NDP constitutions to accept and respect that labour leaders and others will act in accordance with the democratic decisions made by their unions or organizations" (CAW 2006d).

4. Similarly, SEIU Local 2 developed a "swing table" which outlined what it described as the "tight races" in the 2011 federal election and asked its members to vote strategically in order to "deny a Tory majority" (SEIU Local 2 2011).

6. LABOUR AND THE POLITICS OF VOTING SYSTEM REFORM IN CANADA

Dennis Pilon

Over the past century organized labour in Canada has lobbied for and against all manner of voting system reform. Labour representatives have sometimes energetically promoted the introduction of a new voting system at the municipal, provincial and federal levels, while at other times condemned such proposals, opposed their introduction and worked for their defeat or repeal. Unravelling these shifting positions requires attention to divisions both within and outside the ranks of organized labour. These divisions often reflected struggles within the labour movement over political strategy, specifically how best to influence the state's regulation of unions, work and social life more generally. But they also reflected labour's assessment of the tactics adopted by their opponents, whether in the workplace, civil society or in government. Thus labour positions on the "right," "fair" or "most democratic" form of voting were seldom the result of an abstract evaluation of values or ideals. Instead, they were worked out with an appreciation of power, particularly the dramatic power inequalities concretely present in Canada's capitalist democracy.

The Canadian labour movement's positions on voting system change can be divided into three distinct periods: the struggle over independent political action from 1890 to 1931 (pro-reform); the "take power" strategy of 1932 to roughly 1992 (anti-reform); and the "resisting neoliberalism" phase from 1993 on (pro-reform). In the first period, organized labour struggled over just how to enter politics, either through influencing conventional parties, forming independent political parties (be they labour or socialist) or taking direct action to influence or control the political sphere (Heron 1984; Palmer 1992). Interestingly, at different times, proponents of all sides took up the mantle of voting system reform, though often for different reasons. From 1935, and particularly from 1944, a significant group in labour opted to support the Co-operative Commonwealth Federation (CCF) provincially and federally (barring Québec) and opposed any voting system reform that might weaken its electoral chances. This position was reinforced by their opponents' often sudden and zealous advocacy of voting system reforms wherever the CCF appeared close to winning power. Craft workers in the national

Trades and Labour Congress who remained partial to the Liberal Party reinforced this anti-reform sentiment. Labour's hostility to reform only began to weaken with the seemingly constant advance of neoliberal policies in the 1990s, even under allegedly labour-friendly New Democratic Party (NDP) provincial governments in BC, Saskatchewan, Manitoba and Ontario. The meltdown of NDP support in the 1993 federal election and the sagging electoral fortunes of NDP provincial sections, particularly in Ontario, opened space for activists in both labour and the party to raise the issue as a strategy to slow the neoliberal assault.

To clarify, "voting system" refers to how votes cast in an election are converted into representation. Canadians have generally used a voting system known as plurality or "first-past-the-post" in single- or multi-member ridings. This means the candidate with the most votes wins, regardless of what proportion of the vote that represents. For instance, with three evenly matched candidates, one could gain election with just 34 percent of the votes. Plurality has been defended as both stable and decisive in its workings because usually one party will gain a majority of seats. Conversely, it has been criticized as unrepresentative and unresponsive for basically the same reasons (Pilon 2007: 30–1). The two key alternatives to plurality are majority and proportional voting systems. Majority systems usually ensure that a winning candidate has secured a majority of the votes by some means. Proportional systems tend to create roughly mirror-like results between the percentages of votes cast for different parties and the percentage of seats they win. In Canada, the majority system promoted and used was the alternative vote (AV) while the traditional choice of proportional representation (PR) was the single transferable vote (STV). More recently, a mixed-member proportional (MMP) version of PR has also been promoted (Pilon 2009). The functional details of these systems are less important than the political implications that people thought might flow from their workings. As such, we will attend mostly to why people supported or opposed different systems, and what they thought they might gain or feared they might lose.

THE STRUGGLE OVER INDEPENDENT POLITICAL ACTION, 1890–1931

Late nineteenth-century Canada witnessed a rapid development of the country and its economy. Under impetus from the Conservatives' National Policy, both manufacturing and resource exploitation expanded rapidly. Unions too expanded and struggled for recognition. Though initially hostile to organized labour, both national political parties eventually saw the potential in mobilizing working-class support. The Conservatives moved first, opening up the franchise to better-off workers and passing the Trade Unions Act, which decriminalized union membership (Kealey 1995: 420–1). The Liberals went further, essentially enfranchising all white working men by 1900. By the turn of the century, skilled labour had basically become part of the national Liberal coalition along with farmers and various reformers. A number of union officials were eventually elected as "Lib-Lab" politicians (Heron 1984: 52–3; Palmer 1992: 177–8). In response to labour's efforts within the party, Wilfrid Laurier's federal Liberal government established the first Minister of Labour and passed the Industrial Disputes Investigation Act in 1905, further solidifying the state's toleration of organized labour as a semi-legitimate force in Canadian society (Kealey 1995: 423–4). Labour had established itself as a constituency worth courting and mobilizing.

Despite this attention, critics within the labour movement complained that the Liberal government too often sided with business interests when strikes occurred or labour sought policy changes. Labour's legitimacy in political terms seemed predicated on accepting whatever business and government were prepared to offer. For these critics the answer was for labour to run its own candidates and/or create an independent political party. Only then could labour use the state to change anti-labour laws or introduce pro-worker policies. This debate emerged repeatedly before the First World War, often pitting conservative craft unions and skilled workers against resource and industrial unions representing unskilled workers. Though a number of independent labour or socialist candidates ran for (and occasionally won) office before the war, labour leaders effectively resisted calls for a labour party for fear of diminishing their influence, such as it was, with federal and provincial Liberal parties (Heron 1984: 52–62; Palmer 1992: 176–86).

These debates over political action influenced early discussions over voting system reform amongst labour activists. Some of the earliest public calls for proportional voting occurred at the municipal level in Canada, precisely because the use of official political party labels was frowned upon (Anderson 1972). Labour had its earliest electoral successes at the municipal level prior to the First World War (Palmer 1992: 178–9), though its role remained controversial and opposed by business elites (Anderson 1972: 18). This nominally non-partisan setting avoided conflict with union hierarchies committed to working with the Liberals federally or provincially.

Initially, voting system reform seemed to make headway within unions as part of a larger set of social and institutional reforms touted in the late nineteenth century (Hoag and Hallett 1926). Often to their surprise, middle-class reformers found unions hospitable spaces for detailed discussions of democratic reform. As a result, some unions began promoting the issue. By 1894, the topic began appearing in a number of Canadian labour papers (*PR Review* December 1894: 62; March 1895: 94). In 1899, the Ottawa Trades and Labour Council lobbied Queen's Park to allow PR for local elections in Ontario, a sentiment echoed by the Hamilton Trades and Labour Council in 1902 (Phillips 1976: 413). Some labour bodies, such as the Toronto Trades and Labour Council, promoted PR for their internal elections as well; others, such as the BC Federation of Labour in 1913, did so to address deep divisions within their ranks (Phillips 1976: 116; *British Columbia Federationist*, February 21 and 28, 1913).

Still, prior to the First World War, neither independent labour politics nor voting system reform had made much progress. Yet on the eve of war in 1914, during a debate on the Dominion Election Act, Conservative MP W.F. MacLean foreshadowed what was to come when he warned that PR must be considered to open parliament to the "minorities and… the great classes that now are not represented," specifically naming labour (*Hansard* February 17, 1914: 856). MacLean's warning went unheeded at the time.

Wartime would change all of this. The production demands of a wartime economy improved the bargaining position of organized labour and contributed to greater unity in its ranks. Labour tried to continue working within conventional political forces but the compromises became harder to sell as war dragged on. Reforms of all kinds became popular again, including changes to voting systems. Ottawa added PR voting to municipal elections in a plebiscite in 1915 and organized labour was a key force in the coalition behind the successful adoption of PR in Calgary in 1916 (*PR Review* 1916: 41–2; Masson 1985: 327).

But the key event that would shift the terrain of labour politics was the battle over conscription. With the election in 1917 of a Union government committed to the conscription of working men, opposition within labour's ranks to independent political action evaporated. One labour convention approving the formation of a labour party shortly thereafter was likened to a "revival" meeting (Robin 1968: 147–9). PR took on even more importance at this juncture, as a new party would need all the help it could get. Yet as quickly as this new consensus was reached it slipped away, with a sizable group of labour activists now calling for the increased use of direct action and general strikes as a political weapon (Palmer 1992: 196–200). And strikes got results, at least during wartime. By 1917, 60 percent of strikes ended in victory or compromises favourable to workers (Kealey 1995: 368–72). Inspired by this, many of the radical elements within organized labour would eventually form the One Big Union (OBU) with the express purpose of organizing a giant strike to topple the capitalist system. Federal authorities took these claims very seriously and worried enough about radical organizing in Vancouver to twice request a British naval cruiser to help put down any possible uprising (Penner 1977: 70).

In the early post-war period, it remained unclear whether labour would move to the streets or the ballot box. The war's end sparked new economic insecurity as returning soldiers swelled the ranks of those competing for jobs just as the war economy was winding down. Though soldiers initially buttressed the forces of reaction, unemployment and government indifference to their problems quickly led many to switch sides to back labour's demands. As more soldiers returned home in 1918–19, economic conditions worsened. The situation culminated in the Winnipeg General Strike of May 1919, a largely peaceful event where organized labour and its supporters took over the administration of a major Canadian city. General strikes in sympathy with the Winnipeg actions soon spread to other cities (Kealey 1994). Though only six weeks in duration, the Winnipeg General Strike shook the Canadian establishment out of its complacency. Conventional political elites suddenly proclaimed the need to take the grievances of the "reasonable labour man" seriously. A royal commission was struck to examine the conditions leading to the strike and the historic National Industrial Conference was organized for September 1919, which would bring representatives of business and labour together to work out their differences (Pilon 2006: 144). However, little was actually accomplished.

The next steps were electoral. Farmers decided to strike out on their own, winning by-elections in early 1919. Labour too turned away from the mainstream parties. In the fall of 1919 Winnipeg's labour movement did not seem discouraged in the aftermath of the strike. Indeed, labour candidates won seven seats in the fall municipal elections, gaining control of half of council, a major breakthrough. Farmers and labour then surprised political elites by winning the Ontario provincial election in October 1919, a shocking result (Naylor 1991: 127). Farmers, with labour allies, would go on to win electoral victories in Alberta, Manitoba and Nova Scotia over the next year and make an impressive breakthrough at the federal level in 1921. Traditional elites were deeply disturbed by these developments, and many sought ways of including the more conservative elements of these new political forces as a means of restoring political order. The solution they discovered to co-opt, contain or marginalize them was PR (Pilon 2006: 145–6).

The voting system reform issue had taken off in Canada around 1915 as wartime spurred the forces of middle-class reformism. But after a few small-town conversions in western Canada it had pretty much run its course by 1918. Indeed, a number of reformed towns were clamouring to return to the previous simpler plurality systems. Yet just a year later formerly skeptical news commentators and political veterans were championing PR as the key to labour peace by accommodating and representing labour (Pilon 2006: 142, 145). The Mathers Royal Commission on the Winnipeg General Strike recommended it, the opposing forces of business and labour at the National Industrial Conference could agree on little else but the desirability of PR, and the federal Liberals invited organized labour and farmers to attend their 1919 leadership convention to review their platform, which also included PR (Royal Commission on Industrial Relations 1919; Hopkins 1920: 509–14; Gerber 1991: 42–65). Legislation was rushed through the Manitoba Legislature in early 1920 introducing PR for local and provincial elections in Winnipeg out of fear that labour would sweep the city at both levels of government (Lightbody 1978: 317; Phillips 1976: 142). Though newspaper editors often wrote as if advocating PR was simply about including labour's perspective, other motives sometimes surfaced, as when the *Winnipeg Free Press* recommended PR federally to limit labour's political influence and the spread of socialism (Phillips 1976: 150).

Between 1919 and 1921 conservative elements in the labour movement promoted independent political action and PR to counter the revolutionary sentiments of the OBU and various brands of socialism. Appearing before a parliamentary committee examining voting system reform prior to the 1921 election, a labour delegation argued that had PR been widely in use in Canada in 1919 it would have weakened the more radical elements of the labour movement (Phillips 1976: 140). The 1921 federal election result appeared to make the adoption of PR imminent as three of the four parties elected (together comprising a majority of votes in the House of Commons) had endorsed it. But Liberal interest in the reform quickly waned with the decline of the post-war upheaval (Pilon 2006: 146–7). In a free vote on the question in the House of Commons in 1923, the prime minister, the minister of labour and the minister of agriculture, along with a handful of other progressive Liberals, voted for PR, along with the labour and farmer MPs (Phillips 1976: 178). In the context of a minority government, the Liberals had to show some solidarity with their former labour and farmer allies in the hopes of wooing them back into the fold. But the PR motion failed when the bulk of the Liberal caucus, particularly the Québec members, and all the Conservative MPs voted against it (Pilon 2006: 147).

Into the 1920s organized labour remained deeply divided, despite the apparent consensus over independent political action in elections. The defeat of the OBU and the Winnipeg General Strike channelled labour radicalism back into elections and the struggle to establish a viable, competitive national labour party. Tensions between revolutionaries and reformists, between socialists and reform liberals, remained (Young 1976–77; Isitt 2009), yet both sides could agree that PR was a necessary part of that electoral strategy. From 1920 to 1930 PR would figure as one of the key requests made by organized labour in its annual list of demands submitted to Parliament (*Canadian Annual Review* 1920, 471; *Labour Gazette,* September 1921, 1135, March 1922, 264, February 1924, 126, April 1926, 337, December 1927, 1313, January 1928, 39 and January 1929, 37). The federal "ginger group" of labour-identified MPs continued to press for the introduction of PR throughout the 1920s and into the 1930s (Woodsworth 1926; Phillips 1976: 198–9). But the electoral weakness of labour made the status quo politicians coy, promising reform when they found themselves under threat, as the Liberals did in 1925 and again in 1933–34, but ignoring such promises when the crisis passed (Pilon 2006: 147, 149–50).

THE "TAKE POWER" STRATEGY, 1932–92

Labour's consensus for PR began to give way as a national party of the left finally emerged from the depths of the Great Depression. Over the course of fifteen years, labour's political strategy would change from one focused on simply gaining representation and a voice in national affairs to one committed to gaining office. Various voices, international and domestic, now argued that labour should use the conventional electoral machinery for its ends by gaining a majority of seats, taking power and using such complete control to introduce its agenda unencumbered by deals or resistance from the conventional parties. At the same time, as this new left thinking solidified, so did right-wing interest in manipulating electoral rules to prevent the left from carrying out such a vision. Still, this new view of voting systems would take some time to become the dominant one in the labour movement. Well into the 1940s, there were unions and left politicians still supporting PR.

The first key shift in labour thinking on the issue occurred at the inaugural policy convention of Canada's new left-wing national party, the CCF, in 1933. Former farmer MP and longtime PR supporter W.C. Good travelled to Regina to make the case, supported by labour MPs J.S. Woodsworth and William Irvine, but those present refused to add it to the *Regina Manifesto* (Phillips 1976: 214–5). Similar conflicting assessments of progressive priorities emerged in the wake of the federal election in 1935. Left-wing professor Frank Underhill complained in the *Canadian Forum* that the CCF was unfairly punished by the plurality system and that the adoption of PR was a key progressive priority (Underhill 1935). But when the League for Social Reconstruction (LSR), a left-wing policy group, presented its recommendations for progressive legislation, PR was not on the list, despite Underhill's participation. Other members of the LSR had apparently outvoted Underhill on the voting system reform issue because they were no longer convinced it was either possible or desirable (Phillips 1976: 215–6).

These shifts in thinking about voting systems amongst labour and the left in Canada were in line with debates and experiences elsewhere. Herman Finer summarized these views in a 1924 Fabian tract that argued that the UK Labour Party would actually require the inflated majorities typically produced by plurality voting if the party was ever going to be able to introduce its policies against the combined opposition of the other parties and their opponents in civil society. Only the unassailable majorities produced by plurality, argued Finer, would give Labour policies a chance to work by granting them some breathing room from their opponents' unrelenting opposition (Finer 1924). In Canada, Ontario CCF member Herbert Orliffe made a similar argument (Orliffe 1938). That PR might be used to limit the left was not an entirely new theme in Canada. John McQueen was an early left critic of PR's deployment in Winnipeg, complaining that it was just another strategy to contain labour's influence on politics (Lightbody 1978: 317).

By the late 1930s Canada's left had no consistent position on the issue. The 1936 federal parliamentary committee looking into voting system reform rejected PR, with CCF member A.A. Heaps allowing that while its use in Winnipeg had worked out, the system was not appropriate for the country as a whole. Meanwhile, Tommy Douglas' provincial CCF regularly promoted PR in the Saskatchewan legislature into the early 1940s (Phillips 1976: 262). The shift away from PR and towards plurality was finally settled when the Douglas and the CCF won a majority government in Saskatchewan in 1944.

As the left became more committed to a take power strategy that would require the retention of a plurality voting system, the right discovered the virtues of voting system reform, particularly majority voting systems. At the federal level, a shift to majority voting was raised by a number of Liberals, Conservatives and national business organizations whenever CCF fortunes appeared to be on the rise. The surprising defeat of Conservative leader Arthur Meighen by a CCF candidate in a 1942 by-election ignited interest in the reform as politicians feared that centre-right competition might split the vote and allow the CCF to "come up the middle." Just before both the 1945 and 1948 elections, the fear of vote splitting had federal politicians debating the merits of changing the voting system. In the end, the feared CCF breakthrough did not materialize in either election and the interest in the reform waned (Pilon 2006: 151–2). But at the provincial level, the debate over majority voting would go much further.

Both Alberta and Manitoba had introduced the alternative vote for provincial contests in rural districts in the 1920s, largely to benefit their farmer governments (Pilon 2006: 147–8). In British Columbia, majority voting became a serious issue in the late 1940s as the successful Liberal-Conservative coalition government came under strain. Though effectively stitched together as a governing coalition after the 1941 provincial election where the CCF came first in the popular vote, the Conservatives and Liberals did not like working together. Balancing the different political interests proved tricky and a provincial coalition interfered with federal party competition (Alper 1977). Activists within both parties settled upon the majoritarian alternative vote as a way out of coalition but not necessarily into a CCF government. The thinking was that the transferable approach to voting under AV would allow coalition government supporters to mark their first choice for one member of the coalition and their second choice for the other, thus assuring that the CCF would not benefit from any vote splits (Pilon 2010a: 94–5).

Media quickly seized on the reform as a necessary democratic initiative, though the strategic political benefits were not overlooked either. As the *Vancouver News Herald* noted, reform either through PR or majority voting would "diminish the undue influence of the marginal floating vote." This was important, the paper argued, because: "So long as a majority of people in Canada remain opposed to socialism, the P.R. system will give full protection against minority socialist governments" (*Vancouver News Herald* July 12, 1948: 8). The *News Herald* would continue its advocacy of voting system reforms, though by 1949 it was prepared to forgo PR for majority voting if it would prevent the CCF from gaining power. As the editors reminded their readers, "The menace of minority government is real and should be guarded against. The [alternative] vote is a somewhat halting and halfhearted means of dealing with it, but it is probably less controversial" (*Vancouver News Herald* February 18, 1949: 9). The papers would go back and forth on these themes of democracy versus more blunt political strategy, sometimes chortling that majority voting might freeze out the CCF altogether, preventing the party from winning many seats, while at others intoning that the new system was a "much needed and healthy democratic measure" (*Vancouver News Herald* June 6, 1950: 1; October 23, 1950: 4). BC's other major newspapers echoed these sentiments (*Victoria Daily Colonist*, October 23, 1950).

The BC CCF leader Harold Winch denounced the reform as a trick and a swindle, designed to give free enterprise supporters more influence (*Victoria Daily Times* October 25, 1950: 1). Organized labour also condemned AV as undemocratic, claiming that it was designed to eliminate minority representation (*Victoria Daily Colonist* February 22, 1951: 27). Media chided the CCF for its opposition, claiming that it betrayed a totalitarian mindset (*Vancouver News Herald* November 28, 1950: 4). But as a CCF letter writer would later point out, the left's opposition had less to do with democratic reform than the obvious self-interest behind the initiative. As any fair-minded person could see, the reform was a blatant attempt to marginalize the CCF (Frank Snowsell, *Victoria Daily Times*, April 19, 1952: 4). In the end, AV failed to re-elect the coalition parties but it did arguably keep the CCF from power. Instead, an upstart populist right-wing party, Social Credit, gained power and became the new dominant centre-right political choice. The "stolen" election of 1952 would powerfully shape labour and left-wing thinking on voting systems in Canada for decades to come. When Social Credit proposed scrapping AV in 1953 the BC CCF and its labour allies quickly agreed (Pilon 2010a: 94–5).

The 1950s would also see the repeal of the voting system reforms used in Alberta and Manitoba. Labour supported the repeal in the latter but opposed it in the former, largely because opponents of the Social Credit government were finally learning how to use it effectively (Hesketh 1987). But with the return to plurality everywhere, both right and left, business and labour largely forgot about voting system reform. The issue resurfaced in Québec in the late 1960s as Québec unions and the upstart Parti Québecois (PQ) called for voting system reform to increase their influence (Doody and Milner 2004: 267–8). Ironically, the PQ's majority win in 1976 also put PR on the agenda for the rest of the country, as a number of analysts called for PR to better represent the regional diversity of the country and aid Canadian unity. But attempts to shift the left's position on the issue in English Canada failed (Seidle 1996). A 1975 survey of NDP MPs showed them hostile to any voting system reforms, no doubt in part because AV was being touted once again in BC to defeat the NDP provincially (Phillips 1976: 385; Pilon 2010a: 95–6). Federal NDP leader Ed Broadbent tried to float a modest PR proposal in both 1978 and 1981 to increase the federal party's influence nationally, only to have such suggestions vetoed by the provincial sections (with labour support) that had gained office by plurality rules (Blight 1981; Seidle 1996: 294). Attempts to reopen the question within the NDP in the late 1980s and early 1990s also failed.

THE "RESISTING NEOLIBERALISM" PHASE, 1993 ON

For four decades the NDP remained a perennial third party at the federal level. Despite this, faith that the party would someday overtake the Liberals as a left governing alternative remained strong amongst party elites. Only when the party fell to fifth place in the popular vote after the 1993 federal election did this confidence begin to slip. Internally, labour's party was having difficulties maintaining unity amongst its varied constituencies. White-collar middle-class professionals increasingly dominated the party, while the party's voting base shifted to include a broader swathe of liberal, postmaterial voters and lifestyle issues. Stints in provincial government for the NDP were proving fractious and unsatisfying. Faced with unremitting hostility from business and the media, NDP governments in BC, Saskatchewan, Manitoba and Ontario tried to distance themselves from traditional supporters like the labour movement and social justice activists, instead adopting what amounted to "neoliberal-lite" policies in a bid to curry favour with the perceived political mainstream. But such initiatives usually demobilized support for the government without gaining any new supporters, which ultimately led to defeat (Carroll and Ratner 2007). Facing such a dead end, some labour and left activists began exploring how to change the game. PR emerged as one possible alternative.

By the late 1990s, discussions of voting system reform began appearing at union and NDP conventions. The Ontario NDP consulted broadly on the question throughout 1996 and 1997, voting to support the introduction of PR in Ontario at its convention in 1998 (Pilon 2004: 252). The BC NDP also studied the issue in the late 1990s, eventually endorsing an MMP form of PR at its 1999 convention (Pilon 2010b: 79). Federal NDP MP Lorne Nystrom championed the issue in the party and the House of Commons, leading to a federal party commitment to seek PR in the late 1990s. At a historic renewal convention for the party in 2000, there was little agreement about which direction the NDP should take, but all sides agreed that getting PR federally was a key priority (Hartviksen 2001). Unions also debated PR, with the United Steelworkers, Communications Energy and Paperworkers Union and the Canadian Union of Public Employees (CUPE) Ontario adopting resolutions for it both federally and provincially. In an appearance before the Ontario NDP's PR task force, Ontario Federation of Labour president Wayne Samuelson noted that the provincial labour body had endorsed PR officially in 1999 because it feared that non-elite views were being shut out of Canadian politics (Ontario NDP 2002). A number of unions also became key players in the country's new national voting system advocacy organization, Fair Vote Canada (FVC). According to former FVC treasurer John Deverell, this increasing level of union support for voting system reform culminated in a 2002 resolution from the Canadian Labour Congress (CLC) endorsing Fair Vote Canada's campaign (Deverell 2011, interview with the author). However, there were holdouts. The CAW studied the question but did not produce a clear policy on the issue, and a number of unions in BC like CUPE remained hostile to voting system reform out of fear that it might interfere with the BC NDP gaining power (Pilon 2010b).

The left and unions were not the only ones reassessing voting system reforms. With a balkanized party system, and declining rates of Canadian participation in elections, PR would emerge as one of a host of possible reforms to address what Liberal Paul Martin dubbed Canada's "democratic deficit" (Seidle 2007: 305–6). The Law Commission of Canada recommended PR to the House of Commons in 2002, and in 2004 the Liberal minority government acceded to an NDP request for a parliamentary committee to study the issue (Seidle 2007). Provincially, voting system reform emerged as an issue in five provinces at the start of the new century. Liberals in BC, Ontario and Québec all made promises to study the question when they were in opposition. BC and Québec Liberals had both recently suffered under the plurality system, losing elections in the 1990s despite getting more votes than the eventual winner. Ontario's Liberals had long suffered under plurality, rarely gaining office in the twentieth century despite almost always being the key opposition party. At the same time, Maritime Conservatives in Prince Edward Island and New Brunswick turned to voting system reform to improve the embarrassing exclusion or near exclusion of opposition voices from their legislatures, results that challenged the legitimacy of their democratic institutions.

As these various parties gained office at the provincial level, they began to move on their commitments to examine the issue. BC and Ontario Liberals both eventually established innovative citizens' assemblies to examine the question. In Québec, an Estates General was organized to examine various alternative voting schemes. In PEI and New Brunswick, Conservative premiers established commissions to explore the issue and make recommendations (Seidle 2007).

The results of these various processes were remarkably different and similar in important ways. First, nearly all committed to a process but not a result. BC and Ontario's processes eventually produced recommendations for PR, though by different means. BC's Citizens' Assembly called for the adoption of the STV form of PR while Ontario's recommended an MMP model. The two Conservative commissions both recommended a form of MMP for their provinces. Yet despite these differences in process and proposals, the politics surrounding them across jurisdictions became strikingly uniform. In each case, political elites sounded committed to an open and fair consideration of the proposals, with a strong role for the public in making the final decision through a referendum, but behind the scenes those same elites rigged the rules against the possibility of change. Whether through the imposition of super-majority rules to secure change, or the lack of public education about the proposals, or via manipulation of election administration or the question wording, conventional elites signalled their opposition to voting system reform (Pilon 2010b).

In Québec, the minority provincial Liberals stalled on the recommendations of the Estates General and, despite the appearance of an all-party consensus for change in the previous election, neither the right-wing Action démocratique du Québec (ADQ) nor the PQ seemed determined to press the issue. When the Liberals did bring forward a highly disproportional mixed model, it was quickly scuttled in the legislature. In the end, the ADQ, hoping to displace either the Liberals or the PQ as a major party, misjudged the strategic situation and lost support in the next election, contributing to a majority for the Liberals and an end to voting systems discussions. In New Brunswick, the Conservative government had promised a referendum on the MMP proposal but decided instead to hold a general election. When they lost, the new government abandoned the Commission report and its promised referendum vote (Seidle 2007).

Meanwhile, at the federal level, elite opposition was more direct. The defeat of Paul Martin's minority Liberal government in 2006 sank the initiative to reconsider Canada's voting system. The new Conservative government acted on Parliament's promise to investigate it by awarding a research contract to the Frontier Centre, a right-wing think tank with a solid record of opposition to voting system reform. Not surprisingly, the report it produced recommended against any change (Tanguay 2009: 243).

Still, despite elite interference in all cases, the decisions in PEI, BC and Ontario would be decided by referenda and even the best-laid plans by elites could still go awry. Labour was all over the map in terms of its responses to these initiatives. Unions appeared to strongly support voting system change at the federal level, and came out in support of the MMP proposals in Ontario, PEI and Québec. They remained much more suspicious of STV as proposed in BC. Labour's response partly reflected the provincial NDP's ambivalence on the question. The BC NDP had passed a resolution in 1999 favouring the introduction of MMP for provincial elections. This in itself was a major breakthrough, given how the 1950s use of the majoritarian alternative vote had soured the province's left on any voting system reforms. But the commitment was largely a deathbed conversion from a party and government desperate to keep some supporters mobilized. Despite the party's punishing defeat in the 2001 election where it was reduced to just two seats in the BC legislature, the province's union and NDP leadership could not bring themselves to support the STV proposal. Their stated rationale was that they preferred another form of PR (MMP), but many thought that they simply were holding out for a return to the province's political status quo, one characterized by a fairly evenly matched two-party system and a potential return to government for the NDP in the future (Deverell 2011, interview with the author). By contrast, unions and provincial NDP elites in Ontario and PEI had no such illusions about gaining power and as such faced no similar dilemma in supporting voting system reform.

When the referendum campaign in BC got underway in the spring of 2005, a number of unions spoke out against the adoption of STV, claiming it would prevent the NDP from winning power and that it would do nothing to help the election of women. CUPE BC and the British Columbia Government Employees Union (BCGEU) came out strongly against the proposal, incorporating anti-STV messages into their election outreach to members. This was not entirely unexpected. When FVC had announced its support for STV months earlier, a number of BC unions used their influence at the national level to reverse CLC support for FVC and its campaigns (Deverell 2011, interview with the author). According to former FVC executive director Larry Gordon, CLC president Ken Georgetti resigned from the FVC national advisory board in protest, and union financial contributions to the organization tapered off markedly (Gordon 2011, interview with the author). Voters, however, disagreed, with nearly 58 percent for opting for the change, a figure that included an overwhelming majority of NDP supporters. Only the government's super-majority rules arguably prevented STV from being implemented at that time.

Labour support for voting system reform rebounded in 2007 as unions appeared much more supportive of the MMP model proposed for Ontario. The Ontario Public Service Employees Union (OPSEU), the Ontario Secondary School Teachers Federation (OSSTF), the Communication, Energy and Paperworkers Union (CEP), the National Union of Public and General Employees (NUPGE) and CUPE Ontario, among others, all contributed money to the MMP campaign in the referendum to varying degrees (Gordon 2011, interview with the author), and a few unions encouraged their members to vote "Yes to MMP" (PSAC 2007).

However, the CAW refused to endorse MMP when approached (Deverell 2011, interview with the author). Despite some private sector union support for MMP (e.g., the Steelworkers), an emerging public/private split was apparent. Private sector unions seemed reluctant to move away from single party majority governments, where they would know with whom they were dealing. In contrast, public sector unions were more keen to slow or even reverse neoliberal policies by making minority governments more likely. Either way, labour support or opposition did not appear to be decisive in the Ontario campaign as the MMP proposal was decisively defeated, primarily due to public indifference (Pilon 2009). When the BC referendum was rerun in 2009, a few unions had changed their minds but many remained hostile. Attempts to gain public endorsements from labour for the STV proposal were not any more successful than previously (Deverell 2011, interview with the author). This time the result in BC was decisively against change (Pilon 2010b), though, again, a majority of NDP voters were supportive.

By 2010, all the provincial voting system reform processes had ended in failure, with reformers convinced that the issue was dead for at least a generation. Some held out hope that federal level reform might be possible, particularly as the likelihood of any single party gaining a majority of seats seemed remote. But breakthroughs for the Conservative party (in capturing a majority government) and the NDP (overtaking the Liberals to become the official opposition) in the 2011 federal election have decisively altered all parties' strategic calculations. Though the NDP campaigned on a promise to bring forward PR, their historic rise to second place in federal politics will likely diminish the enthusiasm of both the party and its union allies for voting system reform.

CONCLUSION

Organized labour has responded in many ways to proposals for voting system reform. At times, unions have championed reform and urged their chosen political party or the state directly to introduce changes, usually some form of proportional representation. At other times, they have defended the status quo plurality system and condemned attempts to replace it with something else. In both kinds of campaigns, unions have remained fairly consistent in their advocacy of deepening Canadian democracy and furthering the goals of working people. The shifts in their positions therefore have reflected their assessments of the contexts in which reform was occurring, the political goals of their opponents and divisions within their ranks about assessing the way forward. Thus labour's debates over institutions like voting systems were not merely informed by abstract values or theories of institutional design (though these often formed jumping-off points for discussions). Instead, they have reflected an engagement with the concrete inequality of Canadian democracy, such as it is and has been, an inequality rooted in workplace relations and the structure of the Canadian economy and a recognition that such inequalities are held in place or put under challenge through political action aimed at the state.

Part III

THE PROSPECTS OF EXTRA-PARLIAMENTARY ACTIVISM

7. UNIONS, GENDER EQUITY AND NEOCONSERVATIVE POLITICS

Amanda Coles and Charlotte A.B. Yates

Neoconservative governments are hostile to equity politics. With a socially conservative agenda that emphasizes "traditional family values," neoconservatives deny the existence of, and consequently state responsibility for, systemic political, economic and social inequalities. Recent neoconservative governments in Canada have pushed back against more than thirty years of gains fought for and won by the women's movement and other equity-seeking groups. This has been most evident at the federal level since 2006, when the Harper Conservative government began changing policy, cutting programs and de-funding equity-seeking groups in attempts to depoliticize equity issues and advocacy groups. These tactics have, as Brodie (2008: 158) argues, "cut the transmission lines that had been cultivated between the women's movement and the federal state." Neoconservative attacks on women's groups and issues have been made easier by neoliberal economic rationales, which emphasize market forces, individual risk and responsibility, and the fragmentation of the women's movement itself.

However, the depoliticization of gender equity has not gone uncontested. As government undermines the institutional foundations of the women's movement and, by extension, its ability to identify and advocate an equity agenda at the political level, several feminist non-governmental organizations (NGOs) and civil society groups have called on their long-time allies in the labour movement for more support.

This chapter analyzes the role played by organized labour in advancing women's equity issues in the political arena, with particular focus on the period since the 2006 election of the Conservative government. We argue that the labour movement is playing an important leadership role in feminist mobilizing and political advocacy in an effort to keep equity issues on the political agenda in the face of hostile governments. The historical relationship between the women's movement and labour movement in Canada, increases in women's labour market participation and union membership, and labour's self-financed structure are critical factors explaining why the women's movement has turned to the labour movement as a key ally. Yet unions have complex, sometimes contradictory, relationships to the pursuit of women's and equity issues. They are often resistant to the formation of coalitions in which unions pay the bills but do not control the agenda (Tattersall 2010). Unions are also constrained by their legal and structural position as workplace and collective bargaining institutions. These roles shape their prioritization of which gender issues to pursue and whether political action, rather than collective bargaining, is the best strategy to adopt. These internal and external constraints underscore the importance of an independent organized women's movement to maintaining the labour movement's focus on gender equity.

IS THIS WHAT EQUALITY LOOKS LIKE?

> We have to understand that if women are continually told that they are not equal, they will continue to believe that. We say that everyone in Canada is equal. —Bev Oda, Minister of Canadian Heritage and Status of Women (Canada, House of Commons Debates, November 10, 2006)

Despite Oda's assertion to the contrary, women continue to face an economy that systematically discriminates against them on the basis of gender. Women's labour force participation has risen steadily in the post-war period, especially amongst women with children, but remains slightly lower than men's. Women continue to be segregated in a range of occupations that draw on "traditional" female skills such as nursing, child and elder care. They also make up the majority of part-time workers as well as a growing share of employees holding more than one job (Statistics Canada 2011).

Despite increasing labour force participation, women still face systemic employment and pay barriers. The gender pay gap for full-time, full-year workers persists, reaching its lowest level in the 1980s when women were paid 73 percent of men's wages. Thereafter the gender pay gap stagnated until the 2008 financial crisis, when it began once again to widen (World Economic Forum 2010). The Canadian Labour Congress's (CLC) 2008 report on the gender pay gap demonstrates that, although more women are gaining post-secondary educations and significantly higher wages as a result, the pay gap between educated young women and men rose sharply over a ten-year period, from 12 percent in 1991 to 18 percent in 2001 (CLC 2008: 13).

Particular groups of women face additional inequalities. Female single parents are less likely to be employed than mothers in two-parent families. In 2008, female single-parent families had the lowest average total income of all family types, $42,300, or 70 percent of the $60,400 earned by male single-parent families. Racialized women, especially recent immigrants, experience higher rates of poverty and are often stuck in precarious, low-paying jobs. According to 2001 census data, racialized women earned on average $22,301 compared to average annual earnings of all women at $24,390. Women immigrants who had come to Canada in the previous five years earned on average only $18,113 annually (CLC 2008: 17). Immigrant women were also disproportionately affected by the fallout of the 2008 financial crisis. In 2009, the female immigrant unemployment rate reached 9.6 percent — up from 7.4 percent in 2008 — while the rate for Canadian-born women was 6.3 percent — up from 5.2 percent in 2008 (Statistics Canada 2011).

These trends, combined with women's disproportionate role in child rearing, explain why women are less likely than men to qualify for Employment Insurance (EI) when they lose their job and, when they are eligible, qualify for lower rates than men (Porter 2003: 211–30). Since the 1996 reforms that transformed the unemployment insurance system and increased the minimum number of hours worked to qualify, "only 32% of unemployed women qualify for regular EI benefits, compared to 40% of men who are unemployed" (CLC 2008: 19). In the face of this evidence, it is unsurprising that women and women's groups have rejected claims that they have achieved equality.

FEMINISM AND THE TRANSFORMATION OF THE CANADIAN LABOUR MOVEMENT

Women have long demanded an end to their unequal treatment by employers, and have had to fight to garner labour's support for these demands. Starting in the early 1900s, women struggled for sixty years with employers and unions for better wages, equal access to unemployment insurance and improved working conditions (Briskin and McDermott 1993; Creese 1999; Porter 2003). Early demands for equal pay were met with derision. When unions did take up this call during wartime and again in the 1950s, they usually did so in order to prevent low-wage competition from women and ensure that employers had little reason to hire women rather than men, thus cutting women out of good jobs (Sugiman 1994a and 1994b; Creese 1999). But a plethora of changes in politics and the labour market in the late 1960s and 1970s led to the transformation of the Canadian labour movement by women, resulting in unions taking up the call for women's equality.

Women streamed into the paid labour force in growing numbers beginning in the 1960s (White 1993). This coincided with the expansion of the welfare state as large numbers of women found employment in the public sector, at the same time swelling the ranks of newly formed public sector unions. But women's increased labour force participation also coincided with the gathering momentum of social movement politics, at the leading edge of which stood the women's movement. The labour movement, which had hitherto been dominated in membership and leadership by white men, experienced pressure from feminist activists working inside unions, communities and the political arena who demanded that unions embrace women's demands for equality. Large numbers of women expected unions to become vehicles for social and political-economic change, transforming the conditions under which women worked. Most feminists believed that women's equality relied, at least in part, on women gaining economic independence through decent paid work. Unions were therefore critical to this struggle.

Luxton (2001: 64) rejects the popular idea that the women's movement in Canada is a struggle of middle-class liberal feminists, arguing this obscures the "existence of a union-based, working-class feminism that has been a key player in the women's movement, the labour movement and the left since the late 1960s and early 1970s." Luxton connects the swell of women's labour market participation during this period to the growing strength of women in Canadian unions. Furthermore, Luxton argues that women's workplace and union-based equity struggles helped fuel the women's movement in Canada. Feminism provided working women with the tools to make sense of the systemic discrimination and marginalization they faced at home, at work and in their unions, where they faced the double day, employment barriers, wage gaps and exclusion from leadership positions.

In the late 1970s, feminist groups marched on picket lines with striking women workers in numerous workplaces to gain the same rights and workplace representation as men. Collective agreements were renegotiated to secure women's access to pensions, dental care, seniority, job security, extended maternity leave and other benefits that many non-union women still do not have. In the 1990s, unions negotiated a growing range of family-friendly policies, reflecting their recognition of women's disproportionate role in unpaid social reproduction and its impact on their paid work (Bentham 2007). Simultaneously, unions successfully bargained for gay and lesbian families to secure equal access to family benefits (Rayside 2007). By 2000, gender equity through collective bargaining had been entrenched in many, including male-dominated, unions. Many of these gains were the result of alliances between the women's movement and unions.

Many union women also fought to establish women's committees, host women's conferences and establish union equity and human rights offices, seeing these as critical to institutionalizing the collective recognition of women and raising the consciousness of both women and men in the labour movement. From the 1970s to the present, there has been tremendous cultural, symbolic and, to a lesser degree, structural change within the labour movement itself. Unions shifted to gender-neutral language at conventions and in collective agreements, removed many of the overt forms of gender discrimination in collective agreements (such as separate sex-based seniority lists, job classifications and pay rates), and frowned upon open sexism. More women were accorded public recognition for their union activism (Rebick 2005; Briskin 2006a).

Women still have more difficulty than men in securing elected union leadership positions. Where they are elected, these tend to be in smaller locals in female-dominated occupations. When appointed, women are disproportionately found in areas such as health and safety and education (Kaminski and Yakura 2006). Men are frequently reluctant to give up their positions of power, and women lack the resources, membership power base and leadership training to succeed in election bids. Recognizing these obstacles to women's leadership, in the mid-1980s the CLC and many provincial labour federations designated seats for women on their executive boards. Nonetheless, leadership of labour federations remains male-dominated. Women who have succeeded in becoming union leaders have been concentrated in female-dominated unions, especially in the public sector and amongst white-collar workers. Yet women's leadership has made a significant difference. When they have been elected, women union leaders like Grace Hartman, Shirley Carr, Nancy Riche and Madeleine Parent successfully shifted their unions' priorities and internal cultures, modelled new leadership styles, and moved forward the equity agenda both in the workplace and in the political sphere for women and other equity-seeking groups (Briskin 2006b).

FEMINIST POLITICS AS UNION POLITICS

Extra-parliamentary advocacy, a key aspect of both union and feminist politics, has encouraged the emergence of collaborative working relationships between the two movements. Judy Darcy, Canadian Union of Public Employees (CUPE) national president from 1991–2003, articulates the deep relationship between the feminist and Canadian labour movements:

> The role of women in the Canadian labour movement is recognized all over the world. The union women organizing around affirmative action and choice were women who saw themselves as feminists. They saw themselves as active in the women's movement.... It was the alliance with the women's movement that showed the first organizational commitment of the labour movement to social unionism. We were able to build recognition in the labour movement that the women's movement was a major ally. During the Eaton's strike [in 1984–85], there was a rallying cry around women's issues. The Fleck strike [in 1978], too, was an important landmark where people in the labour movement came to understand that there was another movement out there that could be an ally. It gave us a whole other perspective on the issues we were fighting for. (quoted in Rebick 2005: 99)

Often women looked outside their unions to form coalitions in the hope of making more rapid progress on equity issues. Pat and Hugh Armstrong (1990) argue that union women were frustrated at the slow progress on the issue of pay equity at the bargaining table. Consequently, in Ontario, women from a variety of unions joined with others from community groups, business and professional organizations to form the Equal Pay Coalition, aimed at forcing legislative change to address pay equity. This coalition relied heavily on unions for financial and strategic support. The pressure mounted by this coalition came at an opportune political moment when the economy was booming. In 1985, the Ontario New Democratic Party (NDP) made pay equity legislation a condition for its parliamentary support for a Liberal minority provincial government. The result was the passage in 1987 of the Ontario Pay Equity Act, one year after Manitoba had passed the first pay equity legislation in the country. The majority of provinces soon followed suit in large part because of the joint efforts of women and labour movements.

One of the most significant linkages between the labour movement and feminist political organizing was labour's ties with the National Action Committee on the Status of Women (NAC), Canada's leading national feminist advocacy group from the early 1970s until the late 1990s. At its height, NAC membership included over six hundred women's organizations from across Canada and a large number of unions which had been present since NAC's inception in 1971 (Luxton 2001: 81). NAC's executive structure included feminist union leaders such as Madeline Parent, Laurel Ritchie and Grace Hartman in key positions. Unions provided office space, publicity and political connections for NAC campaigns (Luxton 2001: 80). Union support and leadership ensured that working-class feminism informed many of NAC's advocacy campaigns, which focused on violence against women, child care, poverty, minority rights, abortion, pay and employment equity, constitutional politics, reproductive rights and free trade agreements.

Through the 1980s and into the early 1990s, women's equity politics gained momentum. The 1980s brought pay equity legislation across most of the country, as well as some employment equity measures aimed at improving employment opportunities for designated groups such as Aboriginals, women, the disabled and "visible minorities." Paid maternity leave was introduced in 1971 through the unemployment insurance system and significantly expanded in 1990 (Porter 2003: 124, 203). For their part, unions mobilized behind equality and human rights demands, both as political allies and at the bargaining table (White 1993; Hunt and Rayside 2007; Forrest 2009).

WOMEN AND LABOUR UNDER NEOCONSERVATISM

The recession of 1990–92 precipitated a seismic political and ideological shift in Canada that had hit other countries much earlier, such as Great Britain under Margaret Thatcher and the United States under Ronald Reagan (Bashevkin 1996; McBride 2001). Liberal government priorities shifted from making Canada a "just society" to one driven by market imperatives and fiscal restraint. Deficit reduction, relentlessly promoted by business think tanks and corporate leaders, became governments' primary focus. Reducing the size and role of the state and restructuring government programs was central to economic reform. This included cuts to transfers for education and health, restricting income supports and social policies and cutting funding to women's agencies, all of which had a particular and disproportionate impact on women.

Because of the large number of women employed in public services, cutbacks hit women through lay-offs and the declining availability of "good" jobs characterized by decent pay, benefits and job security. Because of their lower wages and disproportionate role in social reproduction, women's greater dependence on government income-support programs made them more vulnerable when these were cut. For example, the 1996 restructuring of the unemployment insurance program ignored women's distinctive work patterns and hence excluded them in greater numbers from qualifying for benefits (Porter 2003). These and other changes contributed to women's deteriorating incomes and reduced capacity to look after their families.

At the federal level, the attack on feminist organizations was quite direct. In 1992, the Mulroney Conservative government cut funding to NAC, justified through the rhetoric of deficit reduction but also arguably because of NAC's opposition to the proposed Charlottetown Accord (Bashevkin 1996: 235; Rebick 2005: 193). In 1998, under the Chrétien Liberal government, Status of Women Canada stopped core funding to all women's organizations, critically damaging NAC's ability to continue its day-to-day operations. NAC all but ceased to exist in the late 1990s. While the organization attempted to regroup largely through private donations, it was a much less powerful and influential body (Brodie 2008). The loss of NAC's voice in federal politics was a major setback for the women's movement in Canada.

At the provincial level, equity measures also came under attack. Funding for human rights tribunals was cut in many provinces, as was support for legal aid, social welfare and labour market training. When the Ontario Progressive Conservatives took power in 1995 under the leadership of Mike Harris, one of their first acts was to rescind provincial employment equity legislation (Bakan and Kobayashi 2007). The Harris government also narrowed the coverage of pay equity legislation, thus taking away the rights of women in heavily female-dominated sectors to pursue pay equity claims. Unionized women bargaining for pay equity found themselves confronted with having to make trade-offs between securing a pay equity claim and keeping their public sector jobs.

For their part, during the recession of the early 1990s unions were hit hard by job losses and wage cuts, and under attack by neoliberal governments who blamed unions for declining productivity and growing budget deficits. Union density (the proportion of workers who belong to a union) began to decline, dropping from 37.6 percent in 1981 to 29.6 percent in 2010 (Statistics Canada 2010b), in part because economic restructuring gutted the manufacturing sector, where large union memberships were concentrated.

Both the women's movement and the labour movement fought back against these economic and political changes. However, when women's organizations protested, governments cut their funding and sidelined them from political consultations, arguing that policy had become captive to "special interests." Unions responded with political mobilization, equity-focused collective bargaining and a high strategic priority throughout the 1990s on recruiting new members amongst unorganized workers (Yates 2007). However, anti-union labour law reforms in most provinces made it more difficult for working people to join unions (Martinello 2000). Organizing results have thus been mixed. Although breakthroughs in retail and restaurant chains such as Walmart and McDonald's have been missing, unions have been quite successful in organizing workers employed in home care, auxiliary hospital services, university support staff, security guards and casinos, many of which are female-dominated sectors. Union membership growth has stabilized union density, which has hovered around 30 percent since 2001, and has been disproportionately amongst women, those with relatively high levels of education and workers over thirty-five years of age. In fact, in 2004, women's union density rose for the first time to a level higher than that of men's, a trend that has continued to the present (Yates 2006; Statistics Canada 2011).

Organizing the unorganized has meant growing diversity in union memberships, posing the challenge of reconciling the demands of aging, often male, members who expect the union to protect their benefits with those of new members who are more likely to be women and/or racialized minorities. Both feminist organizing within the labour movement and the increase in the numbers of women and racialized minorities who are union members have combined to produce a noticeable, albeit contested, shift in union politics. Gender equity issues as union issues have moved from a frame of basic economic equality for women to fundamentally challenging the gendered division of labour in the context of work-life balance and human rights in the workplace.

Unions have also successfully used the courts to fight the retrenchment of equity politics. In 2003, a coalition of unions challenged the Ontario Conservative government's rescind of pay equity legislation as discriminatory and won, paving the way to a mediated settlement that allocated hundreds of millions of dollars in pay equity funding to roughly 100,000 women workers (CUPE 2003).

Somewhat contradictorily, the growing centrality of equity politics in union bargaining and political activity occurred when the women's movement in Canada, and NAC in particular, was spending considerable time wrestling with issues related to power and influence within the movement itself. In 1991, NAC adopted affirmative action policies for its executive, allocating positions for women of colour, immigrant women, Aboriginal women and women with disabilities (Rebick 2005: 236). The change in NAC's executive structure also produced a shift in its political priorities that generated considerable debate and fractures within the organization. According to Sunera Thobani, NAC's first non-white president:

> We were trying to do something in the women's movement that nobody else was trying to do in the whole of Canadian society. We were grappling with issues of power, representation, who gets to speak for whom. We were dealing with issues of "diversity" in a profound way. (quoted in Rebick 2005: 241)

Judy Rebick, NAC president from 1991–93, connects these internal conflicts over strategic direction to the broader political economic environment, arguing that "as neoliberal globalization increased the gap between rich and poor, the challenge of maintaining a common vision among women became much greater. The backlash against feminism and the funding cuts to women's groups made dealing with these difficulties even harder" (Rebick 2005: 254–5). NAC's internal divisions emerged at a time when it also faced enormous external pressures, the result of which was a serious weakening of this umbrella organization that for more than twenty-five years had led the women's movement.

The combination of a besieged women's movement and rising female union membership resulted in a shift in labour-women's movement politics in which unions began to play a more central leadership role. Some women channelled their energies into single-issue groups, many of which had existed for years but acquired a new prominence in the post-NAC era. Child-care coalitions had particular success in mobilizing support, largely from women but also from growing numbers of men. With women entering the labour market in ever-increasing numbers, the question of who should look after the kids and kin became increasingly difficult to answer. Child-care coalitions across the country mobilized with the strong support of several unions, including the Canadian Auto Workers (CAW), British Columbia Government Employees Union (BCGEU) and CUPE, all of which ran their own campaigns in support of affordable and accessible child care. Mounting political pressure on Paul Martin's minority federal Liberal government paid off, if only briefly. Supported by the NDP, the Liberal government changed regulations governing Employment Insurance to allow caregivers to take paid time off to look after gravely ill relatives. The Martin Liberals also introduced a national child-care strategy, but the plan was shelved once the government was defeated and the Harper Conservatives assumed office in 2006, making the situation measurably worse for equity-seeking groups in general and feminists in particular.

In place of the national child-care program proposed by the previous government, the Conservatives offered tax credits and a $1200 subsidy so parents could "choose" how to care for their children. The Conservatives defended this policy as equalizing the choices for all women, including allowing parents (namely middle-class mothers) to stay at home to care for their children. The Conservative government also eliminated all funding for equity claims under the Court Challenges Program, which provided financial assistance for Charter challenges related to constitutionally entrenched language and equality rights. The Harper government further cut the operating budget for Status of Women Canada (SWC), closed twelve of its sixteen offices and eliminated its independent Policy Research Fund. The government's decision to prohibit use of federal funds for advocacy at any level of government resulted in the denial of federal funds supporting more than twenty women's groups, including several focused on child-care advocacy and women's health issues.

The Conservative government has also actively involved itself in discursive politics, attempting to shift the equity paradigm away from any explicit recognition of women and inequality. This was most evident in the unsuccessful attempt to remove the goal of equality from Status of Women Canada's mandate and funding program guidelines. A more subtle but more devastating change came with the introduction of the Public Sector Equitable Compensation Act. Following the Public Service Alliance of Canada's (PSAC) 2010 pay equity victory in the courts, the federal government changed the goals from pay equity to "equitable compensation," with a stronger emphasis on a role for the very market forces that reinforce gender inequalities. This Act significantly reduced the scope of persons covered by the legislation, thus denying thousands of women the right to claim equitable compensation (PSAC 2011).

Driven by calls for help by women's organizations undercut by neoconservative ideas and political attacks, the labour movement's relationship to equity politics has entered a new stage. While unions have historically been important partners in gender equity politics, they have been pushed into leadership roles in recent political advocacy campaigns focusing on gender equity issues.

THE AD HOC COALITION FOR WOMEN'S EQUALITY AND HUMAN RIGHTS

The Ad Hoc Coalition for Women's Equality and Human Rights is comprised of thirty-five women's groups, unions and human rights organizations that advocate for gender equality and human rights in Canada. The coalition came together in 2006 to resist the Harper government's attack on women's organizations and rights. As an umbrella organization, the coalition serves as a shelter to the women's movement in Canada. Since 2006, they have generated public awareness and political pressure through petitions, letter-writing and media campaigns on issues including child care, pay equity, funding for women's groups, the long-gun registry, the Status of Women Act, family planning and abortion, Employment Insurance, the Court Challenges Program and the federal budget. The coalition offers an explicitly feminist critique of Conservative Party politics. Echoing many of NAC's principles, the organization seeks to "coordinate on a pan-Canadian level the activities of organizations and groups intent on advancing women's equality and advocating for the full participation of women in decision making at all levels" (Ad Hoc Coalition for Women's Equality and Human Rights 2011).

As with NAC, unions play a key role in the coalition. In 2006, the Ontario Federation of Labour, the Communications, Energy and Paperworkers Union, PSAC, CUPW, CUPE and the CLC pledged three years of financial support to allow the coalition to develop as an organization and establish a political presence in Ottawa. These labour groups became part of the coalition's core group members, identifying issues, developing proposals and doing strategic planning for advocacy campaigns. Labour's relationship with the NDP has helped get issues on the political agenda, although the coalition has attempted to remain non-partisan.

Given the explicitly hostile relationship between the Harper Conservatives and feminist groups, it is unsurprising that the coalition's political demands go largely unheeded. However, they have succeeded in framing numerous political issues through a feminist lens in the mainstream media. Coalition media releases were picked up in major daily newspapers and over newswires, particularly around framing gun control as an issue of violence against women but also linking changes to federal pay equity legislation to women's poverty, and funding cuts to women's groups as threats to democracy. This organized resistance to the discursive depoliticization of gender equity in the public sphere is an attempt to challenge the structural dismantling of the political arm of the feminist movement.

While there are similarities between the two federal feminist advocacy groups, the significant differences between the coalition and NAC are its funding model and its relationship to organized labour. NAC relied heavily on state funding, as did most women's groups, whereas the coalition is entirely funded by unions. State funding had been longstanding and, according to Bashvekin (1996), allowed the Canadian women's movement to advance a more militant politics than its counterparts in the U.S. and Britain. In contrast, labour's funding of the coalition was short-lived. In May 2011, financial support from labour groups ceased, as unions argued they had insufficient funds available to support the coalition's ongoing activities. This reveals the difficulty for women's organizations of relying exclusively on the financial support of unions that have other priorities, commitments and constraints. Comparing this case with gender equity politics of the Alberta Federation of Labour (AFL) provides us with a way of understanding why this happened and its implications for labour's role in equity politics.

EQUITY POLITICS IN ALBERTA

In 2008, the AFL decided to formalize its political advocacy efforts through lobby days.[1] The Women's Committee of the AFL, which dates back to the early 1960s, identified the need to situate women's equity as a primary focus of lobbying activity. Despite a history of feminist political activism that saw women elected to the Alberta legislature before women received the federal franchise, and consistently (relatively) high levels of political representation in provincial politics, Alberta has a long history of fiscally and socially conservative governments hostile to claims from equity-seeking groups (Rankin and Vickers 1998; Harder 2003). Alberta is the only Canadian province without a provincial ministry, women's directorate or advisory council on the status of women. The gender pay gap in Alberta is the largest in the country, with women working full-time, full-year making 66 percent of what men earn. Two-thirds of minimum wage earners and 70 percent of the part-time workforce in Alberta are women. Since 2003, Alberta allocates the lowest number of per capita dollars for child care, with only 17 percent of children under six in Alberta having access to a regulated child-care spaces (Phillips 2010).

On March 16, 2011, over forty Alberta Federation of Labour affiliates lobbied more than a dozen government members of the Legislative Assembly — including three Cabinet ministers — and members of the opposition, calling on the government to appoint a minister responsible for the status of women as a first step towards taking action on pay equity and child care, framing these two specific issues as major barriers to women's social and economic equality (AFL 2011). The lobbying day was timed to coincide with International Women's Day and build on the media profile accorded gender equity issues at that time of year. The AFL successfully secured a meeting with Lindsay Blackett, Minister of Culture and Community Spirit, who expressed interest in referring this issue to a committee for review. According to Nancy Furlong, AFL Secretary Treasurer, unions' "acceptance and enthusiasm [for this campaign] is palpable," and plans are underway for continued political lobbying on gender issues.

Gender equity is a key aspect of the AFL's long-term political agenda and has been framed consciously in ways to garner active support from union men. Consistent with the strategies of many unions engaged in political advocacy on equity issues, Nancy Furlong argues that framing gender inequality as issues that affect whole families and society at large means that "the guys buy in" (personal communication with the authors, 2011). Although the AFL Women's Committee must actively fight for its share of the political action budget, funding for the gender equity campaign is likely more stable than that for the Ad Hoc Coalition because this campaign is entirely organized and controlled by the labour movement with financial contributions from more than twenty unions and labour organizations.

The AFL is actively working to develop a province-wide coalition with other women's groups and equity advocates in building a "solidarity core" around gender equity. This is challenging, since the lack of equity policy at the provincial level combines with the structural and discursive attacks on feminist groups at the federal level to leave a scattered and disorganized women's movement across the province that is largely focused on local service delivery rather than political advocacy. This is what prompted the AFL Women's Committee to return to addressing the big picture on root causes of systemic inequality, which necessarily requires framing the issues as political problems. Labour, Furlong argues, is best positioned to influence the people who cause or support inequality (interview with the authors, April 14, 2011).

Whereas union funding of the Ad Hoc Coalition allowed feminist groups to continue their advocacy work as part of a larger umbrella organization, the Alberta example is one where the labour movement itself is taking on gender equity as a political issue. These two examples of labour's involvement in equity politics point to some of the complexities in labour's new leadership role in advancing gender equity. The Ad Hoc Coalition was supported by only six labour organizations, two of which were labour federations with weak financial bases. In Alberta, the funding and institutional base within the labour movement may prove to be a more sustainable model for a long-term strategic advocacy campaign. In both cases, however, funding is constrained by declining membership dues and competition over the scarce resources in organizations where men continue to dominate. These divergent patterns of financial support are also likely related to the different roles played by labour in each of these organizations. Whereas unions were actively involved in the Ad Hoc Coalition, its governance structure was relatively flat, with decision-making on a consensus basis, meaning that labour's influence was limited. This differs from the Alberta example, where the activities and organization being created are part of the AFL and subject to strong control by labour leaders and activists. Unions have long been uneasy about coalitions that they fund but do not control, in part because of concerns over accountability for membership dues expenditures but also because of the danger that unions may end up funding initiatives that come back to bite them (Tattersall 2010). For their part, women's organizations have also preferred to be independent for the same reason. Finally, unions and labour federations are structurally and legally organized around a primary role for collective bargaining and a focus on workplace issues. Whereas the Ad Hoc Coalition's agenda of equity issues is far-reaching, the AFL is sticking closer to an economic inequality agenda that aligns more clearly with union goals.

CONCLUSION

The depoliticization and privatization of equity issues under neoconservative governments exaggerates power imbalances between unions and employers in collective bargaining by taking away the legislative supports unions use to push equity issues ahead at the bargaining table. As public policy is a key element in pressuring both employers and unions to keep equity issues on the table during bargaining, regressive changes to equity legislation encourage unions to engage in political advocacy on equity issues. There have also been significant shifts in the labour movement, including growing numbers of women members and large numbers of men who prioritize women's pay equity given that two-wage earning families are now essential to maintain standards of living. But engaging in equity politics is internally fraught as unions continue to rely heavily on resources from higher-paid male-dominated jobs, which are now disappearing. Union leadership also continues to be male-dominated. While issues such as pay equity and child care are clearly linked to the workplace, many unions continue to see a broader engagement in gender equity politics as outside their purview. Yet the active attacks on feminist advocacy groups leaves few voices left to articulate gender equity at the political level.

The importance of both the Ad Hoc Coalition and the AFL gender equity campaign lies in the role they play in resisting the aggressive depoliticization of gender equity under Conservative governments. Unions are, in both cases, core supporters whose organizational and financial support are crucial, but whose political commitment to equity also signals, by nature of their membership base, that gender equity continues to be working-class politics. The framing of gender equity as working-class politics fundamentally resists claims that we are "all equal now" while acknowledging that class is further shaped by other factors, including gender. The degree to which unions commit to gender equity as working-class politics is complex and fragile, yet crucially important to both the labour movement and the (tattered and torn) feminist movement in Canada. As Forrest (2009: 98) argues:

> Periods of union renewal are those in which organized labour self-consciously acts as an equality-seeking movement; concomitantly, renewal stalls when this vision fades and unions focus their energy on protecting the relatively privileged positions of the already organized…. Unions … "deepen their grip on public life" — when they have a clear social purpose and become vulnerable when motivated by materialism. When organized labour acts for its members only, when it turns its vested-interest face to the public, it can "no longer count on anything but its own power to withstand assault."

Although labour is crucial to advancing equity issues as political issues, it seems likely that many unions will concentrate their efforts on workplace issues, often narrowly defined, through collective bargaining. Although strategies such as wage solidarity offer hope of significant gains for women through bargaining (Warskett 1990), these gains are limited to unionized women, who constitute only 30 percent of working women in Canada. Moreover, Judy Haiven's (2007) analysis of the backlash against pay equity in a union local is a reminder of the continued battles faced by women looking to advance equality through unions. The fragility of women's progress in unions was highlighted during the recent financial crisis. Widespread job loss in male-dominated sectors since 2008 shifted union attentions away from equity issues, which became a "luxury" to be addressed only when jobs were not at stake (Walby 2009). Yet unions cannot be expected to carry the full burden of advocating and leading on all women's issues. This goes beyond their mandate, resources and discursive repertoire. An independent women's movement has been critical to pushing labour forward, a role that will be jeopardized if it is dependent entirely on labour support. For the time being, however, the women's movement needs unions to actively resist a neoconservative push to re-privatize gender equity. Unions must continue their dialogue with and support of feminist activists in developing long-term strategy for how the labour movement will play a proactive leadership role in ensuring that gender equity remains firmly anchored in public discourse and on the political agenda.

Notes

The authors gratefully acknowledge Claire Tremblay, Coordinator for the Ad Hoc Coalition for Women's Equality and Human Rights, and Nancy Furlong, General Secretary-Treasurer for the Alberta Federation of Labour, for their important contributions to this paper.

1. Labour organizations have lobbied governments since the turn of the nineteenth century with limited success in influencing government decisions. Labour's lobbying effectiveness is limited as it depends upon access to political insiders and financial resources that unions do not have in ready supply. Yet the absence of alternative political strategies for those unions unable or unwilling to engage in more mobilizational politics make lobbying the continued strategic choice of many unions.

8. SOCIAL UNIONISM, PARTNERSHIP AND CONFLICT: UNION ENGAGEMENT WITH ABORIGINAL PEOPLES IN CANADA

Suzanne E. Mills and Tyler McCreary

Through the 1990s and early 2000s, many unions in Canada began to develop structures and strategies to better organize and represent Aboriginal workers and show solidarity with Aboriginal struggles for self-determination. Whatever the shortcomings of their approaches to Aboriginal engagement, unions' increasing attention to Aboriginal peoples' concerns suggested that some sections of the labour movement were making an effort to redress the negative effects of colonialism on Aboriginal workers and communities. Equally, it implied that at least some unionists were morally compelled to support Aboriginal peoples in their struggles for Aboriginal rights. Yet in many cases political necessity rather than moral compunction has governed union relations with Aboriginal peoples.[1]

Seeking to remain relevant and rejuvenate their memberships, some unions have grounded an engagement with Aboriginal peoples in justice-oriented commitments to social unionism. As the approach to union renewal commonly advocated by critical labour scholars and community activists, social movement unionism situates worker representation and union militancy within a broader quest for social and economic justice (Moody 1997). Although there are several examples of social movement unionism in the global south, in the north, unions have typically combined social justice pursuits with more traditional member servicing and representation (Ross 2008). In Canada, social unionism describes this approach, denoting unions who participate in social justice struggles outside of the workplace such as anti-poverty initiatives, living wage campaigns and the struggles of social groups marginalized on a basis other than class (Sadler 2004; Fine 2005). Unions have often combined external union strategies with changes to their internal structure to better represent marginalized groups in union decision-making (Briskin and McDermott 1993; Leah 1999; Hunt and Eaton 2007). Since Aboriginal peoples have been economically, socially and culturally marginalized through colonialism, some unions have initiated Aboriginal strategies under the rubric of social unionism.

But other unions have often reactively engaged with Aboriginal peoples in response to shifting Aboriginal rights frameworks in Canada. In particular, many unions find they must engage with Aboriginal peoples and concerns because of advances in Aboriginal struggles for rights to self-determination and territory across the country. These changes have resulted in a new jurisdictional context for union activity on state-recognized Aboriginal territories and in areas of actively contested land claims. This context has necessitated that unions increasingly engage with Aboriginal governments' goals for greater employment among their memberships, for involvement in decision-making in their territories and for royalties and business opportunities stemming from developments on their lands.

Drawing on secondary sources as well as primary research we conducted in several distinct projects, in this chapter we discuss and problematize the labour movement's selective engagement with Aboriginal peoples. We begin by presenting some early examples of alliances between unions and Aboriginal peoples that indicate a genuine engagement with anti-colonial struggle. These early examples are contrasted with the now-prevalent forms of social union engagement with Aboriginal peoples. We then turn to Aboriginal political developments from the 1970s to the present, discussing how these developments have created a more complex and contradictory terrain for union engagement and emphasizing the necessity of valuing reciprocal relations and engagement.

EARLY SOCIAL UNIONISM AND ABORIGINAL PEOPLES

Notwithstanding the racism Aboriginal people experienced in the labour market and their frequent segregation into distinct jobs, Aboriginal people were active members of several unions in the early twentieth century. Iroquois ironworkers from Southern Ontario, renowned for their skill on the high steel, were early members of the International Association of Bridges, Structural, and Ornamental Iron Workers (Mitchell 1960). On the West Coast, First Nations were members of early stevedore unions and the International Woodworkers of America and active participants in strikes and job actions (Newfeld and Parnaby 2000; Parnaby 2006, 2008). First Nations fishers and canners banded together to fight for better wages, participating in both separate native organizations and in the ethnically inclusive United Fishermen and Allied Workers Union (Knight 1978; Wright 2008). Particularly during the period 1927 to 1951, when Aboriginal land claims activity was outlawed, Native Brotherhoods on the West Coast functioned as Aboriginal unions, fighting for the rights of First Nations fishers (Drucker 1958; Tennant 1990). This rich and largely understudied history of Aboriginal involvement in early industrial unions created the foundation for unionists to become allies in Aboriginal movements' anti-colonial struggle.

One example of early collaboration that linked union activity to anti-colonial movements occurred at the Northwest Study Conference in British Columbia in the mid-1970s. The conference was organized to address the New Democratic

Party (NDP) provincial government's continued courting of foreign capital and failure to address local social and environmental concerns. The invitation to delegates argued that "because the Northwest of BC is slated for massive industrial expansion, affecting the physical and social environment of the area, the Indian land claims and northern lifestyles," trade unionists, environmentalists, Indian and non-Indian people needed to work together to ensure that development would "benefit all local residents" (Steering Committee Northwest Study Session 1975: 1). The government's refusal to negotiate treaties with First Nations and its failure to involve local communities in planning and decision-making were key concerns. First Nations wanted recognition of their title claims so they could both exercise greater control over and receive a greater share of the benefits from the industrial development of their resources and lands. Unions similarly desired greater involvement in the province's industrial development plans and in drafting labour legislation, such as the BC Labour Code amendments the government was developing. Local unions and First Nations found commonality in their opposition to a pro-industry government that was not addressing the concerns of either group. Organized labour had invested considerably in social democratic politics. When the provincial NDP's 1972 victory failed to translate into increased self-determination in the British Columbian north, unions began to formalize alliances with other regional organizations (Jensen 2010, interview with the authors). On March 8, 1975, twenty organizations representing Aboriginal peoples, unions and community groups adopted a resolution to create a conference focused on local control over decision-making in the Northwest (*Terrace Herald* 1975).

At the Northwest Study Conference in May 1975, 175 delegates representing Aboriginal, labour, environmental, church and community organizations met in Terrace to discuss building a movement for regional self-determination (Coward and Garrod 1975). Business and government representatives were excluded from participating as voting delegates. The principal achievement of the meeting was a solidarity pact between unions and Aboriginal groups. John Jensen, secretary of the Terrace-Kitimat Labour Council, argued for union solidarity with Aboriginal peoples on the basis that just as workers had the right to hold a contract and have it respected, so did First Nations. In his opinion, advancing development without treaties was akin to forcing workers to work without a contract (Jensen 2010, interview with the authors). In a labour movement paper, Jensen was quoted as saying "Under these conditions we are wholeheartedly in support of native people. We will stand shoulder to shoulder with them" (*Western Voice* 1975: 1). Mel Watkins, a keynote speaker at the conference, told the *Prince Rupert Daily News* (1975: 1): "We have to work together to get political recognition of the north and this involves an alliance between Indians and workers."

The conference passed a series of resolutions in support of local involvement in planning, provincial control over key industries and recognition of Aboriginal rights (Northwest Study Conference 1975). There were calls for northern industrial development to be accompanied by comprehensive environmental impact studies, community and worker representation in decision-making, preferential hiring of local people and government ownership of a majority share of key industries. In relation to Aboriginal peoples, resolutions demanded that the government address First Nations' land claims; replace lands unjustly cut off reserves; provide First Nations peoples with access to salmon licences for commercial fishing; and allow Indian women who married non-Indian men to reclaim their status. Delegates also supported the Nisga'a resistance to the renewal of forestry licences on their territory and the Stuart Trembleur band (Tl'azt'en) blockade of BC Rail. Rod Robinson, vice-president of the Nisga'a Tribal Council and an International Woodworkers of America shop steward, described how "when we, the native leaders, go back to our respective villages, we will tell the people that... we have the people, all the labour organizations and people from all walks of life, standing behind us" (quoted in Northwest Study Conference 1975: 9).

The highly politicized context of Aboriginal struggle during this period was not confined to northwestern British Columbia. Unionists in other regions were also integrating Aboriginal issues into their campaigns. A strike by Québec teachers in 1965 protested the colonization of northern Aboriginal communities through the educational system (Corporation des Enseignants du Québec 1973), and in 1972, the Ontario Teachers' Federation provided funds to investigate the images of Aboriginal peoples portrayed in school (McCue 1994). These attempts to forge bonds of solidarity between labour and Aboriginal peoples, however, remained limited. The initial optimism of the Northwest Indian-labour Pact was dulled as the provincial labour federation and national union offices rebuffed attempts to reconstruct the meaning of labour solidarity to include a broader vision of social justice. Early Aboriginal-labour coalitions often pledged commitment to the ideal of solidarity between movements, but lacked a clear program to enhance the power of labour and Aboriginal communities, either locally or nationally.

Further, there remained in many sectors of the labour movement an entrenched racism that inhibited coalition work. Union of BC Indian Chiefs representative George Watts described some of the deep divisions between labour in resource-based industries and First Nations peoples attempting to exercise control over resources in their territories:

> In the south, some of the first people to oppose us [First Nations] were the labour unions. Guys were saying they couldn't take off 5 days for some roadblock. They were pitting bread and butter against land claims. Blockades bring rednecks out of the woodwork, and they make a strong stand against us, show their hatred for us. (quoted in Coward and Garrod 1975: 7)

Unionists' prioritization of "bread and butter" issues over land rights points to the entrenched belief that equity and Aboriginal rights concerns remain separate from and less important than workers' struggle for economic justice.

The separation of bread-and-butter union issues from Aboriginal claims to territorial rights reflects the different trajectories and commitments of each movement. For Aboriginal peoples, impoverished by the transfer of their lands to settlers, struggles for control over resource wealth have sought to reverse earlier patterns of dispossession by reasserting ownership of traditional lands. For the non-Aboriginal working class, economic disadvantage stems from exploitation in waged labour. Their key aim has been to reduce this exploitation by increasing wages and advancing workers' control over the labour process. Since unionists primarily orient themselves against the owning class, it matters little whether this class is Aboriginal or non-Aboriginal. Tensions sometimes arise when workers' desires for employment and development overlap and conflict with Aboriginal peoples' territorial claims.

Aboriginal peoples' assertions that their indigeneity is a critical difference distinguishing them from other workers and/or owners of land has often conflicted with unionists' visions of worker solidarity (Menzies 2010). Tensions between Aboriginal and union trajectories are further revealed when the question of who inhabits the category of "worker" is posed. Dunk's (1994) research on white unionized manufacturing workers and Guard's (2004) study of the 1964 Lanark strike[2] both document the white working class's propensity to portray Aboriginal workers as non-workers. The bracketing of Aboriginal peoples' struggles for lands, resources and rights to governance as less important than the "working-class" concerns of settler workers contributes to the representation of Aboriginal peoples as outside of the working class. When many private sector unions are losing their manufacturing base and public sector unions are on the defensive, positioning equity concerns as unrelated to worker interests has often served to justify a narrow focus on servicing and organizing traditionally unionized workplaces.

CHANGING UNION CULTURE

Even in unions with a leadership professing social unionism, the belief that Aboriginal issues are tangential to workers' struggles and only apply to Aboriginal workers slows the introduction of Aboriginal solidarity initiatives. Despite these challenges, Aboriginal activists within several unions have worked to increase Aboriginal representation in the staff and governing structures. Greater representation in union decision-making structures allowed Aboriginal unionists to push for other changes to union activities such as the implementation of Aboriginal awareness education programs and symbolic demonstrations of solidarity with Aboriginal struggles. However, unlike the early grassroots coalitions cited above, many contemporary strategies for inclusion are internal to the union and therefore distanced from Aboriginal communities and governments. The unions most active in advancing strategies for Aboriginal inclusion and labour-Aboriginal solidarity have been public sector unions and private sector unions professing social unionism. These union engagements with Aboriginal peoples can be understood to fit within the social union belief that unions "have a broad responsibility to working people extending beyond the workplace" (Ross 2008: 135). Initiatives to bring Aboriginal workers' concerns into union activities imbue a more holistic understanding of workers' lives that recognizes the concerns of Aboriginal workers who may have greater allegiance to anti-colonial struggles or to their communities than to their identities as unionists.

Unions' efforts to support Aboriginal struggles have included public endorsement of campaigns for Aboriginal rights and the elimination of racism, public policy reform to enhance Aboriginal self-determination and increased funding to First Nations (Mills and Clarke 2009). Symbolic displays of solidarity with Aboriginal protests and actions often aim to increase cultural understanding and recognition of Aboriginal peoples, such as the Canadian Union of Public Employees' (CUPE) annual participation in the canoe trip to the Back to Batoche celebrations put on by Métis Nation–Saskatchewan (CUPE 2010). Such initiatives increase union visibility in Aboriginal communities and bring Aboriginal culture into union activities. However, while important, these activities are predominantly implemented at the national level or in select jurisdictions and do not challenge racism towards Aboriginal peoples amongst rank-and-file union members, nor do they require major changes to union structures and practices. Moreover, the inclusion of Aboriginal culture in union activities, such as the use of pow-wow dancers as entertainment at conventions, can further tokenize Aboriginal union members if not accompanied by genuine empowerment of Aboriginal peoples. Such practices, particularly when initiated by and according to the design of non-Aboriginal people, risk re-inscribing pre-existing stereotypes of Aboriginal peoples as "historic" and "traditional," thereby further alienating Aboriginal workers (Mills and McCreary 2006).

For these reasons, Aboriginal activists within CUPE and the Public Service Alliance of Canada (PSAC) interviewed in 2009 were often more concerned with increasing the representation and influence of Aboriginal members within unions and with anti-racist educational initiatives than with symbolic demonstrations of solidarity. Strategies to increase Aboriginal union members' influence in union activities have loosely followed those of other equity-seeking groups (Coles and Yates, this volume). Aboriginal people's struggles for human rights and an end to discrimination in non-Aboriginal communities and workplaces often effectively sync with broader anti-racism campaigns (Biolsi 2005). CUPE and PSAC have national-level committees for Aboriginal members to articulate their issues, named the National Aboriginal Circle and National Aboriginal Peoples' Network respectively. Other unions include Aboriginal peoples within committees for workers of colour such as the Canadian Auto Workers' (CAW) Aboriginal Workers and Workers of Colour committee. CUPE and the CAW have seats on their national executives reserved for representatives of Aboriginal committees. In order to facilitate the movement of Aboriginal members into union leadership positions, both PSAC and the CAW have Aboriginal leadership development programs. Aboriginal union activists also felt that ensuring that unions hired Aboriginal staff, particularly if they were engaging in Aboriginal organizing initiatives, was critical to increasing the influence of Aboriginal peoples within unions (Mills and Clarke 2009).

Aboriginal representation within union structures is often critical to getting Aboriginal awareness and anti-racist training on the agenda. "Unionism on Turtle Island," the most comprehensive Aboriginal awareness training course, is offered by CUPE, the Saskatchewan Government and General Employees' Union and many labour federations. Developed by a network of Aboriginal union activists through the Saskatchewan Federation of Labour, the course provides a history of how colonial practices and beliefs in Canada have affected Aboriginal and settler workers. By taking a historical approach, the course helps to dispel racism towards Aboriginal peoples rooted in the belief that Aboriginal peoples' inherent and treaty rights constitute unfair privileges. "Unionism on Turtle Island" has transcended some inter-union barriers. However, very few union locals have implemented mandatory Aboriginal awareness training, something that could make significant strides in creating a safe and supportive environment for Aboriginal workers.

These strategies are valuable and important to the lives of Aboriginal union members since they help to address the discrimination and disadvantage they face. Since many unions support human rights struggles for a variety of marginalized groups, supporting the struggles of Aboriginal individuals to combat racism, sexism and other forms of discrimination fits within their approaches to social unionism. However, since the above approaches are aimed at changing unions' internal culture and public self-representations, they often take place at a physical distance from Aboriginal communities, in urban locations or industrial development sites. These approaches do not require union engagement with the class politics within Aboriginal communities or with the issues that activities in Aboriginal jurisdictions would raise. Moving beyond this safer form of social unionism requires engagement with Aboriginal politics and the history of Aboriginal peoples' struggles for recognition of their distinct rights.

ABORIGINAL STRUGGLES

Over the past three decades, Aboriginal peoples have seen many positive developments, obtaining greater state, corporate and public recognition of their rights to lands and resources and self-determination. New legal precedents recognize Aboriginal rights and Crown duties to consult and accommodate Aboriginal peoples. Further political change has occurred through both formal political negotiations (through Comprehensive Land Claims Agreements, for instance) and policy changes resulting from court rulings and the findings of government commissions and inquiries. Thus, there is now increased state recognition of Aboriginal powers of governance on reserves, treaty settlement lands and claimed traditional territories. In addition to the formation of new Aboriginal governments through Comprehensive Claims or modern-day treaties, Aboriginal development corporations and businesses are increasingly involved in economic activities on Aboriginal territories. The underlying motivations of Aboriginal political institutions diverge from those of unions since they are grounded in Aboriginal assertions of nationhood, title and territorial rights. These developments, increasing access to resources and ability to self-govern, have conditioned labour's evolving relationship with Aboriginal workers and governments.

While Aboriginal peoples have contested colonial policies for generations, the last half-century has seen significant change in terms of state recognition of Aboriginal peoples' distinct relationship to their territories. In the late 1960s and early 1970s, Aboriginal peoples began reasserting their claims to their traditional territories in the courts. In the *Calder* case, the Nisga'a people in northwestern British Columbia sought a declaration that their title had never been extinguished (Godlewska and Webber 2007). The 1973 Supreme Court of Canada (SCC) decision split on the extinguishment of Aboriginal title and the deciding justice dismissed the case on procedural grounds. However, the SCC recognized the validity of the concept of Aboriginal title in law, and the *Calder* decision formed a basis for the development of the modern federal land claims process. Facing hydroelectric development on their lands, Cree and Inuit of James Bay in northern Québec were also asserting their claims in the early 1970s, and the 1975 James Bay and Northern Québec Agreement became Canada's first modern-day treaty. Subsequent comprehensive land claims have created a proliferation of Aboriginal treaty settlement lands and Aboriginal governance institutions across the north (Usher 2003), and the 1982 patriation of the Constitution included recognition of Aboriginal and treaty rights (Henderson 2006).

Other Aboriginal peoples used occupations and blockades to challenge the imposition of Crown regimes of land use onto pre-existing systems of Aboriginal tenure (Borrows 2005). Land conflicts at Oka in 1990 and Ipperwash in 1995 became flashpoint events that confronted the public with the fundamental mistreatment of Aboriginal peoples in Canada, helping to create political pressure to change governing policy orientations (Russell 2010). This set into motion both the Royal Commission on Aboriginal Peoples (1996) and the Ipperwash Inquiry (2007). Blockades have also been an effective tool of First Nations economic resistance, dissuading investment and pressuring governments to address Aboriginal claims (Blomley 1996; Morris and Fondahl 2002).

Aboriginal peoples have accrued further political and economic leverage as court victories recognized government duties to deal honourably with Aborginal peoples. In the 1997 *Delgamuukw* case, the Supreme Court recognized the contemporary validity of Aboriginal title, generating government responsibilities to reconcile Aboriginal claims with Crown title (Slattery 2006). Subsequent decisions have further clarified Crown duties to consult with Aboriginal peoples and accommodate their interests in developments on their claimed traditional lands, historic treaty lands and contemporary land claims territories.

Legal victories, comprehensive land claims and the devolution of specific authorities to Aboriginal peoples have reshaped the political geography of Canada's northern and Aboriginal spaces. As a result of these developments, Aboriginal peoples have increasingly been able to influence corporate activities on their territories. Corporations now attempt to negotiate legal agreements with communities that exceed their Crown obligations to accommodate Aboriginal interests, thereby decreasing the likelihood of disruptive Aboriginal protests or litigation and increasing the profile of the company as socially responsible and secure for investors (Gogal et al. 2005). The legal agreements documenting how companies seeking to exploit resources on traditional or treaty lands will compensate local Aboriginal peoples for development on their lands are termed Impact Benefit Agreements (IBAs). These twin developments of state recognition and direct involvement in economic development through corporate partnership and Aboriginal businesses create a complex environment for union activities.

UNIONS REACTING TO ABORIGINAL EMPOWERMENT

Unions' engagement at the local level on Aboriginal lands or in Aboriginal workplaces[3] has had to contend with complex political environments resulting from Aboriginal peoples' desires to enhance their effective jurisdiction on the one hand, and to promote economic development on their lands and in their communities on the other. Aboriginal efforts to meaningfully extend the exercise of Aboriginal sovereignty and class dynamics on Aboriginal lands and in Aboriginal workplaces have created a complex and often contradictory environment for labour organizing. Traditional union organizing assumes the jurisdiction of the Canadian state since it relies on provincial or federal labour legislation. Since unions aim to unite the working class over spatial boundaries and across ethnicities, they often organize with limited sensitivity to Aboriginal workers' and some community members' particular allegiances to employers who are Aboriginal or who have partnered with Aboriginal businesses or governments. Since economic development in Aboriginal territories often contributes to the collective wealth of the Aboriginal community, it complicates workers' allegiances, even when it is capitalist in form or driven by transnational investors.

Since unions traditionally represent workers in sectors where Aboriginal employers have made inroads, they have had to engage with this changing jurisdictional and political landscape. However, union motivations for engaging with local Aboriginal empowerment are mixed. In some cases, unions are simply resisting these changes, while in others they are adapting their organizing and representation strategies to increase Aboriginal peoples' access to collective bargaining. In neither case can union changes be called social unionism, but instead should be seen as reactions to Aboriginal peoples' growing influence in employment. Two main conflicts include industry-Aboriginal agreements overriding union hiring halls, seniority systems and delineations of merit, and the reorganization of the nature of service sector work in line with Aboriginal community interests and desires. We will discuss two examples where unions have taken reactive stances to Aboriginal empowerment: first, a case of Building and Construction Trades Unions' (BCTU) involvement in resource development in an Aboriginal settlement area; and, second, a case where a union representing academic staff at a small college[4] did not show support for an employer-driven program to indigenize their workplace. In each of these cases adaptations to the needs and desires of Aboriginal governments and workers were necessary for the union to carry out their normal activities rather than outcomes of a commitment to equity.

The construction of the Voisey's Bay nickel mine in traditional Inuit territories in Labrador provides an example of how corporate-Aboriginal partnerships create a challenging institutional environment for union activities, a situation which is amplified when unions are reactive or resistant to adapting to new employment structures. Soon after the discovery of a high quality nickel deposit in 1993, Voisey's Bay Nickel Company (VBNC) began consulting and building relationships with the Innu Nation and the Labrador Inuit Association (LIA). The LIA was able to use the discovery of mineral resources and the threat of halting the extraction to leverage a Comprehensive Land Claim Agreement and an Impact Benefit Agreement (IBA), the negotiations for which began in 1993 and ended in 2002, with mine construction beginning immediately after. While Comprehensive Land Claim Agreements are negotiated with federal and provincial or territorial governments, IBAs are confidential contracts with corporations wherein Aboriginal groups trade permission to develop their lands for cash, royalties, mitigation of environmental harm, opportunities for business development and employment and training opportunities.

Impact Benefit Agreements have evolved to become the principal mechanism Aboriginal governments use to ensure their members gain jobs and training from resource development on their territories. The IBA between the LIA and VBNC included provisions for the employment and training of LIA members during the construction and operations phases of the mine, as well as coordinator positions to ensure the future Inuit government (Nunatsiavut) would be able to enforce the IBA provisions. The Resource Development Trades Council of Newfoundland and Labrador (RDC)[5] and the Labrador Inuit Association only had contact with one another after construction had begun. References to the IBA in the Special Project Collective Labour Agreement between the RDC and Labrador and Voisey's Bay Employer Association signed in 2002 were limited to a stipulation that contractors had to follow IBA provisions for hiring and layoffs and that the unions, contractors and owners would work together to ensure that Inuit and Innu workers were trained and hired (SPCLA 2002).

The building trades unions had done minimal organizing in Labrador, particularly in remote coastal communities, and all of the union training centres and offices were located in Newfoundland. As a result, most unions had few if any Innu or Inuit members at the start of the Voisey's Bay project and there was no Aboriginal worker representation during the bargaining of the collective agreement. Furthermore, with a primarily non-Aboriginal membership, local unions sought to minimize Aboriginal hiring so their members could get work. This bias towards established, non-Aboriginal members was reinforced by the union perception that new Aboriginal members would not retain union membership after project completion. When Aboriginal people were hired on site, the RDC made little effort to integrate them into the union. Moreover, although the RDC was in an ideal position to facilitate the training of Inuit and Innu workers, they did not initiate any training partnerships. Thus, union contact with the Nunatsiavut government was predominantly antagonistic, with each group fighting for the employment of their members (Mills 2011).

Another instance where unions were faced with a changing political environment as a result of increasing recognition of Aboriginal peoples is in the case of the indigenization of a small public sector college in British Columbia. Indigenization is a term used to describe increasing Aboriginal control over the design and implementation of activities impacting the economic, political, social, cultural and ecological landscape of their territories. However, the indigenization of public sector work was influenced by the neoliberalization of the public sector as much as Aboriginal empowerment. As a result, public sector unions with an established social unionist tradition struggled with how to respond to indigenization. While desirous of increased justice for Aboriginal peoples, the college unions also sought to mitigate workplace reforms that were detrimental to their members. Lacking a comprehensive strategy to address the workplace changes brought on by increased Aboriginal control in a period of neoliberalism, unions again adopted a reactive posture, this time negotiating between a desire to protect established member interests and support for Aboriginal empowerment.

Indigenization was fiscally desirable for the college because of a changing post-secondary funding context that favoured shifting from base funding to targeted funding pools, implementing extended accountability measures, increasing partnership with Aboriginal communities and channelling funding through Aboriginal governments and organizations. Within the college, indigenization provided new committees for increased Aboriginal influence over post-secondary education in their region, as well as new staff positions to better support Aboriginal students and curriculum and programming changes to better represent Aboriginal concerns and community needs. However, these changes resulted in prioritizing technical and trades over academic programming and reorganizing the geography of educational delivery to increase access in Aboriginal communities. These changes increased instructors' workloads, as they were asked to increase student support, and threatened their academic freedom by constraining their ability to determine course content. While many of these initiatives allowed the college to access new funding pools, they also sought to further maximize the college's exploitation of instructors' labour, undermined instructors' autonomy and introduced new increasingly flexible and mobile regimes of work.

Thus, two union locals representing academic instructors and technical and trades instructors had an ambivalent response to an administration-led initiative to indigenize their workplace. Despite union rhetoric and policy promoting Aboriginal self-determination, the unions did not endorse the indigenization of their workplace as the Aboriginal inclusion strategies were accompanied by undesirable outcomes for their members. Instead the union selectively responded to and resisted particular changes through collective bargaining and grievances. Despite the fact that an efficiency-maximizing approach to educational reform at times conflicted with the needs and desires of the Aboriginal community, the unions' defensive posture through this period of neoliberal restructuring inhibited the development of union-Aboriginal alliances that could articulate an alternative vision for the reorganization of education reflecting the interests of workers and Aboriginal communities. However, while established unions sometimes struggled to adapt to the changing environment of Aboriginal control, in other cases unions have invested considerable resources in organizing Aboriginal workers.

ABORIGINAL ORGANIZING FOR EQUALITY

Despite the challenges presented by the intersection of Aboriginal empowerment with corporate interests and the neoliberal state, several unions are taking more proactive approaches to Aboriginal engagement at the local level. One promising area is new organizing strategies in Aboriginal communities or territories. Aboriginal organizing draws on the proposition that collective representation is critical to equity since it is the best way to increase the wages, benefits and work conditions of the most marginalized sectors of the workforce (Blackett and Sheppard 2003). Unions organizing in Aboriginal communities and workplaces often tailor their strategies to account for cultural and political differences. Unions recognize that they are often organizing workers who want or need to have solidarity with their employers in anti-colonial struggles.

Some of the organizing innovations implemented by CUPE include having a presence in the community prior to organizing, using Aboriginal organizers and ensuring that organizers are knowledgeable about cultural protocols. In some cases, union staff and activists have been able to build a relationship with the community and gain wider support for the union drive. PSAC's longstanding organizing efforts in Inuit hamlets throughout the north have used consensus decision-making to determine if workers want union representation. In their more recent Aboriginal organizing initiatives, PSAC has translated all union materials and incorporated Elder participation in union activities.

Despite these changes, however, union organizing in Aboriginal workplaces and on Aboriginal territories has often created tensions between Aboriginal leadership (who are often employers), Aboriginal workers and settler-dominated unions. Although Aboriginal employers may oppose union organizing for reasons that are similar to those of non-Aboriginal employers, their anti-union sentiment is interwoven with the desire for economic self-reliance as a key element of self-determination and a mistrust of settler-dominated unions. Regardless of whether they actually believe that unionization will hamper their ability to attain economic self-reliance, some Aboriginal employers fight unionization with a rhetoric that unions are colonial and against Aboriginal traditions (Newhouse 1993; Tourand 2004).

Aboriginal leadership has also mounted court cases opposing the validity of federal and provincial labour legislation on Aboriginal territories. The federal government has primary jurisdiction over the northern territories, reserve lands and Status Indians. Thus, workers on reserves generally fall under federal labour legislation provided they are conducting activities that are "Indian" in nature or related to "Indian lands." Federal jurisdiction therefore applies to band workers, teachers and health-care workers on reserves in the provinces. On- and off-reserve Aboriginal businesses often fall under provincial labour legislation. Challenging the applicability of labour relations legislation was most pronounced through the 1990s. The Assembly of First Nations passed a resolution stating that "First Nations have the right to conduct their labour relations without interference by other governments or their laws" (AFN 1999; Burton 1999). However, the Supreme Court of Canada upheld the applicability of the Canada Labour Code on reserves and in the northern territories in all cases it heard regarding its applicability to Aboriginal workers.

Aboriginal-owned casinos are another area of significant labour relations tension between Aboriginal management, workers and unions. Since casinos are generally a heavily organized sector, and since workers at Aboriginal casinos are just as likely to face workplace stresses as other casino workers, Aboriginal casinos have been targeted for organizing by unions. In his book on Aboriginal gaming, Belanger (2006) documents the Saskatchewan Indian Gaming Authority's (SIGA) use of common anti-union tactics such as firing union organizers and threats to employees to prevent the certifications filed by the CAW, PSAC and the Retail, Wholesale and Department Store Union in casinos throughout the province. The First Nations employers, however, also used jurisdictional ambiguities to try to dispel union activity. SIGA tried to nullify the certification of four casinos by the Saskatchewan Labour Relations Board in 1999, arguing that the casinos were under federal jurisdiction. Despite numerous organizing attempts, Belanger cites only one example of a successful union campaign to organize an Aboriginal-managed casino: the Great Blue Heron Charity Casino, where, after an Ontario Labour Relations Board decision determined that the casino was under the authority of the Ontario Labour Relations Act, the workers became represented by the CAW.

Aboriginal workers themselves are often skeptical of unions and retain mixed allegiances in unionized workplaces. After a history of exclusion from many unionized forms of employment, it is unsurprising that many Aboriginal workers view unions as a "white man's tool" and look to their own governments to secure their employment. Others, however, have seen unions as a means for caring for the collective well-being of Aboriginal workers and therefore as consistent with the valuing of Indigenous knowledge. For example, an Aboriginal activist in CUPE wanted to help organize the band workers in her community because she felt they were being treated in ways that were inconsistent with traditional teachings. When presented with union activities in workplaces owned or managed by their nation or located in their territories, Aboriginal workers must negotiate whether they feel their interests are best represented through their own leadership or through affiliation with largely settler-dominated unions. When organizing and representing workers on Aboriginal territories, the United Steelworkers' strategy has been to try to harmonize collective agreements with

Aboriginal employment provisions contained in IBAs. The logic is that collective agreements can strengthen the language around IBA promises, which the union can then help to enforce. This approach supports Aboriginal peoples' role in regulating employment while also recognizing a place for unions to represent Aboriginal workers.

A major concern, however, is that, in a period of neoliberal attack on organized labour, unions may curtail new organizing campaigns and focus on minimizing losses in the face of state and corporate austerity. As they are weakened by political-economic and cultural shifts, unions are increasingly reluctant to divert funds and efforts to new initiatives not associated with their "core" functions. There is a substantial concern that unions may decrease or cease efforts to expand unionization to further include Aboriginal workers and Aboriginal workplaces, as the cost of these new organizing campaigns often far exceeds the expected returns in membership dues. This is a serious problem because of the important role that collective bargaining can play in raising the wages, benefits and security of the lowest-paid and most precarious members of the workforce.

CONCLUSION

There is a complex geography informing the relationships between Aboriginal peoples and organized labour in Canada. In settler-dominated workplaces in the urbanized south of Canada, anti-racist and Aboriginal awareness campaigns have been key strategies to combat racism and ensure equitable treatment to Aboriginal peoples, although these programs operate on a scale that too often remains distant from the everyday experiences of rank-and-file members and the local practices of everyday discrimination in the workplace. Other social unionist initiatives have sought to link with Aboriginal struggles, although these efforts too have been limited and are often treated as tangential to core labour concerns.

Tensions between unions and Aboriginal peoples continue to be exacerbated by many unions' defensive posture towards Aboriginal peoples' anti-colonial struggles for greater economic self-sufficiency. The prioritization of non-Aboriginal members' interests has tended to prevail despite some promising efforts to adapt organizing and representation to the specificities of Aboriginal or indigenizing workplaces. For their part, Aboriginal governments and employers have at times adopted anti-union positions as a result of their desire to prioritize capitalist economic development in their communities. Moreover, the centrality of cultural and historical distinctiveness to Aboriginal struggles does not always mesh easily with union frames that emphasize the commonality of diverse workers in the struggle against capital. The fact that only a minority of both unionists and Aboriginal community members are at the same time anti-capitalist and anti-colonial unquestionably constrains efforts to build union-Aboriginal relationships capable of integrating the trajectories of their respective organizations.

In his submission to the Royal Commission on Aboriginal Peoples, Onondaga scholar David Newhouse raised the question of whether capitalist economic development was consistent with Indigenous cultural values and concluded that Aboriginal cultures' adaptability allows them to integrate their values into market economy forms (Newhouse 1993; Anderson 1999). However, if Indigenous values can integrate with the market economy, they can also be compatible with the traditions of labour organizing, as evidenced by the history of Aboriginal involvement in and with unions. Since the labour movement and Aboriginal values are often concerned with equity, unions can be seen as a way to guard against worker exploitation when multinational companies operate in Aboriginal lands and in partnership with Aboriginal enterprises.

A common desire for social justice offers significant possibilities for building reciprocal relationships between settler workers and Aboriginal peoples, some of which we have described above. Opposing environmentally and socially destructive manifestations of contemporary capitalist development, such as the building of the Mackenzie pipeline and the commodification of water, have historically been and can continue to be a point of political convergence and relationship-building between Aboriginal activists and non-Aboriginal labour activists. Unions can also learn much from the Aboriginal communities with which they engage. Within Aboriginal communities, there are increasing efforts to look towards Aboriginal frameworks for solutions (Battiste 2000; Garroutte 2003; Kuokkanen 2007; Wilson 2008). The language of reciprocity, reflecting traditional practices of building and maintaining relationships through the mutual exchange of gifts, expresses an alternative model for social solidarity. Integrating these traditions into Aboriginal labour organizing both recognizes the significance of Aboriginal identities to Aboriginal workers and also presents new opportunities to link labour organizing with established Aboriginal community practices and networks.

Ultimately, given that Aboriginal struggles and concerns are critical to advancing social justice in Canada, unions will continue to be asked to support Aboriginal peoples in their struggles for their rights and sovereignty as distinct peoples. Recognizing that, unions will need to extend their activities beyond the traditional concerns of organized labour to substantively engage with these Aboriginal struggles. Unions must develop differential modes of organizing that move between positions and employ multiple techniques of resistance (Sandoval 2000). Rather than adhering to a singular strategy, organizers need to link different paths of struggle, using the pull of different trajectories and the tensions between them to reorganize the terrain of politics. Building upon approaches to both connect to Aboriginal people as workers and as Aboriginal peoples, and to support Aboriginal communities in their struggles, offers possibilities for a social unionism both revitalized and reframed through reciprocal relationships to the cause of Aboriginal self-determination.

Notes

1. We use the term "Aboriginal" in its legal sense to denote the prior occupants of the territory known as Canada. This term is inclusive of First Nations, Metis and Inuit peoples. "Indian" is the established legal term for First Nations in Canada as defined

by the Indian Act, and we use it in particular instances as the appropriate legal or historical frame. However, we also use the term "First Nations," which many prefer, to denote band governments as well as people who identify as Indian, regardless of whether or not they have Indian Status. The term "Indigenous" is a designation for colonized first peoples world wide.

2. Lanark Manufacturing was an auto parts plant in Dunnville, Ontario, that employed approximately fifty women. The 1964 strike involved significant militancy on the part of the primarily white female workforce, but also saw Native women crossing the picket line to "scab."

3. We use the term "Aboriginal workplaces" broadly to refer to those situations where Aboriginal governments, organizations or businesses are the employer, as well as those situations where Aboriginal people predominate among the service-users or workers.

4. We have not used the name of the college to protect the confidentiality of the research participants.

5. The Resource Development Trades Council of Newfoundland and Labrador represents fifteen Building and Construction Trades Unions locals in the province. Each union is represented by their business manager and by one representative from their union international. The organization exists for the purpose of negotiating special project agreements for resource development projects in Newfoundland and Labrador.

9. CANADIAN LABOUR AND THE ENVIRONMENT: ADDRESSING THE VALUE-ACTION GAP

Dennis Soron

In recent decades, much debate in environmental policy circles has been devoted to analyzing what has come to be known as the "value-action gap." In its most common usage, this term refers to the discrepancy that often exists between people's professed concern about the natural environment and their continued involvement in unsustainable ways of life. While typically applied to individual behaviour, the term also readily lends itself to an analysis of the mismatch between environmental word and deed that prevails within dominant economic and political institutions. The most craven contemporary examples can be found in the area of corporate "greenwashing," through which business interests have sought to craft an upbeat green image even as they continue to engage in ecologically destructive activities and fight against effective government regulation. Governments and political institutions that affirm their commitment to sustainability while doing little to ensure its realization also provide an illustration of the value-action gap. In Canada, this duplicity is evident in the country's so-called "Kyoto Gap." In 2002, to much public fanfare from mainstream environmentalists and howls of protest from business groups, Canada formally ratified the Kyoto Protocol, committing itself to reducing the country's greenhouse gas (GHG) emissions to 6 percent below 1990 levels. Ten years later, national emissions have risen to well over 30 percent above the country's Kyoto targets. Despite successive federal governments' claims to global environmental leadership, Canada's GHG emissions have risen faster than those of any other industrial country, including those that have not even ratified Kyoto, like the United States (Flynn 2009; Rivers and Jaccard 2009). In December 2011, the federal government announced that Canada was withdrawing from Kyoto altogether.

The notion of the value-action gap also offers an interesting window into the Canadian labour movement's own complicated relationship to ecological sustainability. At the level of expressed values, official statements and policy documents, the movement as a whole has been a consistent advocate of progressive environmental reform. That said, as Nugent (2011: 71) has argued, the movement increasingly exhibits an "apparent contradiction between policy and practice" when it comes to the environment. Overall, while unions have undertaken a variety of green initiatives and established tactical alliances with environmental groups around a range of important issues, the ideals expressed in their policy statements have been inadequately integrated into their ongoing bargaining priorities, forms of political action and worker education and mobilization efforts. While the movement has done important ideological work challenging the "jobs versus the environment" frame exploited by business to undermine popular support for environmental regulations, it has also found itself pulled toward pragmatic positions that are inconsistent with labour's own stated principles and the public's broader interest in a healthy and sustainable environment.

Addressing this gap, and considering how to overcome it, forces us to reconsider the limits and possibilities of established labour strategies for confronting the challenges posed by contemporary environmental crises. It also leads us to consider some of the reasons that the generally pro-environmental ethos of unions in Canada has not translated into an effective program of action, or into durable alliances with progressive segments of the environmental movement. To some extent, this involves clarifying the basic principles of progressive unionism, but it necessarily goes beyond a simple moralistic critique of the apparent hypocrisy of unions or the personal failings of labour bureaucrats.

Instead of naively assuming that behaviours flow simply and directly from values, the notion of the value-action gap enables an analysis of the wide range of constraints and incentives that encircle individuals and shape their habitual patterns of action in ways that are out of alignment with the values they hold or claim to hold. Similarly, our analysis of labour's environmental strategy needs to be tempered by an awareness of the structural context of union action and mobilization; of the economic, political and cultural pressures that shape the terrain within which labour operates; and, more broadly, of labour's contradictory positioning within the overall system of capitalist production. In recent decades, a variety of developments in Canada have weakened labour's structural power, political leverage and capacity for mobilization: neoliberal economic restructuring; the liberalization of international trade and investment; attacks on the welfare state and social protections that shield workers from the volatility of the market; declining rates of unionization, alongside concerted attacks on labour rights and freedoms; and — most recently — global economic recession, financial crisis and the deepening crisis of the Canadian manufacturing sector. Taken together, such developments have led some labour organizations into defensive positions that draw them into greater alignment with employers and mainstream political parties, dilute their practical commitment to struggles beyond the workplace and generate conflict with progressive allies beyond the labour movement. In this context, labour's alliance with the broader environmental movement remains complicated and uneasy, and its capacity to play a constructive role in this movement faces a number of challenges that are often insufficiently appreciated by those anxious to witness the emergence of a more dynamic form of green unionism.

THE AMBIGUOUS PROMISE OF GREEN UNIONISM

For those hoping to see greater cooperation between the labour and environmental movements, the spectacle of Teamster members enthusiastically marching en masse alongside Sierra Club activists dressed as sea turtles at the 1999 World Trade Organization protests in Seattle provided an iconic moment. While heartening in many ways, such fleeting instances of symbolic convergence can belie the abiding conflicts, ideological tensions and institutional pressures that reproduce the familiar divide between labour and environmental struggles and undermine the development of a meaningful "blue-green" alliance.[1] For some critics (Burrows 1998; Gottlieb 2001; Foster 2002), the mainstream environmental movement has helped to perpetuate this divide by largely skirting around issues of work, class and economic power, crafting a single-issue form of green politics that aims to preserve nature without being mindful of the interests, anxieties and cultural self-understandings of workers whose livelihoods may be entwined with ecologically damaging forms of production and consumption. This failure to link the pursuit of ecological sustainability with sustainable livelihoods and economic justice is one of the key reasons that workers and their unions have often remained hostile toward environmentalists and susceptible to the "environmental job blackmail" tactics of employers (Kazis and Grossman, 1991).

While blue-green alliances have been impeded by the mainstream environmental movement's historical blindness to social class, this is only one part of the story. Indeed, we have perhaps arrived at a point where maintaining this focus upon environmentalists' haughty disregard for ordinary workers merely distracts union activists from deeper reflection on the labour movement's own ambivalent relationship to the quest for environmental sustainability. While the Sierra Club, Greenpeace and other international environmental organizations have come some distance in the years since the Seattle protests in integrating workers' concerns into their official platforms and campaigns (Greenpeace International and EREC 2009; Sierra Club 2009; Smith 2011), many key labour organizations have not made a comparable effort. Despite the possibilities suggested by Teamsters and Turtles marching together in Seattle, most influential segments of the American labour movement have remained fickle and opportunistic regarding environmental protection, paying tribute to it when expedient to do so and disregarding it when it appears to conflict with the immediate economic interests of union members. The American Federation of Labor and Congress of Industrial Organizations (AFL-CIO) and some of its key affiliates not only campaigned against Kyoto ratification, but have lobbied aggressively for the expansion of environmentally destructive activities like Arctic drilling and the commissioning of new nuclear and coal-fired power plants, remaining hostile to environmental regulations that might curtail employment in specific sectors, harm U.S. competitiveness or slow economic growth (Ness 2003).

While, as Silverman (2006: 193) argues, the emergence of a dynamic form of green unionism is an enticing political possibility in this era of ascendant corporate power and fractured progressive opposition, it must be acknowledged that this runs against the grain of labour's traditional association with "an instrumental view of nature and the belief that more jobs, more goods, and more wealth, whatever the environmental cost, are the solutions to workers' needs." Proponents of green unionism today need to openly confront the ways in which economism, sectionalism and productivism within the labour movement have traditionally marginalized the goal of environmental sustainability and curtailed the development of broad-based alliances with environmentalists.[2] As many green thinkers have emphasized, bringing an ecological perspective to bear upon economic life helps to reformulate our understanding of the antagonism between labour and capital (Porritt 1984; Porritt and Winner 1988). While labour and capital may differ strongly over the distribution of the fruits of production and workplace authority, this conflict need not imply any corresponding differences over the scale, intensity or ecological impact of economic activity. Indeed, unions' desire to improve wages, enhance consumption and secure workers a larger share of society's aggregate wealth often gives them a direct interest in the perpetuation of unsustainable economic growth and environmentally destructive firms and industries. In some cases, this orientation leads labour into positions that may narrowly serve the short-term economic interests of particular workers, but contradict broader principles of social, economic and environmental justice. The Québec labour movement's continued support for the production and export of asbestos is one prime example of this tendency (Dobbin 2010).

While labour's green commitments are often vulnerable to the pull of economism and sectionalism, we need to remember that workers' interests are not necessarily counterposed to environmental improvement. While mainstream media outlets focus disproportionately upon sensationalistic instances of conflict between workers and environmentalists, this downplays the ground they do share and the many ways they can and do work together for common goals. For example, as Mayer (2009: 7) argues, "concerns about health play a major role in the history and current activities of both the labor and environmental movements," providing one means of overcoming the divisive "jobs versus the environment" script and fostering deeper forms of blue-green cooperation. As former Canadian Labour Congress (CLC) official David Bennett (2011: 32) asserts, health issues can provide a bridge between workplace and community concerns, for "the pollutants that poison workers are also the toxins which erode community health and degrade the physical environment."

Even in a narrow economic sense, workers' interests are often well served by environmental regulations that help to create jobs, preserve the resources upon which local economies rely or force employers to adopt more labour-intensive production methods. In this light, Obach (2002) sees promise in what he calls the "Baptists and Bootleggers" model, whereby blue-green cooperation emerges at strategic points where the material self-interest of workers and the moral ideals of environmentalists happen to intersect. Of course, labour's relationship to the environment need not be purely opportunistic. Hrynyshyn and Ross (2011: 5) write, because working-class people are "more than simply wage-earners, but are also citizens with a wide range of other identities, they have experiences, problems, and therefore interests that extend beyond the workplace." Indeed, they suggest, it is precisely this more extensive notion of workers' interests that has underpinned the ethos of social unionism in Canada, and has inspired many unions to attempt to transcend the limits of conventional business unionism by developing a progressive position on the environment that speaks directly to matters of broad community concern.

GREENING THE CANADIAN LABOUR MOVEMENT

In line with its broadly social unionist ethos, the Canadian labour movement's engagement with environmental matters has generally been more expansive than that of its cousin to the immediate south. However, the history of this engage-ment reveals a number of contradictory pulls and unresolved tensions that have manifested themselves in an increasingly apparent value-action gap. From the fledgling efforts of labour occupational health and safety activists in the 1970s to address questions of pollution and community health, to the widespread formation of union environmental committees in the 1980s, to the labour-led development of green-work alliances in the 1990s, there have been many posi-tive efforts among unions in Canada to develop a social unionist approach to the environment and establish practical bridges between workers' interests and the pursuit of sustainability. Despite the country's relatively high proportion of workers in the energy, automotive, mining, forestry and other environmentally sensitive sectors, the CLC and many of its affiliates have been vocal public pro-ponents of Kyoto and other progressive environmental measures.

To the extent that labour organizations and the workers they represented benefited directly from the fruits of the post-war economic boom, unions in Canada were, throughout much of the 1950s and 1960s, largely caught up in an optimistic view of economic growth, technological development and mass consumerism, and hence at a significant distance from the practical concerns and counter-cultural ethos of the emergent modern environmental movement (Palmer 1992; McInnis 2002). While flare-ups of outright conflict between unions and the environmental movement, as happened in British Columbia between timber workers and Greenpeace activists in the 1990s (Harter 2004), have garnered a great deal of media and academic attention, the real story of Canadian labour's engagement with environmental concerns is much more nuanced and complex.

As David Bennett (2011) has chronicled, the origins of labour environmental-ism in Canada can be found in the worker-led health and safety activism of the 1970s. Concerned with the effects of industrial toxins upon people within and beyond the workplace, activists in many economic sectors, including most notably the mining and chemical industries, succeeded in incorporating some primary concerns of the environmental movement into the established repertoire of union activity, giving them a more pronounced human slant. In contrast to the more disinterested goals of protecting virgin forests or safeguarding threatened animal species, the threats posed by chemical hazards in the workplace and community meshed more easily with interest-based labour activism. Such activism, including wildcat strikes by miners in northern Ontario over toxic exposures and other militant measures, is today seldom given its due credit for spurring the creation of more stringent provincial and federal occupational health and safety legislation, including workers' right to know about chemical hazards and other workplace dangers and right to refuse unsafe work (Storey 2004). By leveraging its strategic power in the workplace to address questions of environmental health, labour has often been able to recast its negative public image, break down political barriers and establish alliances with a range of other community actors. Even in the midst of the divisive timber wars of the 1990s, unions in BC were able to spearhead a unified campaign with First Nations groups, public heath organizations and environmentalists for tougher dioxin discharge regulations for the pulp and paper industry. Such early collaborations around environmental health and toxics reduction helped to establish the groundwork for the emergence of larger scale and more durable alliances, such as the Labour Environment Alliance Society (LEAS), in the latter half of the 1990s (LEAS n.d.).

Throughout the 1980s and 1990s, environmental issues gradually acquired a higher profile within the policies and practices of much of the Canadian labour movement. Bennett (2011: 32) credits much of this institutional change to the tireless pioneering efforts of early "labour environmentalists" from a range of public and private sector unions, all of whom "saw environmental protection as a moral or political issue where workers have an interest, since workers were both polluters and the victims of pollution." Further opportunities for the development of cross-movement solidarity and activism were afforded by the fight against free trade from the late 1980s onward, with labour and environmental activists working together under the banner of groups such as the Pro-Canada Network and, later, the Action Canada Network (Bleyer 2001).

Perceiving that environmental issues were of growing concern to many union members and the Canadian public at large, and anxious to stake out a leadership position on them, the CLC, the Canadian Auto Workers (CAW), the United Steelworkers (USW), and other unions became more proactive in drafting environmental policy, forming environmental committees, undertaking innovative workplace initiatives and fostering working alliances with environmental groups. The CLC Environment Committee, beginning as a subcommittee of the Occupational Health and Safety Committee in 1989, became a standing committee of the CLC in its own right in the early 1990s, leading in turn to the development of an Environmental Liaison Group, which brought together labour activists and representatives from national environmental groups (Bennett

2007: 3, 5). Beginning in the mid-1980s, the CAW began to take a leading role in developing a social unionist approach to environmental and transportation policy, taking out memberships in a variety of environmental organizations, participating in a range of environmental hearings and roundtables, and revising the by-laws of its national constitution so as to require each local to have its own standing committee on the environment (Adkin 1998: 230). In 1990, the USW expanded its International Health and Safety Department to include environmental concerns, going on to become one of the country's leading forces in the development of blue-green policy and alliances with the environmental community (USW 2006).

Although reversing ecological decline will require a dramatic reinvigoration and expansion of the public sector and the non-market collective goods it provides, public sector unions in Canada to date have not played an especially important role in the advancement of labour environmentalism, in spite of their growing stature and importance within the labour movement as a whole. Perhaps because of their perceived sense of distance from the most overtly ecologically destructive sectors of economic activity, the environmental positions of such unions have tended to be quite weak and muted. Large public sector unions have until recently steered around any serious engagement with climate change and other key spheres of environmental policy, choosing instead to prioritize limited efforts to green their own workplaces through reductions in paper use, recycling, workplace energy audits and so on. The Canadian Union of Public Employees' (CUPE) 2007 green workplace guide, for instance, is largely focused on encouraging workers to engage in environmentally virtuous individual behaviours like biking to work, using public transit, not idling one's car during morning commutes, and turning off equipment when it is not being used. In other instances, as in the Canadian Union of Postal Workers' fight against increased private vehicle use for postal delivery, or in CUPE's campaign to ban bottled water, or in various transit unions' efforts to highlight their industry's green credentials, the environmental arguments invoked by unions have often seemed designed to simply bolster their own numbers or their members' own bargaining positions, rather than express any deeper commitment that applies to other environmental issues or spills over into other areas of union activity.

While it is beyond the scope of this chapter to provide a detailed historical account of all the various environmental initiatives and policies undertaken by different segments of the Canadian labour movement, it is fair to say that the majority of such activity over the past couple of decades has coalesced around the twin themes of "Just Transition" and "Green Jobs." Associated initially with the pioneering work of American labour leaders like Tony Mazzocchi of the Oil, Chemical and Atomic Workers in the 1970s, the notion of Just Transition was taken up early in Canada by unions such as the Energy and Chemical Workers Union, gradually becoming a central feature of labour-environmentalist discourse in the country and the focal point of some solid union policy documents (CLC 1999; CEP 2000). The real strength of the Just Transition model promoted by the CLC, Communications, Energy, and Paperworkers' Union (CEP) and other labour groups has been its ability to move ideologically beyond the "jobs versus the environment" stalemate. It acknowledges that job losses in certain sectors will occur in the transition to a more sustainable economy, but insists that the burdens of ecological reform should not simply be offloaded onto workers. Accordingly, displaced workers should have access to income protection, education and retraining opportunities and alternative employment. Of equal importance, disproportionately affected communities should garner targeted government investment for new sustainable industries and services, and be given preferential consideration for new public sector jobs.

While similarly addressed at easing workers' fears, the green jobs agenda that has emerged within key sectors of the Canadian labour movement has been more optimistic in tone than the Just Transition model, presenting environmental reform not as a harm to be mitigated but as an opportunity to be embraced. While business groups typically exploit worker anxieties by linking environmental action to massive job loss, a CLC (2008: 3) document on climate change and green jobs argues that Canada actually "has an unprecedented opportunity to create new and better jobs as part of a planned transition to a much more energy efficient and environmentally sustainable economy." The CLC's Green Job Creation Project, initiated in 1999 and formally adopted in 2003, along with the ongoing work of CEP and BlueGreen Canada, a formal alliance between the Canadian branch of USW and the group Environmental Defence begun in 1999, have helped to establish the green jobs agenda as the cornerstone of much contemporary environmental policy and debate in the Canadian labour movement. From the outset, as in the innovative work done by groups such as the Green Work Alliance and the Coalition for a Green Economic Recovery in the 1990s, this agenda has been framed as a means of counteracting the historical problem of rising industrial unemployment by re-employing existing industrial capacity and worker skills toward sustainable, socially useful production. That said, this initial focus has expanded in recent years as labour activists and thinkers have begun to connect the green jobs agenda to potential job growth in the public sector, the female-dominated service sector and other areas of the economy (Harden-Donahue and Peart 2009; Stevens et al. 2009).

Although the Just Transition and green jobs agendas have functioned mostly as hypothetical possibilities and have yet to bear much fruit in any practical sense, they have had important indirect effects. Indeed, it can be convincingly argued that the Canadian labour movement's laudable support for the Kyoto accord was itself enabled by its longstanding work on the Just Transition model and on the opportunities for increased employment in burgeoning sectors of the emergent green economy. In the lead-up to Canada's ratification of the Kyoto Protocol, alarmist job blackmail tactics were widely employed by business lobby groups such as the Canadian Manufacturers and Exporters, who argued that Kyoto would lead to massive job loss and cost increases for ordinary Canadians. Canadian labour's support for Kyoto, focusing on the key themes of Just Transition and green jobs, played a very important public pedagogical role in countering this quasi-populist fear campaign and bolstering public support for public action against climate change (Nugent 2011).

IT'S NOT EASY BEING GREEN

While the Canadian labour movement's work in support of Kyoto was undeniably a critical contribution to national environmental debate, Nugent (2011: 65) has argued that "labour environmental activists have struggled — especially since Kyoto ratification — to implement concrete initiatives." Indeed, in some cases the very unions that had previously been the most vocal supporters of Kyoto — such as the CAW — have drifted towards more ambiguous positions, supporting environmental goals in the abstract but resisting efforts to implement Kyoto targets or to apply more stringent environmental standards to particular industries where the spectre of job loss has loomed increasingly large. This value-action gap surrounding Kyoto mirrors the broader problem that the Canadian labour movement has had in translating the pro-environmental principles outlined in declarations, policy papers and speeches into any kind of coherent and sustained environmental strategy.

While Canadian labour groups, especially when set against the uninspiring example of the U.S. labour movement, are rightfully proud of the pro-environmental stands and initiatives they have adopted in recent decades, they clearly still have a long way to go. Part of the reason that established labour strategies for addressing environmental sustainability have not gained any significant political traction is external in nature. Economic crises, political assaults on unions, declining rates of union density and other factors that have tilted the playing field decisively towards employers have all made environmental commitments harder to sustain in practice, and have highlighted fissures even within unions committed to social unionist principles. While external influences have played an important part in the impasse of green unionism, the relative stagnation of labour-based environmentalism has also been a reflection of the lack of resources and mobilization devoted to environmental education and action within unions, the abiding gulf between immediate bargaining priorities and ostensible social unionist commitments, conflicts within the broader labour movement, organizational maintenance issues and — to some extent — flaws in labour's chosen strategies. Instead of simply restating the broad environmental ideals with which labour has associated itself historically, union activists today need to consider why various key initiatives in the past have not borne fruit in any significant way.

Rank-and-file occupational health and safety activism, for instance, has not provided the foundation for wider labour mobilization around environmental issues relevant to the broader community, and is considered by many unionists to be stagnant and constrained by labour-management bureaucratic bodies (Storey 2004). While the institutionalization and co-optation of rank-and-file activism has played a part in this process, it is also true that Bennett, Mayer and others have seriously underestimated the barriers that frequently prevent workplace health concerns from being translated into community-oriented environmental action. Indeed, in many instances — in the nuclear, uranium and coal industries, for example — claims about worker safety on the job site, bolstered by employer-backed scientific research, often provide a means for workers' groups to downplay or dismiss community environmental and health concerns. Laurie Adkin's (1998) trenchant study of the Energy and Chemical Workers Union and its relationship to the petrochemical industry, for instance, reveals the extent to which relatively affluent unionized workers in dangerous, highly polluting industries can be reluctant to challenge their employers on health or environmental grounds, and quite hostile to the meddling of "outsiders" in the broader community.

It also bears mentioning that the immediate dangers experienced by workers on the job are not always equivalent, in a qualitative or quantitative sense, to the externalized costs of production imposed upon others beyond the job site. Indeed, in many cases such costs are significantly displaced across time and space. Workers involved in energy-intensive industries today, for instance, do not suffer in any direct way from the greenhouse gases their industries generate, although such emissions are leading cumulatively to dire problems for future generations. Similarly, workers involved in industrial operations in urbanized areas may be quite insulated from the health and environmental problems experienced by remote mining towns, First Nations populations and hinterland resource communities located elsewhere along an industry's long production chain. Because workers are often distanced psychologically, geographically and temporally from the full effects of the industries in which they are involved, their experiences on the job site do not necessarily provide any basis for understanding or acting upon broader environmental issues that impact others. All of this is not to suggest that, historically, unions in Canada and beyond have not attempted in earnest to integrate ecological goals and perspectives into their own strategies and institutional practices, but that such efforts have often tended to be undercut by countervailing institutional, material and ideological pressures. This is borne out in many instances in the contemporary Canadian labour movement, even in the cases of unions that have consistently attempted to transcend business unionism's narrow economism and sectionalism by explicitly adopting an ethos of social unionism.

If, as Derek Hrynyshyn and Stephanie Ross (2011: 6) have argued, "in many ways, environmental protection is the quintessential social unionist issue," then the relative political ineffectiveness of labour environmentalism to date also offers an especially revealing window into many of the abiding tensions within contemporary forms of social unionism. Hrynyshyn and Ross have offered an excellent illustration of the contradictions within social unionist approaches to the environment in their analysis of the growing gap between the CAW's principled support for progressive environmental reform and its increasingly problematic defence — in the context of mass layoffs and economic crisis — of the North American auto industry, the jobs it provides and automobility more generally. Apart from its short-lived involvement in the Green Car Industrial Strategy alliance with Greenpeace, the David Suzuki Foundation and the New Democratic Party (CAW 2003), the CAW has tended to focus upon environmental issues that are disconnected from the auto industry itself and its manifold impacts upon collective life, and has not adequately integrated environmental goals into the demands it places upon employers. In this light, Hrynyshyn and Ross (2011: 2) suggest social unionist principles can often simply be "an add-on rather than a fundamental reorientation of a union's role and purpose." This add-on logic helps to explain the disappointing trajectory of the CAW's once-heralded local environmental committees, which have now mostly fallen stagnant, restricting their activities to symbolic gestures like sending small delegations to annual Earth Day festivities. To the extent that such committees were mandated from above by the CAW's national leadership as an expression of its social unionist principles, they have lacked any organic link with rank-and-file activism from below, remaining quite uncertain about their mandate and timid in their relations with management.

In other cases, such tensions are also apparent in the limited, tactical partnerships that unions often form with environmental groups around particular issues to advance their own economic goals. One instance of this "business unionism by other means" is the alliance between Greenpeace Canada and the CEP surrounding opposition to the Keystone XL pipeline (intended to carry unrefined oil from the tar sands to the US). While much of the campaign material produced by this alliance has focused on the potential environmental effects of this pipeline (potential oil spills and disruption to habitat), the environmental message seems muted and half-formed, papering over the misalignment between Greenpeace's goal of radically curtailing the tar sands and the CEP's own goal of preserving jobs in the non-renewable energy sector. In the case of central labour bodies, this tension is evident in the delicate balancing act of maintaining fidelity to certain universal social unionist principles regarding the environment while simultaneously striving to accommodate the sectional interests of workers in existing industries, which often clash with such principles. This dynamic has meant that organizations like the CLC, for the purposes of organizational maintenance, have either simply steered clear of particular "hot" issues (such as forestry), or gradually weakened their principled opposition to specific industries (such as nuclear power) subsequent to sectionalist pressure (Savage and Soron 2011). What results in such cases is an increasingly apparent gap between the high-minded environmental ideals to which labour claims allegiance and the weak, compromised or even regressive positions that it actually adopts in practice.

While the Just Transition strategy proposes a way for labour to transcend many of the pragmatic compromises it is currently compelled to make, this strategy has also arrived at an impasse. Unfortunately, as even CLC insiders like David Bennett (2011: 35, 67) have come to acknowledge, this strategy has "remained largely a slogan and a well articulated theoretical program" rather than a sustained and focused political project. In the absence of government commitment to transitional measures, and of a more proactive and mobilizing approach on the part of labour, Just Transition arguments can often function defensively, reinforcing the status quo by implying that even the most urgent environmental reforms can only be contemplated if they come along with guarantees that they will not have a negative effect on workers in existing industries (Adkin 1998). To this extent, Just Transition discourse — much like the jobs versus the environment discourse wielded by employers — tends to uniquely position environmental reform as a source of job loss, even though it is in many cases a net generator of jobs (Kazis and Grossman 1991; Renner et al. 2008). In recent decades, even in the absence of stringent environmental regulation, many sectors of the Canadian economy (including some heavily unionized ones) have seen massive job loss thanks to free trade, technological change, consolidation, outsourcing, capital flight, financial crisis and other forms of profit-driven restructuring. In the first decade of the twenty-first century, hundreds of thousands of manufacturing jobs have been lost in Canada, creating dire circumstances for many workers who continue to lack adequate access to Employment Insurance, education and re-training opportunities, and other resources to help them transition into new types of work that compare favorably in terms of wages and benefits to their old jobs.

As the CLC (1999: 18) itself has acknowledged, "it is difficult in principle to justify providing extraordinary adjustment assistance to workers affected by societal decisions with respect to the environment and not to workers affected by other societal decisions." In the absence of a broad-based labour effort to ensure that workers have social protections to safeguard their livelihoods from a variety of looming threats, particularly those related to the actions of employers and the business community more generally, Just Transition arguments about the effects of hypothetical environmental reforms seem strangely out of place and extremely selectively applied. Such arguments are also weakened to the extent that they are not integrated into unions' ongoing bargaining priorities and public campaigns. As a case in point, the CAW's "Manufacturing Matters" campaign, launched in early 2007, was relatively successful in terms of public education about the human cost of industrial job loss, and in terms of mobilizing public rallies in defence of such jobs in several Ontario cities (Ross 2011). By the same token, however, its blanket defence of manufacturing as an unambiguous public good smacked of a certain nostalgia for post-war Fordism, an era comprising the most environmentally destructive decades in human history. Oriented more towards historical resurrection than transition or transformation, this much-publicized campaign remained surprisingly devoid of any acknowledgement of the environmental or human cost of traditional manufacturing, and of the need to transition away from industrial gigantism and mass consumerism to more sustainable patterns of production and consumption.

While in some ways promising, the Canadian labour movement's commit-ment to the green jobs agenda is also beset with problems and inconsistencies that manifest themselves in an apparent value-action gap. For example, Hrynyshyn and Ross (2011: 12) suggest that solving the current ecological crisis

will require, amongst other things, not just the creation of a "green jobs" sector or the attraction of "green capital" to a particular community or country, but rather a thorough structural transformation of our entire economy involving new forms of production and consumption as well as new relationships between the state and the market…. Moreover, the fight for environmentally sustainable economic activity also implies a challenge to employers' power over investment decisions, product choice and design, the use of technology, and job creation, implicating the labor-management relationship as a terrain of environmental struggle and raising the question of what gets discussed and negotiated there.

The green jobs agenda, as it is currently articulated within dominant sectors of the Canadian labour movement, does not envision any large-scale transformation of economic structures and relationships, reconciling itself to a partnership-based approach in which production and investment priorities remain largely driven by the profit-seeking imperatives of green capital, and workers' jobs, capacities, identities, consumption habits and everyday patterns of life remain largely unaltered.

In this version of "ecological modernization," older, inefficient technologies, production processes and consumer goods are felicitously replaced by ostensibly greener substitutes, without requiring significant change to the overall logic of production, existing power relations or consumerist ways of life. The specific character of these substitutions can often simply displace rather than resolve existing problems, generating a host of new social and ecological crises of their own. As Nugent (2011) suggests, labour's embrace of the green jobs agenda can become the means by which it accedes to capital's effort to steer clear of the kind of state-driven structural change required for true sustainability, and to reshape environmental goals in ways that are compatible with its own interests. While this subordination of environmental reform to the priorities of capital opens the door to pervasive greenwashing, it also enables labour groups like the Power Workers' Union, which has campaigned alongside industry allies for the expansion of "clean coal" and nuclear energy, to ally itself with environmental ideals while remaining safely within the fold of economism and sectionalism (Savage and Soron 2011).

CONCLUSION

While a host of progressive thinkers have called for the further development of a blue-green or red-green political strategy, serious obstacles remain in the way of labour-environmental alliances based on solid principles of economic and environmental justice. Today, at a time of wide-ranging environmental and economic insecurity, an array of internal and external pressures can often lock labour organizations into reactive and short-term forms of thinking, leading them into alliance with industry against environmentalists, or into an embrace of productivist, elite-led "solutions" to current crises that merely displace and perpetuate the social and environmental damage caused by our current socio-economic system. While there are many ways unions can ideologically align themselves with environmental goals and contribute practically to the development of a more sustainable economy, their ability to play an aggressive or leading role in this process is curtailed at present by their loss of structural power and mobilizing ability, their lack of strategic clarity and organizational unity and the heightened economic vulnerability faced by unionized and non-unionized workers.

That said, many of the most valuable things that labour can contribute to the quest for environmental sustainability go beyond its own environmental activities per se, spilling over into the broader political effort to regulate and challenge the authority of capital, enhance the sphere of decommodified public goods, transform the meaning, purpose and duration of paid work, and fight for social and economic rights and protections that render workers less fearful and vulnerable in the face of environmental reform by mitigating their dependency upon the market for survival. Whatever obstacles it may confront, the labour movement has an important responsibility today to help foster, in the ways that it can, a broad-based movement for change that integrates the quest for environmental sustainability with the pursuit of economic equality and social justice. Ultimately, moving beyond today's limited political horizons and toward a genuine solution to our current ecological crisis will require strengthening anti-capitalist currents within the labour and environmental movements, fostering a shared awareness of the systemic origins of both economic and environmental exploitation and injustice.

Notes

1. In recent years, the term "blue-green" has become a popular way of designating a variety of working partnerships between labour and environmental groups, and this usage has spilled over into the formal names of particular groups such as BlueGreen Alliance in the United States and BlueGreen Canada. Blue-green partnerships are typically understood to be more pragmatic and centrist in nature than so-called "red-green" initiatives and coalitions, which are typically associated with a more radical, anti-capitalist orientation.
2. For a discussion of sectionalism and economism, see Swartz and Warskett, this volume.

10. COMMUNITY UNIONISM AND THE CANADIAN LABOUR MOVEMENT

Simon Black

In the Canadian labour movement, discussions concerning union renewal have centred on organizing the unorganized, increasing rank-and-file participation, democratizing decision-making structures within unions and developing new tactics and strategies (Kumar and Schenk 2006). Within this context, new practices of unionism are being explored — some of which draw on past traditions — including global unionism and social movement unionism. In recent years, "community unionism" (CU) has also entered the lexicon of Canadian labour. Yet CU's characteristics have been difficult to pin down, with competing conceptualizations making it an especially slippery concept. Ask any two union activists or labour scholars to define CU and you are likely to get two very different answers.

To clarify, there are essentially two sets of organizing practices (or organizing models) that fall within the rubric of community unionism.[1] One model centres on the coalitions and cooperative partnerships unions forge with community actors in the pursuit of the goals and interests of either or both (Lipsig-Mummé 2003), sometimes referred to as "coalition unionism" (Tattersall 2005 2010). The other model, that of community-based workers' organizations, asks us to look beyond the traditional labour movement and explore new forms of organizing that both challenge contemporary union strategies and also draw on the "repertoires of contention"[2] that have characterized the radical edge of the labour movement in the past. This model is best exemplified in worker centres, which are community-based workers' organizations that address a range of issues, including working conditions and wages, but also concerns such as immigration policy and employment standards legislation (Choudry and Thomas, this volume). Whereas the former model of CU sees the potential for union renewal in union-community linkages, the latter demands that we rethink our ideas about what the labour movement is and should be.

In this chapter, I argue that in both models there lies the potential for building the power necessary to challenge neoliberalism and reverse the decline of working-class fortunes. But first it is helpful to consider the different ways in which labour movement activists and scholars have employed the term "community." I then move to the history and development of community unionism as a concept and practice within the labour movement and the field of community organizing. This requires a brief trip outside Canada to the U.S., where radical movements of the 1960s first experimented with the idea of "community unions." In conclusion, I suggest that Canadian labour needs to explore more fully the power and potential of community unionism.

THE "COMMUNITY" IN COMMUNITY UNIONISM

One of the troubles with defining community unionism stems from the ambiguity of the term "community" (Stewart et al. 2009). In the union renewal literature there are three conceptualizations of community used interchangeably: community as a substitute for the term "community-based organization"; community as a people with a common identity or interest such as the Latino community or low-income communities; and community as a geographical space in which people live, such as a local neighbourhood (Stewart et al. 2009; Tattersall 2010). In most studies of community unionism and community organizing, there is overlap between two or more of these definitions. For instance, the term "low-income communities" refers to people with shared economic circumstances living in a common geographical space and may also imply common interests by virtue of these shared circumstances (e.g., better employment opportunities for residents of the neighbourhood). The Chinese Staff Workers' Association, a worker centre in New York City's Chinatown, organizes Chinese immigrants working in low-wage jobs in the neighbourhood's restaurants, nail salons and garment factories. Here, community is both the geographic site of organizing (i.e., Chinatown) and the constituency being organizing (i.e., low-wage immigrant workers from the Chinese community).

In practice, "community operates as the combination of each of these different structures… these three definitions of community are not mutually exclusive; they are reinforcing and connected" (Stewart et al. 2009: 8). However, it is important to note that the way community is understood theoretically informs how it is acted upon politically and practically (DeFillipis et al. 2006). For this reason, I want to problematize community — recognizing it as a contradictory and contested concept (DeFillipis et al. 2010) — by exploring it in relation to its historical usage on the left; to class and identity; and to the contemporary political economy of neoliberalism.

Before the rise of second-wave feminism, gay liberation and anti-racist movements in the 1960s, there existed a fair bit of romanticization of working-class community in labour history and on the left in general. Communities such as the coal pit towns of northern England and Cape Breton stood as bastions of working-class organizing, radical politics and resistance to the inhumane conditions of industrial capitalism. The confluence of a common class position and shared inhabitance of a particular geographical space produced strong bonds of solidarity amongst working-class people. Workers lived and toiled side by side, sharing the struggles of work and everyday life. Their common interests vis-à-vis their employers and the capitalist state were manifest in their working conditions and wages and in the conditions of their neighbourhoods and communities (reflected in housing, a lack of public services etc.). Cultural institutions such as benevolent societies and working men's clubs cemented working-class solidarity outside the workplace through cultural events and other shared spaces of social interaction. And most unions, before their growth into the large bureaucratic organizations they are today, were much more rooted in the daily lives of workers and their families outside the workplace (Hyman 2002: 7).

According to DeFillipis, Fisher and Shragge (2010: 14) there is a reason that projects of transformative change, from the struggles of workers to those of oppressed racialized groups, have historically been the product of organizing and mobilizing in local communities: "in local communities, as in workplaces, because of shared space and often shared social position, people can be brought together to act." Yet community can have a dark side: it can also be about the suppression of difference and the construction of common interests that excludes or marginalizes the interests of "others" (Young 1990). Working-class families in Cape Breton's coal towns may have had a shared interest in improving wages and working conditions, but what about the interests of women in the community vis-à-vis their husbands and patriarchal household structures? What might such communities have been like for gay and lesbian people given that heteronormativity was the hegemonic mode of sexuality? The assumption of homogeneity of identity or interests in community can work to erase very real differences and power inequalities within that community, whether on the basis of gender, sexuality, race or class.[3]

We must also try to understand contemporary uses of the term community in relation to the political economy of neoliberalism. Since the 1980s, many community organizations have become more collaborative (with the state and capital) and integrated into the neoliberal agenda (DeFillipis et al. 2006). Community organizations in the non-profit sector have increasingly become social service delivery agents as the neoliberal state downloads its responsibilities for social welfare onto cities and communities (DeFillipis et al. 2010). Rather than contest power and make claims on the state, many community organizations seek co-operation and collaboration with neoliberal governments. For DeFillipis, Fisher and Shragge (2006, 2010), community organizing which challenges neoliberalism understands community not as being about a place — i.e., limited by geographic or identity-based boundaries — but within a place, emphasizing local processes that can create linkages beyond the community. If such linkages are not made, then we "should not expect community to be able to engage in anything but working to improve, in a limited way, local conditions" (DeFillipis et al. 2006: 687), leaving broader structures of power and inequality unchallenged.

There are thus two important points to keep in mind as we explore community unionism and community's varied relationship with the labour movement. First, when it comes to political and social struggles, the meaning of community is always open, contested and in the process of becoming. Community organizing, whether independent of unions or in collaboration with them, always involves the social construction of a community's common interests in order to build solidarities and make claims on governments or employers. While common interests are the soil in which solidarity and collective action grow, we must always look out for modes of collective action and claims-making that suppress important differences and inequalities within communities. Second, following DeFillipis, Fisher and Shragge (2006, 2010), community-based organizing that effectively increases working-class power in the neoliberal era looks beyond the local to build solidarity and social movements that connect community issues to broader structures of power and inequality both in theory and in practice.

COMMUNITY UNIONISM: GENEALOGY OF A LABOUR MOVEMENT KEYWORD

The term "community unions" was first used in the United States to describe a new approach to organizing the urban poor. In an influential piece, James O'Connor (1964: 146) predicted that in the future, due to long-term unemployment and the deskilling of work, "the social base for working-class organizations will lie more and more in the community… community unions clearly will be the appropriate mode of working-class organization and struggle." O'Connor argued that if a growing number of workers were unemployed, then new models of working-class organization would have to be developed. Trade unions were modelled on the assumption that workers had long-term attachments to a single employer at a single worksite (in the industrial union model) or to a particular craft, with the portable membership and hiring halls of craft unions. For O'Connor (1964: 146), "since the poor lacked steady jobs… the community rather than the workplace was the logical place to organize them."

O'Connor argued that community unions should focus their energies on improving housing, welfare and public services. He predicted that these new organizations would spring up in deindustrialized towns and urban slums across the United States. His vision was put into practice by Students for a Democratic Society (SDS), one of the key organizations of the American New Left.[4] Looking to build the power of poor communities, SDS sent organizers into the poor neighbourhoods of northern U.S. cities beginning with Newark, New Jersey, in 1963 (Fine 2003a). The Newark Community Union Project was the first of its kind to undertake this experiment in organizing the poor into "unions."

SDS's project was driven not only by a desire for social justice but also the New Left's search for a historical agent of social change to replace the working class. Many on the New Left believed the working class had been disarmed by the post-war culture of consumer capitalism and was led by a labour movement that had become "an ossified mass that tended to follow the tune of the corporate elite" (Ashbolt 2008: 38). Various well-known leftists of the era, from the sociologist C. Wright Mills to the Marxist historian E.P. Thompson, had concluded that the working class as a "class-for-itself" had ceased to exist (Ashbolt 2008). For SDS, the dominance of business unionism (Ross, this volume) signalled the organized working class's thorough incorporation into the modern capitalist system and the state's legalistic management of class conflict (Swartz and Warskett, this volume). In contrast to workers, the poor were fixed at the margins of the system: unemployed, poorly housed and ripe for mobilization — if not revolution. In order to focus on the poor, organizers shifted their attention from the sphere of work to the sphere of community (Ashbolt 2008: 39).

However, critics of this strategy argued that the workplace still presented possibilities for organizing that the community did not. As one such critic stressed, "no force in nature or society throws people together in a social fashion the way that work does" (Ashbolt 2008: 40). As Marx argued, the social relations of work that pitted the common interests of labour against the capitalist boss was unique in fomenting the class consciousness and modes of struggle necessary for the social transformation of the capitalist system (Marx 1990). Community unionists rejected such criticism, arguing that it reflected what C. Wright Mills (1960: 22) called "the labour metaphysic" i.e., Marxists' fixation on the working class as the only true agent of social transformation.

Thus, the theorization of community unions as an instrument of class struggle in part reflected a conscious rejection of organized labour by many on the New Left (Ashbolt 2008: 40). Yet both critics and proponents of community unionism did little to overcome the conceptual dichotomy between "the poor" and "the working class" which has proved so problematic for labour organizing. While the concept of "organized labour" was (and remains) synonymous with unionized workers, the poor were not thought of as workers and their organization into community unions thus fell outside the established boundaries of "the labour movement" (Coulter, this volume). While this dichotomy signalled recognition of long-term or intergenerational unemployment in poor neighbourhoods, it also reflected the labour movement's abandonment of projects to organize the jobless working class, such as the unions of the unemployed established during the Great Depression (Clawson 2003). In Canada, such organizing resulted in the formation of the Relief Camp Workers Union and the On-to-Ottawa Trek in 1935, which built momentum for the development of the Canadian welfare state and the creation of the social wage (Waiser 2003: 261–77). For these reasons, contemporary anti-poverty organizations such as the Ontario Coalition Against Poverty should be understood as community unions (Black 2005; Coulter, this volume).

Not all organizers within the labour movement accepted this dichotomy or rejected the idea of community unions. In the United Auto Workers' (UAW) Industrial Union Department, organizers like Jack T. Conway called for a new model of unionism that built on the example of César Chávez and the United Farm Workers (Fine 2003a: 313). Conway observed that the Farm Workers were developing a new organizational form because "the problems that face farm workers and their families go far beyond the workplace and work relationship, and for an organization to be effective in dealing with these problems it has to deal with the totality of the situation" (Fine 2003a: 313). Conway realized that labour unions did not function in ways that reached the urban poor or some members of the working class, such as migrant farm labourers. Like O'Connor, Conway believed that the labour movement must come to see the community as if it were a factory or workplace. The techniques and tactics of traditional unions could then be employed to organize the community and defend its interests (Fine 2003a).

This conceptualization of CU has strong parallels to what is now called community organizing, broadly defined as the process in which people who live in proximity to each other come together around shared interests (DeFillipis et al. 2010). Indeed, the community union projects of SDS and the UAW built on strong traditions of community organizing in the U.S. dating back to Saul Alinky's Industrial Areas Foundation (Fine 2003a). This connection was evident in organizing other groups of workers in the 1960s, including mothers on welfare, who insisted they were "workers" deserving of a "wage" (in the form of welfare benefits) by virtue of the unpaid care work they did in the home.[5] These mothers organized into the National Welfare Rights Union (NWRU). Local chapters of the NWRU evolved into the largest and arguably most powerful community-based organization in North America, the Association of Community Organizations for Reform Now (ACORN) (Coulter, this volume). While groups like ACORN long ago dropped the union tag, these historical examples show that there is a vibrant tradition of organizing workers in the community, whether employed or unemployed, working in the formal economy or at home.

The other dominant conceptualization of community unionism — the labour-community coalition — has a lineage that can be more immediately traced to the union renewal debates of the 1990s (Banks 1992; Tufts 1998). However, the idea of unions and community groups forging alliances to advance shared interests is nothing new. Indeed, union-community coalitions have a long history in labour organizing. As Piven (2008: 18) notes, the labour movement's "new" strategic emphasis on community "has clear precursors in the efforts early in the 20th century of American unions based in the skilled crafts to organize community boycotts of recalcitrant employers, as well as sympathy strikes or even general strikes." The same can be said of the Canadian labour movement, as struggles such as the Nine-Hour Movement of the 1870s relied on close ties to the community, as did early efforts to win union recognition that employed community participation in boycotts and other measures aimed to force employers to recognize unions and collectively bargain (Heron 1996: 14–5).

The labour movement's (re)discovery of community is thus partly about rediscovering past values, visions, practices and modes of organizing that were central to its success prior to the development of modern systems of industrial relations. This process of rediscovery cannot be divorced from the crisis of the labour movement in the neoliberal era, as unions look for ways to reverse their declining influence and rebuild workers' power, or from the re-emergence of conditions — such as widespread precariousness — that characterized labour markets prior to capitalism's "Golden Age," from 1945 to the late 1970s. The labour movement's growing interest in community — whether in the form of community-union alliances or community-based workers organizations — thus signals an effort to reverse what Piven (2008: 11) has called "the decay of the inherited repertoire of labor strategies," strategies suited to a previous era of capitalism and labour relations but now challenged by neoliberalism and a resurgent capitalist class.

LABOUR-COMMUNITY COALITIONS: CANADIAN EXPERIENCES

In a 2005 report, the Canadian Labour Congress (CLC) highlighted the importance of the labour movement protecting "workers and their families where they live by working with like-minded community allies" (CLC cited in Tattersall 2010: 9). In endorsing labour-community coalitions, the CLC acknowledged the vital role such alliances can play in organizing the unorganized, advancing legislative reform and broadening the reach and influence of the labour movement (Tattersall 2010). In this, the CLC follows labour organizations in the U.S., Europe and Australia in recognizing the potential of alliances with community partners around shared interests and common goals. As one of the leading scholars of labour-community coalitions has argued, "the crisis of the labour movement has made it ever more necessary for unions to unite with other social forces if they are to successfully advance a broad vision of economic and social justice" (Tattersall 2010: 2). In other words, labour cannot turn back the neoliberal tide alone; alliances with social movements and community organizations are essential to rebuilding working-class power.

The historical dynamics of Canadian politics have always made coalition work a necessity for the labour movement (Tattersall 2010: 110). With labour's traditional political ally, the New Democratic Party, historically relegated to third-party status, unions have had to mobilize the non-union public to advance their own as well as broader working-class interests. Although unsuccessful, the struggle against free trade in the late 1980s demonstrated the ability of Canadian labour to work with local communities around a common cause (Black and Silver 2008: 163). More recent alliances, such as those forged during labour's battles against the Campbell government in British Columbia (Isitt and Moroz 2007) and the longstanding cooperation between unions and community groups in alliances such as the Ontario Health Coalition (Mehra 2006), show that community unionism remains an important strategy for the Canadian labour movement.

Coalitions exist when "two or more organizations... build relationships in order to forge a shared common interest agenda to achieve social change in a specific place" (Tattersall 2010: 22). Labour-community coalitions can be formed to advance any number of interests, from living wage campaigns (Fine 2003a) and education reform (Tattersall 2010) to global justice (Acuff 2000) and the prevention of plant closures (Nissen 1995). Unions may look to community allies to support campaigns to organize the unorganized, as in the Service Employees International Union's Justice for Janitors campaign (Banks 1992), and community groups may turn to labour to add organizational muscle and resources to advance their members' interests vis-à-vis local governments, landlords or big corporations.

In one of the first studies of community unionism in Canada, Tufts (1998) outlined two campaigns that saw labour and community groups in cooperation. In the 1980s, the Canadian Union of Postal Workers sought public support for collective bargaining goals by reaching out and mobilizing community allies. Using this strategy, the union was (at least temporarily) able to stem the tide of privatization of rural post offices and preserve union jobs. In the early 1990s, the International Ladies' Garment Workers' Union (ILGWU) sought the support of Toronto's East Asian community in an effort to organize homeworkers in the city's garment sector (who were disproportionately Asian immigrant women). Realizing the obstacles to organizing immigrant homeworkers, which included social and spatial isolation from each other and language barriers between workers and union organizers, the ILGWU worked in and with the Chinese and Vietnamese communities to establish the conditions necessary to build a successful campaign.

These are examples of labour initiating links with community allies in order to achieve what are primarily union goals. Nissen (2004: 72) has critically called such arrangements "vanguard coalitions" where unions treat community groups instrumentally, allowing them little decision-making power but expecting full cooperation with union strategies. However, we cannot assume that community groups in all instances want equal control over coalition resources and decision-making; they may be content working towards goals established by the union in which they also have an interest.

Some of the most powerful examples of CU in Canada are "common-cause coalitions" (Nissen 2004: 72), in which community and labour have converging and often long-term interests. Such coalitions develop joint (community-union) leadership and decision-making bodies and allow participating organizations to "buy in" to the coalition's mission through active participation (Nissen 2004: 83). The Ontario Health Coalition (OHC) is one such coalition, with a network of over four hundred community organizations, including unions, tasked with a mandate to defend public health care. Health sector unions, such as the Canadian Union of Public Employees, are founding and active members of the coalition along with a number of private sector unions, including the Canadian Auto Workers (Mehra 2006). The unions work in alliance with a myriad of community groups such as seniors' advocacy organizations, immigrant health centres, women's groups and anti-poverty organizations (ibid.). Founded in the mid-1990s, the OHC has organized local coalitions across Ontario and has played a key role in mobilizations to combat government plans for the privatization of health care, although with varied success.

Some labour-community coalitions do not fit easily into the vanguardist/common-cause dichotomy. For instance, the 2004 Hospital Employees Union (HEU) strike in British Columbia started as a dispute between hospital workers and the provincial government, but quickly emerged as a symbol of the fight for public health care and a lightning rod for multiple community groups and non-health sector unions (Camfield 2006; Isitt and Moroz 2007). As sympathy strikes expressing solidarity with hospital workers spread across BC, community coalitions provided "flying pickets" to evade no-strike language in collective agreements (Isitt and Moroz 2007). And importantly, as Isitt and Moroz (2007: 99) observe, "community coalitions generalized HEU workers' grievances to other sections of society, pulling diverse groups of workers into the strike." The HEU and other public sector workers developed linkages with community groups that "provided a forum for cross-fertilization on a range of issues. Hospital workers supported the demands of anti-poverty groups for social housing and a guaranteed annual income; teachers advocated for seniors and against the closure of women's centers" (Isitt and Moroz 2007: 99). Yet, as is often the case upon the resolution of a labour dispute, such intense coalition work was not sustained.

Coalitions can bring out the best in community organizations and unions, mobilizing complementary resources to launch big campaigns that can confront the neoliberal agenda. Yet successful coalitions tend to require a commitment of resources from all partners to common goals. While campaigns vary widely, the union renewal literature suggests some necessary prerequisites and conditions for successful and sustainable labour-community collaboration, including: establishing relationships of reciprocity, respect and equality between labour and community partners (e.g., in decision-making structures); the presence of "bridge builders" — from both labour and community — to foster relationships and maintain mutual trust between participating groups; the development of goals and strategies that represent common interests; and recognition of the strengths and weaknesses each ally brings to the coalition (Glover and Rose 1999; Clawson 2003; Reynolds 2004; Nissen 2004; Tattersall 2005).

However, factors internal to coalitions are only half of the equation. The structure of political opportunities that any coalition must navigate is often too complex and case-specific to draw any broad generalizations about what works in the coalition model of community unionism. What we can say is that coalitions that do not have the ingredients listed above are unlikely to sustain themselves, advance shared interests and ultimately build workers' and community members' power. I now turn to the other model of community unionism, that of community-based workers' organizations.

COMMUNITY-BASED WORKERS' ORGANIZATIONS IN CANADA

Over the past decade, community-based workers' organizations — often called "worker centres" — have sprouted up in urban centres across North America (Black 2005; Fine 2005; Cranford et al. 2006). Worker centres can now be found in some of Canada's major cities, including Toronto, Montreal and Winnipeg (Choudry and Thomas, this volume). This model of community unionism represents something of a cross between a community organization and a labour union. Like unions, worker centres seek to organize and represent the interests of workers. Like community organizations — and the community unions of the 1960s — worker centres take the community as their primary site of organizing, in contrast to unions' focus on worksites, industries or occupations.

Worker centres use advocacy, lobbying and direct action to win better wages and working conditions for their members and to challenge the regulation of work via public policy. Thus, worker centres do not intervene in the labour market in the traditional manner of organized labour. Unions use their economic power to improve the lives of their members through bargaining and the strike, or political power to advance their interests in the sphere of public policy (Fine 2003a). Worker centres also mobilize political power to lobby governments for legislative changes, as well as use the disruptive power to shame, boycott and protest employers who are in violation of employment standards (Fine 2005). So while they lack official union recognition and status under labour law, worker centres attempt to force employers to "bargain" with their members by employing a wide range of tactics.

The most effective community organizing emphasizes participatory processes and self-organization. Such community work — exemplified by anti-racist organizing, particularly among immigrant women — focuses on personal and community empowerment using methods such as popular education (Cranford et al. 2005). For worker centres, this commitment to empowerment and democratic and participatory practices is rooted in a critique of traditional unionism: unions have failed, in the words of one worker centre, "to keep organization in the hands of its membership and out of the hands of an organizational elite" (NMASS 2011). For worker centre activists, the exercise of workers' collective power is thus intricately linked to organizing practices that allow worker control over their own institutions.

With the growth of precarious employment, worksite-based unionism is unable to address the needs of an ever-growing number of workers (Cranford et al. 2005: 354–5).[6] For many community union activists, their commitment to the worker centre model stems from a frustration with traditional trade unions' adherence to worksite-based unionism and subsequent neglect of workers deemed "hard to organize," such as the precariously employed, undocumented immigrants and migrant workers.[7] And while a number of worker centres receive financial and organizational support from trade unions, many are staunchly independent of the traditional labour movement, relying on individual donations, membership dues or philanthropic foundations for financial stability (Black 2005).

Seeking to overcome the limits of solidarity in the contemporary industrial union model, in which bargaining most frequently takes place between an employer and paid workers in a single workplace, worker centres organize workers regardless of their employment status or occupation.[8] When a worker in an industrial union loses their job, they also lose their union ties and can experience political isolation, losing their identification with a collective whose combined strength is greater than that of any one worker. The industrial union model was not designed for workers who move between multiple small workplaces in competitive sectors and does not provide an incentive for unions to organize these workers (Cranford and Ladd 2003: 51). Some industrial unions aim to maintain relationships with laid-off members through job placement and retraining programs. Yet such practices are not widespread, and even if a worker finds another job, there is no guarantee that it will be in a unionized workplace.

In contrast, worker centres attempt to build solidarity beyond the workplace, organizing workers around their common class interest in fair and just employment. Building this solidarity is never easy. Many worker centres have a two-fold organizing process: first, centres provide services to workers in need of assistance, like help filing an employment standards claim with the Ministry of Labour, assistance with immigration and status issues, English language instruction and providing general information on workers' rights. Combining this service with popular education, worker centres engage the worker in a process "whereby individuals begin to see personal problems as broader political issues and begin to think about how to address those problems collectively" (Cranford and Ladd 2003: 51). Popular education and leadership development programs foster a will to participate in collective action among individual workers as they begin to recognize their experience is one shared by many (Cranford and Ladd 2003: 51). In this way, worker centres move from servicing workers to organizing for the exercise of their collective power.

With regard to worker centres, critics have asked: "Is it really organizing?" While acknowledging their strength, critics claim "worker centers are a worthy project, but no substitute… for a union" (Roman 2010: 2). This critique rests on the observation that centres do not always establish ongoing relationships with the workers they help. Despite the popular education and emphasis on participation and self-organizing, not all workers who pass through a centre will commit to long-term activism after benefiting from its services. Without a sustained and active membership, a worker centre is, in the words of one critic, "a legal clinic with picket signs" (Roman 2010: 2).

On the question of organizing, worker centres acknowledge that sustaining membership is a challenge, just as sustaining rank-and-file activism is a challenge for unions. The usual barriers to collective action also have to be overcome: time and resources, fear and isolation and other impediments to solidarity such as racism, homophobia and sexism. The worker centre model is new and evolving and each centre is experimenting with novel ways of organizing and mobilizing workers. Best practices are beginning to emerge, and many centres have been able to develop strong and committed memberships (Fine 2003a, 2003b, 2005).

Many worker centres collaborate with unions to help organize workers. If a worker approaches a centre about unionizing his or her workplace, organizers will refer them to an appropriate union. Sometimes worker centres lay important organizational groundwork in a community prior to the launch of a union's organizing drive, developing community linkages, getting to know workers and engaging in popular education. Here, worker centres are a complement to unions, not a competitor, and are sometimes established by unions as a "pre-union" formation. But as the growth of precarious employment has illustrated, there is a need for forms of collective representation that are not tied to a single employer at a single worksite (Cranford and Ladd 2003: 51). Above all else, worker centres are trying to fill this gap. As a keen observer of community unionism argues, "while it is tempting to suggest labor organizing be done by unions, the sad fact is that unions are doing little organizing among these [low-wage, immigrant] workers and those few that are have limited resources in terms of meeting the enormous unmet organizing demand" (Fine 2003b: 2). Worker centres' philosophies and practices, based in participatory democracy and popular education, "can contribute to a broader understanding of what a union is" (Cranford and Ladd 2003: 55), redefining the labour movement and expanding its boundaries like the community unions and welfare rights groups of the 1960s.

Established worker centres in Montreal, Toronto and Winnipeg have shown that community unionism can build power among some of the labour market's most precarious workers (Choudry and Thomas, this volume). The model has spread to communities like Windsor and Hamilton, once bastions of industrial unionism where deindustrialization has seen the local labour market shift from providing "good" jobs to the proliferation of low-wage precarious employment. A new worker centre in the suburbs of Toronto hopes to organize ethnic Punjabis in the notoriously exploitative trucking industry, where workers are classified as "independent contractors" and subject to the whims of freight companies who pit truckers against one another in a competitive race to the bottom. With their participatory community organizing philosophy and focus on the most precarious corners of the Canadian labour market, worker centres have proven to be an important model for building workers' power.

CONCLUSION

There is a great diversity of community unionism in Canada, from labour-community coalitions in which unions and community groups defend the public sector to new forms of community-based labour organizing that empower some of the country's most vulnerable workers. Community unionism is combining new approaches to organizing with some tried and true methods that have been key to the labour movement's past successes. As I hope this chapter has illustrated, the union movement needs to take community unionism more seriously as a strategy for renewal.

In a conservative political climate in which the labour movement is consistently bashed by politicians and the corporate media alike, unions must continually struggle to define themselves in both word and deed as defenders of broader working-class interests, not just the narrow interests of their members. Building and sustaining community-labour coalitions are central to this effort. If unions fail to build public support through union-community campaigns, whether in the defence of public services or in a struggle with a private employer, the neoliberal agenda of privatization, deregulation and rule of the market will be difficult to reverse. Through community coalitions, unions can illustrate to non-union workers that their interests are aligned with, and not contrary to, those of the broader public. This is not simply about improving their public image, for when unions act as "swords of justice" rather than just "vested interests" (Flanders 1970; Tattersall 2010) they can make concrete improvements in the lives of working people, both union and non-union, and demonstrate that a progressive politics of collective well-being and solidarity can trump the neoliberal politics of tax cuts and individualism. This understanding of the labour movement as a sword of justice should guide how unions relate to and engage with worker centres and new forms of organizing. In the growing ranks of the precariously employed, or what Guy Standing (2011) has called the "precariat," the labour movement sees a constituency disillusioned with neoliberal labour markets and predisposed to organizing. But unions must acknowledge that their dominant modes of organizing do not necessarily fit the current labour market realities of many workers, nor do they build solidarity beyond narrow sectional interests. In this respect, worker centres have a lot to teach unions, but unions must be willing to learn.

Despite the growth of community unionism in Canada, for every community that has a worker centre or has been impacted by the power of a labour-community coalition, there are many more where the power of alliances between labour and the community remain untapped. For organized labour, realizing the potential of community unionism must become a priority. Yet in an era where partnerships with capital have as much traction with some labour leaders as partnerships with the community, there are serious obstacles to overcome before the labour movement can explore more fully the power of community unionism.

Notes

1. Cranford and Ladd (2003) conceptualize CU as occupying a centre range along a continuum of community organizing and union organizing. While I am sympathetic to this approach to CU, it does not account for community-union coalitions.
2. The term "repertoires of contention" refers to the set of various protest-related tools and actions available to a movement or related organization in a given time frame (Tilly 1978).
3. On class and community, Adolph Reed (2000) has observed that the assumption of a homogeneous Black community in the U.S. has worked to erase differences in class interests amongst African-Americans. Similarly, the politics and discourse of multiculturalism in Canada tends to reproduce this communitarian approach to community, obscuring questions and issues around class relations within the country's various ethno-racial communities.
4. To be distinguished from the "old left" of trade unions, the Democratic Party and the Communist Party USA (Ashbolt 2008).
5. Under capitalism, this unpaid work is necessary for reproducing the labouring population on a daily and intergenerational basis, and thus essential to the reproduction of the capitalist system as a whole (Federici 2004).
6. Precarious employment is employment that lacks standard forms of labour security, typically paid work characterized by limited social benefits and statutory entitlements, job insecurity, low wages and high risks of ill health (Vosko 2006: 4). Precariousness is associated with non-standard employment relationships, such as temporary employment or own-account self-employment.
7. Precarious employment is racialized and gendered, with workers of colour, new immigrants and women disproportionately represented in the ranks of the precariously employed (Vosko 2006).
8. However, radical industrial unions such as the Industrial Workers of the World had systems of transferable membership.

11. ANTI-POVERTY WORK: UNIONS, POOR WORKERS AND COLLECTIVE ACTION IN CANADA

Kendra Coulter

Too many people are poor. In Canada, single mothers, youth, Aboriginals, new immigrants, single seniors, persons with disabilities and racialized workers continue to face the greatest economic deprivation (Bezanson 2006; Wallis and Kwok 2008). Overall, women are more likely to be forced into poverty, but because of the decline in male-dominated industrial and manufacturing work, men now form a greater proportion of the newly unemployed (Hennessy and Yalnizyan 2009; Townson 2009).

Unemployment is a key cause of poverty. Since 1976, the unemployment rate in Canada has fluctuated between 6 and 12 percent (Human Resources and Skills Development Canada 2011). In other words, even at the best of times, 6 percent of Canadian workers have been unable to find waged work. Underemployment also creates poverty and affects workers who seek waged work which is full-time and/or year-round but can only find precarious, contingent work that is part-time, temporary and/or otherwise insecure (Winson and Leach 2002; Vokso 2006). Low-wage employment is another source of poverty. In 2009, 817,000 Canadians earned the minimum wage or less (Statistics Canada 2009). For these workers, even if they are able to find full-time, year-round work, their earnings do not rise above poverty levels. Thus, even paid employment itself is not necessarily an escape from poverty and simplistic right-wing rhetoric that claims poor people should just "get a job" is fundamentally flawed. Inadequate fixed incomes such as disability benefits, social assistance, Employment Insurance and old age security payments are another source of poverty. Moreover, many laid-off workers find they are unable to collect the unemployment insurance for which they paid (Canadian Auto Workers n.d.). Elucidating these different causes of poverty reminds us that the poor are not homogeneous, nor are the causes of poverty singular. At the same time, what unites all forms of poverty is that they result from social, economic and political inequities. Consequently, solutions to poverty must be social, economic and political in nature.

Drawing on interviews with anti-poverty workers and organizers, documentary sources produced by the organizations themselves and the academic literature, this chapter identifies different forms of anti-poverty work being pursued in Canada today and examines the relations among poor people, poverty issues and labour unions. A full study of the connections between labour unions and anti-poverty work in Canada is a large undertaking, beyond the scope of one chapter, and consequently I concentrate on examples of three main intersections of labour union and anti-poverty relations: union organizing of low-wage workers; poor workers' organizations; and multi-organization campaigns and coalitions. Because poor people's collective agency is under-researched, particularly in Canada, I pay the most attention to poor workers' organizations.

The different forms of anti-poverty work highlighted recognize and reflect context-specific causes of poverty and are characterized by both common and divergent goals and tactics, but each type of collective action plays an important role. Because poverty is inextricably linked to wages, their inadequacy or their absence, I argue that effective anti-poverty strategies emphasize the connections among employment, public policy and the distribution of wealth. A holistic and multi-faceted approach to anti-poverty work is necessary, one which recognizes and respects differences, while emphasizing solidarity and connectivity.

ORGANIZING LOW-WAGE WORKERS

Because so many jobs do not pay enough to allow workers to avoid poverty, confronting low-wage work is essential. Union organizing is one key way to tackle poverty-level wages and underemployment. Labour unions were, of course, created to challenge inadequate wages and economic inequality and to fight for dignity and a better standard of living for working-class people. Unions have played a key role in major battles for social and economic justice in Canada and all workers benefit from the political work of unionists fighting for progressive policies and greater equity. At the same time, unionized workers earn higher wages, have better benefits and pensions and enjoy more rights, protections and security than non-union workers (Canadian Labour Congress n.d.). In other words, unions are fundamentally a kind of anti-poverty organization.

Nevertheless, it must be acknowledged that even among unionized workers, there are marked wage differences. While collective bargaining results in better wages for lower-paid members, who earn more than comparable unorganized workers, these better wages may still be only two or three dollars per hour above the minimum wage. Lower-paid unionized workers include hospital cleaners represented by the Canadian Union of Public Employees (CUPE), food service workers in the United Food and Commercial Workers (UFCW), hotel staff belonging to UNITE-HERE, the Canadian Auto Workers (CAW) and the United Steelworkers (USW), among others.

Many unions continue to organize low-wage workers, particularly in the private service sector, where poverty wages and income insecurity are ubiquitous. Historical efforts in Canada to unionize low-wage workers are captured in Sufrin's (1982) consideration of the 1950s drive to organize Eaton's department store and Sangster's (2010) comprehensive analysis of women and work in post-war Canada. Tufts (2007) has explored the more recent unionization of hotel workers in Toronto, and Zuberi (2007), too, has examined UNITE-HERE'S organizing in Vancouver. However, campaigns to organize low-wage workers in Canada are not well studied.

Most unions in Canada are devoting at least some of their efforts to organizing and representing low-wage workers. For instance, the UFCW is currently organizing in retail, food service and among migrant agricultural workers and aiming to double its current Canadian membership of 250,000 by 2018. As part of this ambitious and laudable approach, not only are efforts initiated and driven nationally, but locals commit at least 10 percent of their resources to organizing. The strategy is already translating into results for low-wage workers across Canada. One notable example from the largely unorganized retail sector is the addition of three hundred new members from grocery and hardware stores in Québec, who joined the UFCW in the spring of 2011 (UFCW 2011a: n.p.). Similarly, in 2008, the USW and Migrante-Ontario, a migrant workers' rights organization, partnered to form a new Independent Workers Association for live-in caregivers. In addition to lobbying for improvements to the Temporary Workers Program and the Live-In Caregivers Program, this association provides home workers with legal services, educational programs and discounted access to dental care at the Steelworkers' clinics, among other benefits (USW 2008).

The process of organizing low-wage workers should also include the active and ongoing engagement of unionized workers. In fact, unionizing should be seen as only the beginning of efforts to organize low-wage workers. Union educational programs, campaign building, demonstrations and other kinds of political action can facilitate the building of solidarity and poor workers' power, essential components for the promotion of social change. Ongoing and increased collective action among unionized workers can broaden and deepen poor workers' political consciousness, goals and aspirations, strengthening the unions and working class.

Although not widely characterized as an anti-poverty strategy, in practice union organizing of low-wage workers is undeniably a form of anti-poverty work. The strategy is labour intensive and challenging. High turnover levels, short-term contracts and low levels of existing union density make it difficult for unions to organize private service sector workplaces dominated by low-wage workers (Clark and Warskett 2010). In terms of a strict cost-benefit analysis, certain unions simply reason that it is too expensive and time-consuming to attempt to organize in these sectors (Milkman and Voss 2004; Yates 2004).

Unions and workers must also confront legislative constraints, including laws preventing unionization in particular sectors like agriculture (Choudry and Thomas, this volume; Smith, this volume), and mandatory-vote certification processes. The mandatory vote model used in most jurisdictions in Canada differs from card-based union certification, whereby the signing of a union card is accepted as sufficient indication of a worker's desire to join a union. Mandatory vote models require two steps. In Ontario, for example, at least 40 percent of the employees must sign union cards before the union can file a certification application with the Ontario Labour Relations Board. Filing the application triggers a board-supervised secret ballot vote one week later, in which at least 50 percent plus one of the workers must vote in favour of unionization in order for the union to be certified as their bargaining agent. The effects of this two-stage process with a built-in delay are significant, particularly for small and vulnerable workforces. Employer representatives regularly use the period of time between the filing of the certification application and the secret ballot vote to try and dissuade workers from voting in favour of unionization. Low-wage workers are particularly susceptible to management's union avoidance tactics because they lack power and feel they are easily identified and fired (Coulter 2011). The combination of corporate opposition and legislative framework reduces the success rate of unionization drives (Martinello 2000) and increases the vulnerability of precarious workers, who often fear employer reprisal if they seek to organize and advocate for themselves.

Put simply, organizing low-wage workers is challenging and the results are uncertain. In addition, unions must invest a great deal of resources in an organizing drive knowing that, if successful, the dues collected from lower-waged workers will not be substantial. However, many unions are including low-wage workers as a key part of their organizing efforts today, recognizing the social and political importance of providing vulnerable workers with security and material improvements. The organizing of low-wage workers reduces poverty for those workers who are able to join a union and provides them with increased job security, benefits and a collective voice. Despite the challenges, union organizing is an important kind of anti-poverty work.

Of course, as large numbers of workers earn poverty wages and are without a union, organizing drives must continue to be expanded. As I have argued elsewhere (Coulter 2011), the more unions take poor workers seriously and the greater the improvements workers earn through unions, the more likely low-wage workers will themselves turn to unions as a means to gain collective power, control and a better standard of living. Grassroots worker organizing, union local-driven initiatives and national efforts in concert will contribute to more widespread unionization for poor workers and will reduce poverty. At the same time, unionization efforts should be combined with legislative and other political strategies which will lead to public policies that benefit the entire labour force, unionized or not.

POOR PEOPLE'S ORGANIZATIONS

Poor people have a history of resistance that stretches back for centuries. Some have pursued or participated in unionization efforts, while others have formed organizations which are not centred around a place of work. As Tait (2005: 11) explains, "since poor people's livelihoods commonly fluctuate between earning wages and receiving welfare or unemployment benefits, their labor activism almost always concerns itself with more than just workplace issues." This form of collective action will be the focus of this section.

Not surprisingly, given the overall level of political engagement at the time, the 1960s and 1970s saw a groundswell of organizations focusing on the need to combat poverty. Some were organized exclusively by poor people, while others were alliances between poor people and politically engaged social workers, students, education workers and other progressives (Finkel 2006). In 1971, at a national political conference hosted by poor people in Toronto, the National Anti-Poverty Organization (NAPO) was born as an umbrella for 1,800 different groups. In 1973, the National Council on Welfare produced a directory which listed 5,000 low-income groups (Finkel 2006: 265), and the idea of a guaranteed annual income was widely discussed and debated as a right of citizenship and a key way to help ensure no Canadians were living in poverty. In 2009, NAPO changed its name to Canada Without Poverty–Canada Sans Pauvreté (Canada Without Poverty n.d.) and now focuses on education, research and select case work, emphasizing public policy solutions to poverty. Today, Canada Without Poverty is a member of three anti-poverty coalitions and identifies sixteen organizations as partners, including half a dozen national unions and the Canadian Labour Congress.

Other scattered organizations comprised exclusively or primarily of poor people exist across Canada, including Under Pressure in Ottawa, LIFE*SPIN in London and End Legislated Poverty in Vancouver. Here I focus on two community-based organizations, ACORN Canada (hereafter ACORN) and the Ontario Coalition Against Poverty (OCAP). Overall, these two organizations exemplify two of the dominant models of poor people's organizing seen in North America. OCAP pursues protest and disruptive action, strategies Piven and Cloward (1979) advance as the most effective approach for poor people and a way to avoid the institutionalization of dissent. In contrast, ACORN draws on the history of ACORN USA (Delgado 1986; Fisher 2009) and the organizing model promoted by founder Wade Rathke (2009), which centres on building community-based organizations of low- and moderate-income people. Such an approach is comparable to the poor workers' unions promoted by Tait (2005: 16) as sites where "mobilization and institutionalization can coexist." These are unions which are not centred around a particular workplace or employment sector, but rather are neighbourhood-rooted.

Members of unemployed workers' unions in London and Toronto, Ontario, created OCAP in 1990. The organization is based in Toronto, but fosters and supports broader anti-poverty and anti-racist struggles (OCAP n.d.). There is an executive and a very small staff, and the decision to maintain a permanent organizational structure is where OCAP differs from Piven and Cloward's model (1979). The organization has regular membership meetings, but no fees or mandatory attendance. As such, it is difficult to know how many people are members, although in 2005, estimates were between two hundred and three hundred (Greene 2005). Moreover, many people will turn to OCAP for help when under extreme economic duress or in crisis. Local sub-groups have been created, such as OCAP Women of Etobicoke, but OCAP members are from poor neighbourhoods all across Toronto. People involved with OCAP seem to be motivated by economic necessity or support for the organization's goals and methods or by having received assistance and interventions from OCAP.

OCAP is an explicitly anti-capitalist organization which focuses on organizing, direct action casework — usually the mobilization of dozens of people to physically intervene in a specific case of welfare denial, eviction or deportation — and other kinds of actions, including economic disruption. There is no avoidance of the term "poor" or the material conditions of poverty. The identities of poor people are harnessed and mobilized as a source of power, and their experiences of oppression are accepted and given legitimacy as such. In many ways, OCAP fosters an explicitly lower working-class consciousness, seeking not to make a moral case to those in power, but rather to unapologetically and boldly emphasize the rights of poor people and promote resistance (OCAP n.d.). The organization's analysis is rooted in class conflict and its goals are decidedly transformative. As organizer John Clarke (2002: 384) puts it:

> If the working class is reaching such a level of polarization and a section of it is experiencing such misery and privation, we are in a profoundly dangerous situation. It is this that prompts OCAP to bypass the politics of futile indignation and token protest and to build a massively disruptive form of social resistance which can actually stop the attacks and induce a political crisis.

A key strategy driving OCAP is the need to support and defend poor people while linking their individual situations to larger social inequities, power structures and economic injustices. OCAP gained heightened prominence in the mid- to late 1990s as it fought against the provincial Conservative government's cuts to welfare rates, major cuts to affordable social housing and other punitive policies. Using various protests and marches, squats, mass panhandles, the establishment of tent cities and other direct actions, OCAP both successfully defended many poor people and won tangible expansion of provisions for shelter from Toronto's municipal government (Dominick 1999; Feltes 2001).

OCAP continues to respond to contemporary material conditions of poverty and challenges the systemic causes of poverty and inequality (Clarke 2009). Its ongoing actions include confronting individual cases of eviction, deportation, police violence and welfare denial, and supporting First Nations struggles, working in particular with Tyendinaga Mohawks (OCAP 2007). OCAP and other anti-poverty activists uncovered and promoted a hidden legislative clause which affords a special diet allowance for social assistance recipients through an additional $250 payment when deemed medically necessary. OCAP organized medical clinics where poor people could be assessed by a doctor to determine if they were eligible for the special diet allowance, which succeeded in garnering additional, tangible benefits for hundreds of poor people. Simultaneously, OCAP consistently challenges dominant economic processes and institutions through various means, including boisterous demonstrations of poor people and their allies, where messages such as "Capitalism Is Broken" and "No War But the Class War" are made central.

As an organization of poor people, and one not requiring dues, OCAP has no ready-made source of financing. Historically, the national offices of the CAW, Canadian Union of Postal Workers (CUPW) and CUPE Ontario made annual donations, and various locals provided supplementary financial contributions (Greene 2005). But following increasing tensions in the early 2000s centred around OCAP's militant tactics, labour's financial support for the organization was largely withdrawn (CAW 2001; Clarke 2002). However, CUPE Local 3903, the local representing teaching assistants and contract faculty at York University, continued to support OCAP through various means, including monetary donations. OCAP organizer John Clarke has been both openly critical of labour bureaucrats and union conservatism (e.g., 2009), and more conciliatory (e.g., 2011). In recent years, OCAP has been advancing a "Raise the Rates" campaign to push for social assistance levels which reflect the actual cost of living. OCAP has been actively seeking and gaining support for the campaign from a broad cross-section of labour unions, including the Ontario Nurses Association, the Ottawa and District Labour Council, various CUPE locals and CUPE Ontario. Even the CAW provided a financial contribution to the Raise the Rates campaign in 2011, a promising step after their earlier estrangement (Clarke 2011). These recent developments suggest that certain unions are reviving a relationship of solidarity with OCAP, expressed through targeted material and political support and campaign building, rather than the larger operational donations of the past. Relations between OCAP and unions are tentative and a work in progress.

Unions provide regular support to another poor workers' organization, ACORN. ACORN has been growing in Canada since its founding in 2004 in Toronto and now has chapters in Hamilton, Ottawa and metropolitan Vancouver. ACORN membership is community-rooted rather than workplace-centred, and grounded in neighbourhoods with a high percentage of low-income residents, although the discursive focus is not explicitly on "poor people." It is self-defined as an organization for low- and moderate-income people which builds people's and communities' power. Its current slogan is "Uniting Communities for Justice" (ACORN n.d.). Paid organizers build membership by knocking on doors and asking residents questions about their biggest local concerns. ACORN members pay monthly dues — generally between $10 and $30 per month — and elect local executives. Organizers facilitate the work the executive and membership mandates. The paid staff do much of the labour of membership building, material production and fundraising, and provide the political framework, but the content and specific local pursuits are driven by the members. That said, ACORN emphasizes campaign-based and action-oriented organizing focused on at least one issue of high priority for community residents and on building momentum. Hamilton head organizer James Wardlaw (2010, interview with the author) explains:

> An organizer I knew said once that there were two rules at an ACORN meeting. One is that staff don't talk, and the other is that members have to plan something. In our meetings there has to be something that moves the campaign forward, so an action has to be planned... actions are the lifeblood of this organization.

The actions differ depending on the particular neighbourhood and membership base. This highlights the importance of the local, and the intersections between the public and private spheres. But the targets can be multi-level and cross-sectoral. Recent or current examples from Canadian cities include organizing tenants to urge individual or corporate landlords to undertake building repairs and deal with pest infestations; pushing local government for infrastructure improvements or polling stations inside apartment buildings; and campaigning for landlord licensing, inclusive zoning, affordable housing and the regulation of high-interest lending institutions (ACORN Canada n.d.). Recently, ACORN partnered with the Toronto Environmental Alliance to engage low-income renters in energy conservation programs and train tenant leaders to engage their neighbours. This partnership focused on community development and the integration of environmental consciousness rather than the explicit targeting of an inequity or the structural causes of environmental degradation, but is nevertheless a noteworthy new chapter for both anti-poverty organizing and the environmental movement (Marshall et al. 2010).

ACORN Canada firmly believes that organizing work needs to be done on the ground with people, and that the members should control what goes on. As such, the payment of dues is seen as an important political statement in addition to a needed source of revenue. As ACORN national director Judy Duncan (2010, interview with the author) explains:

> If you look at any of these other groups, where the money comes from is what dictates the style and the model that they are using. Having a membership-owned and -run organization actually enables us to be independent. So it's so important in terms of what our model is.

The collection of dues from approximately thirty thousand members in Canadian communities forms the organization's core revenue (Duncan 2010, interview with the author), but ACORN also relies on funding from grants from non-profit foundations, governments, individual donors and unions. The latter support ACORN in a range of ways, including financial contributions, other forms of in-kind support like the provision of office space and in collaborative campaigns discussed in the next section.

Overall, ACORN is an example of both a community union (Cranford and

Ladd 2003; Black 2005 and this volume) and a poor workers' union (Tait 2005). There is no workplace to use as a focal point, or unified body of labour to withdraw. Most members of a community union would not have a union at their place of paid employment, if they are engaged in waged labour at all. Unions may or may not be organizing in the kinds of workplaces where many ACORN members would be employed. Instead, ACORN's organizing is based on community membership. As such, the approach is clearly well suited to a focus on local issues, locally rooted larger issues and organizing based on electoral politics.

ACORN's community union framework is integral to its efforts and certainly mirrors strategies used by ACORN in the United States and by other poor workers' organizations (Lorence 1996; Groff 1997; Goode 2001). Canadian organizers draw proudly from these kinds of traditions, seeing them as the most effective way to resist inequities. The political right appears to agree and feels threatened by the approach. In the fall of 2010, ACORN USA was forced to file for bankruptcy after a multi-faceted campaign against the organization that included doctored secret video footage, attacks in the right-wing media and various lawsuits. Although ACORN was vindicated, the costs prohibited the organization from continuing its work under that specific institutional arrangement (ACORN USA 2010). No doubt the groundwork laid by decades of poor people's organizing will mean that communities will regroup in another organizational format, but the attacks, too, will likely recommence.

The ACORN USA case serves as a reminder and a warning that poor workers' organizations, even when operating within the mainstream political framework and eschewing militant direct actions of the OCAP sort, are subject to marginalization and destruction. The idea that poor people may organize and take coordinated action, even if initially only to pursue modest reforms, is unacceptable to neoliberals and the ruling class. They recognize that unless checked, co-opted or appropriated, poor people's collective consciousness and action have the potential to build towards a meaningful shift in the economic and social order. I suggest this is particularly true when community organizing is combined with other anti-poverty strategies and when many organizations bind together with the goal of fighting poverty.

MULTI-ORGANIZATION CAMPAIGNS AND COALITIONS

Finkel (2006) argues that, prior to the 1980s, unions would offer rhetorical support for poor people's groups, and certainly combat poverty through their own organizing and bargaining, but not participate in explicit anti-poverty coalitions. Today it is common for unions to lead, participate in and/or support a range of coalitions and campaigns which confront poverty. One main vehicle for such work is through living wage campaigns (Lemieux 2009). This focus confronts poverty wages conceptually and literally, advancing the idea that paid work should not lead to poverty, and instead proposing wages that allow workers to meet the real costs of living (Mackenzie and Stanford 2008). Progressive organizations solidify their partnerships through declarations of common cause and subsequently collaborate through the creation of campaign materials; the organization of meetings, educational and participatory events and actions; and joint lobbying.

A broad-based coalition of unions and other progressive groups (including ACORN) succeeded in winning a historic introduction of a living wage policy for all municipal employees by the New Westminster City Council in British Columbia, the first in Canada (ACORN 2010). In the spring of 2011, the VanCity Credit Union in Vancouver became the largest organization in Canada to adopt a living wage policy. Similarly, collaboration between the Toronto and York Region Labour Council, ACORN, other progressive groups and the Ontario New Democratic Party — which succeeded in winning an unexpected by-election victory in 2007 in the Toronto riding of York South-Weston, centred on the minimum wage — is credited with forcing the Ontario Liberal government to increase the minimum wage to $10 an hour by 2010 (Schwartz 2009). Given that many organizations are focusing on the living wage as a means to reduce low-wage workers' poverty, the strategy makes sense and fosters coordinated action, resource sharing and movement building.

Although not called an anti-poverty strategy, the Toronto and York Region Labour Council's "Good Jobs for All" campaign is another example of a labour-poverty linkage. The campaign engages unionized and non-union workers and promotes the idea that all people should not only have jobs, but well-paying, secure, equitable work that contributes to environmental sustainability. The idea that the public sector should be engaged in active job creation is at the core of the campaign. In other words, this campaign revives the idea of full employment as a means of fostering economic justice and thus fighting poverty (Good Jobs for All Coalition n.d.).

The multi-pronged and multi-level approach at the heart of these campaigns and coalitions allows both independence and cooperation, with organizations contributing in ways which draw on their resources and particular strengths. This approach to social change complements the organizing of low-wage workers and poor workers' own organizing. There is both moral and strategic value in unions playing a role in promoting full employment and legislated living wages for all workers, particularly those low-wage workers who are without the protection and benefits of a union at their workplaces. Such strategies seek cultural and political change, simultaneously confronting the structures and policies which cause unemployment, underemployment and poverty-level wages by positing proactive solutions. If living wages and full employment were provincial or federal policy, all workers would benefit regardless of their access to union membership.

CONCLUSION

The political right has a long history of creating and disseminating gendered and racialized categories of relative pity, (im)morality and disdain to describe poor people, a pattern that has continued in the neoliberal present and, arguably, has been amplified (Little 1998; Mayson 1999; Swanson 2001; Kingfisher 2002; Coulter 2009). By producing and reproducing political cultural, popular cultural and everyday stereotypical notions, the right depicts most poor people as flawed, suspect, lazy, criminal and/or manipulative, while a very small number are heralded as the deserving, moral and hard-working exceptions worthy of charity or, even better, of celebration as individualized success stories. This is hegemonic political cultural work pursued to construct impoverished social subjects whose lives and identities can be harnessed and mobilized in the promotion of class fragmentation, gender and race-based discrimination, competitive individualism and social hostility. This cultural work is integral to the pursuit of right-wing public policy changes. The poor are stigmatized by the right as a separate and problematic social group, disconnected from working people and "taxpayers."

The reality is that people are forced into poverty because of political and economic policies, not individual flaws. Poverty is a social issue which cannot be separated from issues of wages, work and class. People are poor because they cannot find work, they cannot find enough work, they cannot find work that pays a living wage or because they are not able or expected to engage in waged work. But poor people are workers, whether they engage in inadequate waged work and/or unpaid social reproductive labour (Bezanson 2006). In this vein, welfare recipients have pushed to be taken seriously by labour unions, often enlisting the argument that every mother is a working mother, emphasizing the mandated labour required by workfare schemes or highlighting their identities as unemployed workers (Tait 2007). Many have argued that the separation of the poor from the category of working class and the exclusion of poor people from class-based representative organizations has exacerbated social divisions and stigmatization, inhibited organizing and contributed to the further weakening of social policy by constructing it as targeted rather than universal and disconnected rather than integral to the lives of most people (Groff 1997; Marcus 2005). Unions should ensure they do not reproduce these divisions or discourses, but rather build solidarity among all working-class people, including those who are unemployed, underemployed and poorly paid by whatever source. Certainly, strong alliances between more powerful sectors of the labour movement and low-income people and their organizations must be forged to defend and prevent the isolation and targeting of poor workers (Tait 2005).

However, putting all poor people into the single category of working-class or even poor workers can obfuscate varied needs, contexts and causes of poverty, and risks the perpetuation of reductionist thinking which fails to account for and take seriously differential experiences, intersectionality and/or local specificities. For example, even among social assistance recipients, the unpaid workloads of single mothers with young children are more substantial than those people with partners or without children, and this should be recognized (Little 2001). Thus, approaches to anti-poverty work which recognize differential needs but see answers in social solutions present the most promising way forward. Targeted policies that single out the poor are more vulnerable to isolation and removal. Exceptional strategies that only benefit those who happen to live or work in the right place are insufficient.

This chapter has examined the ways labour unions and organized but non-unionized poor workers have sought to counter divisions and collectively tackle the causes of poverty, while recognizing that because poverty has different causes, a range of strategies are needed. Different forms of anti-poverty work may take different shapes, but they are complementary. Because unions mean higher wages, increased unionization of low-wage workers benefits those who can join a union and is an important kind of anti-poverty work, but is insufficient on its own. Because poor workers may choose to bind together in alternative, community-based organizations, the rest of the working class can also support poor people in the political action they deem appropriate given their circumstances and bolster this kind of collective action. Unions can demonstrate solidarity with poor people's organizations through material and financial contributions, through partnerships and collaboration in campaigns and/or through strong declarations which help explain why poor people fight back. Such public pedagogy provides a counter-narrative to the negative, mainstream constructions of poor people and offers alternative ways to understand and speak about economic exploitation and oppression. Unions can, simultaneously, build on the successes of living wage and other anti-poverty campaigns and push for public policy that prioritizes affordable housing, child care and education, universal health, pharma and dental care and an economy which works for people rather than the other way around. Over time, the success of such ambitious but inspiring strategies would make anti-poverty work unnecessary.

In the heyday of anti-poverty activism, militant women of the Just Society Movement like Doris Power engaged in direct action casework and disruptive activities, much as OCAP does today. But the 1960s and 1970s were a different historical moment, a time when poverty was more widely condemned as a social failure and when poor activist mothers were heralded in the mainstream media as heroines (Little 2007). Several decades of neoliberal material and cultural attacks on poor people and unions have changed the political climate and terrain. But it is precisely in the current context that a clear picture of social justice and the political economic steps needed to make it real is most urgent. Poverty is inextricable from inequality, from economic polarization. Canada does not lack wealth or the resources to eliminate poverty, Canada lacks effective wealth distribution. As a result, militant, poor, single mother Doris Power's comments (quoted in Little 2007: 190) to the Senate Committee on Poverty in 1968 continue to provide a powerful guide:

> We demand that if this committee wishes to study anything, it should study wealth, not poverty. We demand that this committee study the nature of oppression in this country — not the oppressed. There are answers to poverty. You refuse to ask the right questions and until you do there will be no right answers — only more deceit.

12. ORGANIZING MIGRANT AND IMMIGRANT WORKERS IN CANADA

Aziz Choudry and Mark Thomas

Since colonization, Canadian society has been built upon the dispossession of Indigenous Peoples and waves of migrant and immigrant labour, including thousands of indentured Chinese workers who endured dangerous working conditions in the railways and mines in the nineteenth century (Annian 2006). As Thobani (2007) has argued, the Canadian nation-state and the creation of a Canadian national identity have always been highly racialized, operating through institutionalized hierarchies of power. Immigrant and migrant workers also have long histories of self-organizing for justice and dignity in Canada. Historically, some sections of organized labour have at times supported struggles of migrant and racialized workers, while others have viewed foreign workers and newcomers as a threat to "Canadian jobs" (Goutor 2007; Walia 2010).

In recent years, temporary labour programs have become increasingly common in high-income capitalist labour markets (Preibisch and Binford 2007). These programs provide states with the means to promote economic openness, deal with labour shortages and resolve political concerns over the permanent settlement of immigrants (Hollifield 2004). Temporary migrant workers generally hold low-wage, insecure jobs that are difficult to fill due to these conditions. These types of programs create forms of economic, political and social exclusion, whereby migrants are granted limited access to a labour market, but with restrictions on residency and citizenship rights, thus creating a form of labour force stratification based on legal status (Engelen 2003; Castles 2004).

In this context, migrant workers, labour organizations and migrant worker allies have engaged in a wide variety of organizing initiatives, ranging from court challenges to grassroots alternatives to traditional forms of unionization. Here we explore the dynamics of labour organizing amongst migrant workers in Canada, focusing on two case studies. First, we examine recent efforts to unionize migrant farmworkers in the Seasonal Agricultural Worker Program (SAWP). Exempt from many basic labour standards, SAWP workers experience seasonal employment characterized by long hours and low wages. As seasonal farmworkers, they are prohibited from unionizing in some provinces. Nonetheless, unions and migrant worker allies have engaged in farmworker organizing initiatives, including legal challenges to secure freedom of association rights. We focus on a series of on-going legal challenges undertaken largely by the United Food and Commercial Workers (UFCW) that began in 1995. We then turn to the case of the Immigrant Workers Centre (IWC) in Montreal, Québec, formed in 2000 to provide a safe place for migrant and racialized immigrant workers to come together around problems they experience in their workplaces. The IWC is engaged in individual rights counselling, as well as popular education and political campaigns that reflect the general issues facing migrant and racialized immigrant workers, including dismissal, immigration status, exploitation by temporary employment agencies and sometimes inadequate representation by their unions. The IWC's activism includes fostering and maintaining alliances with a broad range of community, national and international immigration, labour and social justice movement networks. We explore the possibility of worker centres as a democratic, grassroots alternative or counterpart to traditional forms of unionization. We conclude by assessing the limits and possibilities of these strategies, particularly in terms of the implications for labour organizing amongst the growing number of temporary foreign workers in Canada.

THE EXPANSION OF TEMPORARY FOREIGN LABOUR IN CANADA

The number of temporary foreign workers in Canada has expanded rapidly over the past two decades. Since the mid-1990s there has been a marked shift from entries of workers at high skill levels (occupations requiring university education) to workers at lower skill levels, especially those requiring occupational-specific training or a high school diploma. Workers in lower skilled categories have increased noticeably in this period (Citizenship and Immigration Canada 2010). Moreover, with an increased emphasis on temporary work permits, the number of workers entering Canada as temporary foreign workers has grown significantly in relation to the number entering as permanent residents under the "Skilled Worker" or "Self-Employed" categories (Valiani 2007a), with Ontario and Alberta as the top destinations for temporary foreign workers.

The SAWP, which operates in nine provinces,[1] is considered a "model" temporary foreign worker program by policymakers because of its practice of creating a permanent flow of temporary foreign workers (Basok 2007). The program primarily employs male workers, with the two leading source countries being Mexico and Jamaica (Citizenship and Immigration Canada 2005). The workers' period of employment in Canada ranges from six to forty weeks, with a minimum of forty hours of work per week, though this can often greatly exceed sixty hours. Under the employment agreements that govern the program, farm labourers are paid an hourly wage just over Canadian minimum wage levels, and are provided with health-care coverage throughout their period of employment. Employers are responsible for covering transportation costs for their employees to and from their home country and for providing accommodations. Once their seasonal contract ends, they are required to return home until the next growing season (Gibb 2006; Preibisch and Binford 2007; Thomas 2010). Essentially, the program facilitates the incorporation of migrant workers from the Caribbean and Mexico into seasonal agricultural production as unfree migrant labour (Satzewich 1991), with echoes of earlier indentured migrant labour such as the Chinese railroad workers. Under the SAWP, migrant workers are neither permitted to seek employment outside their specified contract nor to apply for permanent residency within Canada. Through these restrictions, the state is able to secure a labour force that is both seasonal in nature and static in terms of upward mobility. Further, this ensures a labour force that performs physically demanding and low-paying work and that is subject to labour standards exemptions and abuses without effective mechanisms of appeal (Suen 2000; Sharma 2006).

The SAWP provided a model for the Canadian federal government's 2002 expansion of the Temporary Foreign Worker Program. In July 2002, the federal government developed the Low Skilled Worker Pilot Project for occupations requiring either a high-school diploma or a maximum of two years of job-specific training. As part of the program, employers are expected to assist the foreign workers in finding accommodation, and are required to pay full airfare to and from the home country and provide medical coverage until the worker is eligible for provincial health insurance. The Low Skilled Worker Pilot Project initially placed a twelve-month time limit on employment contracts for foreign workers, with the requirement that the worker must return home for a minimum period of four months before applying for another work permit. The length of the employment contract was subsequently increased to periods of up to twenty-four months (HRSDC 2007), and in April 2011 to a maximum of four years.[2] Under the newest regulations, once they have reached the four-year limit, workers must wait four years before they can reapply to the program. In 2009, 80,192 workers were present in Canada working under the Intermediate and Clerical category and 23,633 under the Elemental and Labourers category, excluding SAWP and the Live-in Caregiver Program (LICP) (Citizenship and Immigration Canada 2010).

This expanded program extends the principles established by the SAWP to a wide range of low-skill occupational categories. As with the SAWP, workers are employed under conditions of unfree wage labour as they are not permitted to circulate in the labour market. Nor are they able to apply for permanent residency through the program. Workers in the program become effectively tied to, and marginalized within, a strata of lower-tier employment, without regulatory mechanisms to enforce basic labour rights (Valiani 2007a). The lack of both labour market mobility and capacity for permanent residency means they work under highly precarious conditions. Moreover, the program creates a high degree of labour flexibility for employers, as it is based solely on short-term labour demands. The expansion of the Temporary Foreign Worker Program constitutes another example of the ways in which racialized migrant workers are constructed as highly exploited labour in the contemporary labour market.

THE LEGAL STRUGGLE TO ORGANIZE FARMWORKERS IN ONTARIO

Several factors make labour organizing particularly difficult amongst temporary foreign workers employed in Canada, including those in the SAWP. These include employer repression of organizing drives; employers pitting racialized groups against one another to avoid unionization; and employers repatriating workers who support unionization to their home countries (UFCW 2007; Preibisch 2010). In Ontario, farmworkers have historically been exempt from labour relations legislation that facilitates freedom of association and collective bargaining. This section of the chapter examines the efforts of the UFCW to challenge the exemption of farmworkers from rights to unionization and collective bargaining in Ontario.

Contemporary farmworker organizing in Ontario has its roots in the efforts of the Canadian Farmworkers Union (CFU), formed in 1980 by migrant farmworkers in British Columbia, who have had the legal right to unionize since the 1970s (Bush 1995). The CFU pushed for a minimum wage, maximum hours of work and improved health and safety protections. The CFU organized in BC through the 1980s, and also set up an office in Ontario, though farmworkers there did not have the legal right to organize. The union faced intense resistance from agricultural employers and growing opposition from the Social Credit government that had taken power in British Columbia. By the end of the 1980s, financial constraints forced a scaling back of organizing efforts, including closing the Ontario office.

Since the 1990s, the UFCW has spearheaded a campaign to win the legal right to organize and bargain collectively for agricultural workers in Ontario.[3] While the campaign takes place within the courts, it is accompanied by efforts to organize agricultural workers into certified bargaining units and to negotiate collective agreements with employers if and when certification is achieved.

The federal Industrial Relations and Disputes Investigation Act (1948) and the Ontario Collective Bargaining Act (1943) excluded agricultural workers in Ontario from association and bargaining rights because it was claimed that "farm enterprises had such low profit margins that they could not pay higher wages" (Butovsky and Smith 2007: 81). In Ontario, this was maintained until the 1990s, when the New Democratic Party government introduced the Agricultural Labour Relations Act (ALRA), which gave non-seasonal agricultural workers the right to unionize. It also allowed for dispute settlement through mediation and final offer selection arbitration. This legislation banned strikes, however, because of the risk to perishable produce.

The current legal disputes began in 1995, when the Progressive Conservative (PC) government overturned the ALRA, eliminating the right to unionize for farmworkers. The UFCW had recently organized a group of farmworkers in Leamington, Ontario. In response to the government's actions, the union launched a court challenge claiming that this exemption was a violation of the Charter of Rights and Freedoms. This complaint eventually made its way to the Supreme Court of Canada, which in 2001 ruled that agricultural workers have rights to association under the Charter (*Dunmore vs. Ontario*) (Smith, this volume). The Supreme Court gave the Ontario government eighteen months to draft legislation that would ensure that the constitutional rights of farmworkers would be respected (UFCW 2004).

In 2002, the PC government introduced the Agricultural Employees Protection Act (AEPA). The AEPA established the right of farmworkers to form associations; however, there was no legal obligation for employers to bargain collectively. This effectively undermined the rights that the legal challenge had sought to establish in the first place. In April 2004, three agricultural workers from Rol-Land Farms and the UFCW applied to take the Ontario government to court to defend the right to association, as the employer refused to recognize the union (UFCW 2004).

The protracted path through the courts continued, with cases being heard at both the Ontario Superior Court and the Ontario Court of Appeal. In 2008, the Ontario Court of Appeal supported UFCW Canada's challenge, which claimed the prohibition on farmworker unions was a violation of the Charter. The ruling ordered the now Liberal Ontario government to provide legislation to enable farmworker collective bargaining by November 2009 (UFCW 2009b). This ruling was reinforced by the June 2007 Supreme Court *BC Health Services* decision, which protected collective bargaining as part of the Charter right to freedom of association (UFCW 2010c; Smith, this volume).

The Ontario government appealed the 2008 decision, however, leading to a further legal battle at the Supreme Court. In April 2011 the Court upheld the appeal, finding that the AEPA did not contravene the Charter. The Court stated that labour relations relies on a "meaningful process of engagement that permits employee associations to make representations to employers, which employers must consider and discuss in good faith." In this context, "good faith" negotiation requires that the parties "meet and engage in meaningful dialogue" but it does not impose a specific method of collective bargaining and it does not oblige the parties to reach an agreement.[4] Through this decision, the Court failed to support a process of labour relations that would effectively counter the power dynamics inherent in farm labour that make collective bargaining necessary in the first place.

In conjunction with pursuing legal strategies, the UFCW began organizing campaigns on farms in Québec, Manitoba, Ontario and British Columbia (UFCW 2007; Preibisch 2010). The first collective agreement covering seasonal migrant workers in Canada was ratified by SAWP workers at Mayfair Farms in Portage la Prairie, Manitoba, in June 2008 (UFCW 2008), though this local has since been decertified. A number of organizing drives have also been undertaken in British Columbia. In 2008, workers at Greenaway Farms in Surrey, BC, voted to join the UFCW, as did workers at Floralia Plant Growers in Abbotsford, BC. Finally, in Québec the UFCW has collective agreements at four agricultural operations and is negotiating a first contract at a fifth, with two more certification applications before the labour board (UFCW 2010b). In April 2010, the Québec Labour

Relations Board (QLRB) certified a UFCW bargaining unit at a farm near Mirabel. The decision hinged on the provision in the Québec Labour Code regarding union organizing on farms with three or more workers employed continuously through the year, which excluded many large farms that principally employed seasonal workers. The QLRB found that whether the workers are seasonal or year-round, they should have the constitutional right to organize and bargain collectively.[5]

Standard provisions in the UFCW agricultural worker agreements include: a grievance procedure; the right to be recalled (named) each season based on seniority; workplace health and safety committees and training; and provision of contracts and other workplace documents in the language of the worker. Most importantly, they provide the right to collective bargaining, giving workers' representatives a seat at the table in negotiating working conditions. In some worksites, collective agreements "also oblige the employer to assist the workers in application for permanent status under the Provincial Nominees Program" (UFCW 2011b: 21). For example, in 2009, a new contract for temporary foreign workers at a Maple Leaf meat processing plant in Brandon, Manitoba, was signed. Under the terms of the contract, the company must process the paperwork leading to permanent residency status for workers coming in under the Foreign Worker Provincial Nominee Program, provide translation for workers and an expedited arbitration process for workers who have been terminated, allowing them to stay in Manitoba until the case is heard, thus preventing premature deportation (UFCW 2009a). A recently ratified collective agreement for Springhill Farms packinghouse workers, who come to Manitoba under the province's Foreign Worker Nominee Program, includes similar provisions (UFCW 2010a).

In Alberta and Ontario, farmworkers still do not have collective bargaining rights; thus the decade-and-a-half-long legislative battle continues. For the UFCW, securing legal rights is a primary way to ensure economic justice for these migrant workers. The pursuit of collective bargaining rights through the courts is not without critics, however. Some academics are less sanguine about the potential of such a strategy. For example, Butovsky and Smith (2007: 70) state: "Court challenges, moral suasion, and public education constitute the tactical repertoire of this essentially legalistic and legislative strategy, which accepts as a given the permanence of capitalist exploitation." For Butovsky and Smith, it is the reformist, top-down nature of this strategy that creates real limits in terms of the capacity to truly address the root of the problems faced by migrant workers in Canada. This does not mean completely forgoing a legalistic strategy; however, "an effective, forward-looking policy must subordinate such methods to a strategy centred on the mobilization of labour's ranks in direct mass action" (Butovsky and Smith 2007: 94). The dilemma they highlight is the need to develop grassroots, democratic, worker-centred organizations that can provide the organizational capacity to confront employers and the state to fundamentally challenge the relations of exploitation experienced by migrant workers in the contemporary Canadian economy.

Another critique of the legalistic strategy revolves around the nature of the legal system itself and its structural impact on the organization of trade unions. Specifically, the legacy of the post-war compromise legislation that accorded collective bargaining rights also imposed a web of legal constraints that circumscribed those rights, with the impact being that the scope of both collective bargaining and trade union action became severely narrowed by a hegemonic framework of "responsible unionism," whereby unions traded off demands oriented towards workplace control in favour of income security for union members and organizational security for unions themselves (Wells 1995a and 1995b; Fudge and Tucker 2001; Panitch and Swartz 2003). While this legal framework enabled economic gains for union members and organizational expansion during the post-war years, it also channelled union action away from workplace activism and towards bureaucratization, thereby weakening the capacity of the movement to engage in broader social struggle (Swartz and Warskett, this volume).

WORKERS' CENTRES AND MIGRANT AND IMMIGRANT WORKER ORGANIZING

As an alternative to the top-down approach of legal strategies and the bureaucratic character of many unions, and in response to legacies of exclusion or inadequate representation within some unions, migrant workers and their allies have undertaken alternative forms of organizing through workers' centres (Black, this volume). There is an established network of workers' centres in the U.S. and a growing number in Canada. These centres are meant to provide a democratic space for workers to come together and organize for change. While critiques of legalistic strategies often posit a dichotomy of organizing models between top-down legal approaches versus grassroots, worker-centred initiatives, we present worker centres as an alternative, but one that may sometimes also build on legal strategies to expand the scope of organizing migrant and racialized workers. We now turn to the Immigrant Workers Centre (IWC) in Montreal as an example to illustrate these kinds of initiatives.

Montreal's IWC was set up in 2000 as a community-based workers' organization in Montreal's diverse, working-class neighbourhood of Côte-des-Neiges by some Filipino-Canadian union and former union organizers, and other activist and academic allies. Two of IWC's founders had been union organizers who found that much of their recruitment and education to support a union drive had to happen outside the workplace, which was difficult. The idea of the IWC was to provide a safe place outside of work where workers could discuss their situation. The organizers also critiqued the unions; for them, once the unions got a majority of workers to sign cards and join up, the processes of education and solidarity built into the organizing process were often lost as union "bureaucrats" came to manage the collective agreement. The IWC was intended to operate instead as a community-based workers' organization in which workers themselves would drive the agenda.

The IWC engages in individual rights counselling and casework, as well as popular education and political campaigns that reflect the general issues facing immigrant workers — dismissal, problems with employers and sometimes inadequate representation by their unions. Often these arise from individual cases and form the basis for campaigns and demands which are expressed collectively. Labour education is a priority, targeting organizations in the community and increasing workers' skills and analysis. Workshops on themes such as the history of the labour movement, the Labour Standards Act and collective organizing processes have been presented in many organizations that work with immigrants as well as at the IWC itself. For example, the "Skills for Change" program teaches basic computer literacy, while incorporating workplace analysis and information on labour rights and supporting individuals in becoming more active in defending those rights in their workplaces. Developing leadership among immigrant workers so they can take action on their own behalf is also an important goal for IWC. Support for self-organizing, direct action, coalition-building and campaigning is used to win gains for workers and to build broader awareness of and support for systemic change in relation to their working conditions and, often, immigration status. As IWC organizer Mostafa Henaway (2012) puts it, the Centre

> tries to build from an organizing model that incorporates radical traditions, going back to basics, focusing on outreach, collective organizing, casework, and education. At times, there are many challenges faced in balancing all of these facets in the organization; but each facet has proven to be critically important to the political work of the centre, such as weekly outreach outside Metro [subway] stations, building relationships with both communities and individual immigrant workers, or attempts to collectivize the casework and individual issues faced by workers, and to respond in a politicized way. The foundation of this organizing has come from these principal organizing methods, in addition to a flexibility in tactics and strategy, due to ever-changing economic conditions in Montreal, and globally.

Campaigns are seen as ways to make gains for individual workers as well as to build collective action from these individual cases over the longer term. They serve to educate the wider community about the issues faced by migrant and immigrant workers. Through these campaigns, the IWC also makes claims on the state (where pertinent, municipal, provincial or federal levels of government) and demand that it intervene to improve conditions for marginalized workers. Recently, for example, more and more migrant and racialized immigrant workers have contacted IWC after being hired by temp agencies, only to be laid off by companies which still owe them wages (Calugay et al. 2011). Statistics Canada estimates that, between 1993 and 2008, the number of registered temporary employment agencies grew from 1,191 to 5,077, an increase of 325 percent (Galarneau 2010). Since 2001, the revenue from employment services firms, 60 percent of which comes from temporary staffing agencies, has increased by 80 percent, to $9.2 billion (Statistics Canada 2010a: 2, 4). These figures do not include many unregistered agencies. Temp agency workers' jobs are located in diverse sectors, including health and social services, warehouses, agriculture and landscaping. The IWC and another Montreal-based worker rights group, Au bas de l'échelle, are campaigning for greater government regulation of temp agencies. Key demands are for these agencies to have an operating permit and that both the agency and the employer be jointly responsible for workplace conditions. Registration is one means of forcing temp agencies to be accountable for their actions, and to end fly-by-night operations (Calugay et al. 2011).

IWC sits between traditions of labour unions and community organizing (Black, this volume). Traditionally, work-related issues have been the concern of the labour movement, acting on the assumption that the best way for workers to have a strong voice and bargaining power is through unions. However, while building good relationships with many unions and union activists, the IWC sees that union representation can sometimes be limited because of the difficulties in organizing migrant and racialized immigrant workers. New forms of labour organizing are needed in the current context and require both support for and from trade unions. The IWC works at both levels with the goals of serving, organizing and educating those who are not unionized. At the same time that it supports worker efforts to unionize, it also helps them get adequate services from their unions. The union-community relationship is developed through many of the IWC's activities, including building alliances with younger union activists, and supporting immigrants in organizing and in helping them negotiate conflicts with their trade unions. The relationship between the IWC and traditional unions can be described as being one formed in ambiguity, but one that is growing on terms of mutual respect. The IWC is in a better position than unions to more quickly focus on, identify and react to issues raised by immigrant and migrant workers, and to lead joint campaigns with unions and community organizations around issues of mutual concern. For example, in 2009, the IWC helped to coordinate a public campaign by around fifty workers, mainly from North Africa and Latin America, who had been hired by a cellphone repair company, which had received government funding to integrate new immigrants into the workforce and then closed its doors, owing thousands in wages to the workers. The IWC and the UFCW staged a demonstration in front of Emploi Québec to highlight the situation and supported the lodging of collective complaints for wages owed. The Commission des norms du travail has ruled that the workers are indeed entitled to this money, and, with IWC's support, they have now received 50 percent of the wages owed to them (*Montreal Gazette* November 26, 2009: B1).

Significantly, organizations such as the IWC and the workers' struggles that they support can be key sites of informal and non-formal learning and knowledge production for labour justice struggles. This process occurs through workers' struggles and contestation of their conditions and rights. A recent study of immigrant workers' struggles in Québec notes:

> Individuals that did eventually take action always did so with the support of others, who provided information and other resources to help them in a dispute with an employer. These others can be unions, community

organizations or co-workers or friends with whom they have informal relationships. "Street smarts" and small victories are shared between people: this in turn encourages others to take action. Such learning most often grows out of pre-existing relations with other individuals, peers or friends. However, organizations play a key role. (Choudry et al. 2009: 112)

Learning to question or to resist exists in tension with learning to cope, adapt or get by — as it has in workplace industrial relations since the emergence of capitalism. Sometimes, as Rodriguez (2010) notes, such knowledge forms contest not only the power (and knowledge) produced by governments, but also that of professionalized unions and other non-governmental organizations which purport to speak on behalf of migrant workers. But building alliances with trade unions, through education and supporting internal debates occurring within organized labour to encourage unions to more meaningfully represent the needs and concerns of immigrant and migrant workers is an important aspect of these local and global struggles for justice.

In Canada, there is also alliance-building between im/migrant worker justice organizing and other groups and networks that work more broadly on issues of immigration justice — No One Is Illegal, Solidarity Across Borders, Justicia 4 Migrant Workers and the Immigrant Workers Centre, for example — and others working on issues of racial profiling and security certificates. These groups and movements organize broader campaigns that mobilize across organizations and bring people together to challenge the general condition of migrants. For example, their participation in mobilizations against the 2010 Olympics and G20 meetings served to make connections between local migrant worker concerns and the global structures and dynamics of power. IWC has presented at municipal, provincial and federal hearings about the conditions and needs of migrant and immigrant workers. The IWC also works to educate and mobilize about the interconnections between its casework and its various campaigns. These include: fighting for workers' compensation coverage for domestic workers and new immigrants to Québec; taking cases of laid-off workers to the Commission des normes du travail; supporting immigration/status cases with public campaigns and media work; campaigning for an end to the three-month delay on accessing medicare, imposed by the Québec government on new immigrants and foreign workers; lobbying; and building and sustaining coalitions and networks with other groups that are struggling for a more just future in Montreal, Québec, Canada and internationally. Those connections between the local and the global are key to understanding the context, and breaking the sense of isolation around what sometimes seem like individual cases of abuse, and for strategizing about how to mount and mobilize around effective collective campaigns.

Some of the challenges and limitations of the IWC model arise from the very predicaments of the immigrant and migrant workers with whom it works. Precarious immigration status adds another layer of complexity to labour organizing strategies, as does the often isolated, atomized and non-union nature of the employment in which many of these workers are engaged. It is also difficult to build long-term, collective workers' power among workers on temporary visas, who will return home and perhaps be replaced by new workers, or even among landed immigrant workers labouring for low pay on the margins of Canadian society in precarious, often casual employment. Sometimes a labour victory for migrant workers can be won, but they are forced to leave the country anyway because of their immigration status.

Likewise, organizing outside of the workplace has both strengths and challenges. Its strengths include the fact that such organizing can sometimes build upon pre-existing community networks and involve families in labour struggles in ways that workplace-focused labour union organization rarely does. Challenges include sustaining an organization financially, which until now has entailed a mixture of donations from individuals and labour unions, various small academic and other grant monies and myriad ongoing fundraising initiatives. Supporting the self-organization of workers has also had successes and setbacks. In some labour struggles, such as the protracted L'Amour apparel factory dispute, workers came together as a committee to organize, with IWC organizers and others playing a supporting role. In other cases it has been harder to build and sustain such collective action among workers.

However, the IWC's persistent outreach to immigrant and migrant workers (often through flyers in neighbourhoods and near worksites, cultural events such as MayWorks and word of mouth), its survival for over a decade and its extensive, diverse alliances and networks help give it credibility, as do successful case and campaign work and support for other labour struggles. In 2011, for example, IWC activists were at the forefront of building community support and an *ad hoc* alliance of Montreal social activists organizing solidarity actions during the lockout of postal workers by Canada Post. The IWC is engaged in a long-haul education process to foster understanding about the situation of migrant and immigrant workers, whose styles and traditions of organizing may not fit with traditional forms of contract unionism. As Mathew (2005) notes, migrant and immigrant workers can and do bring their own histories of struggle and organizing strategies from their countries of origin to the new countries in which they labour.

Although there are periodic discussions which revisit this model, the IWC is not a membership-based organization, unlike the New York Taxi Workers' Alliance, in which taxi drivers become paying members and are thus drawn into collective organizing (Mathew 2005). Instead, the Montreal centre relies on activists, volunteers and student interns, as well as a board comprised of academics, labour unionists and activists from different generations, all with strong links to various communities, unions and networks. The IWC works with employees from diverse and often temporary worksites, with differing, sometimes precarious immigration status and complex family lives. Building a membership-based organization in such conditions is a different proposition from that of organizing landed immigrants working primarily in one sector and dealing with one set of working conditions. Hence participation and leadership among migrant and immigrant workers has tended to be based around the collective cases and campaigns which the IWC supports.

With the collective bargaining rights of all workers under renewed attack, are there lessons to be learned from the flexible tactics and strategies of the IWC for wider labour struggles? Can centres like IWC create sustained structured relationships among workers that enable them to assert control over working conditions, wages and the social conditions of working-class life? The IWC both supports building unions and maintains a commitment to different modes of organizing that are less constrained by union bureaucracy, and that have a presence in community spaces and struggles not always integrated into the workplace focus of traditional union organizers. Furthermore, it is active in building a political movement that not only straddles domestic labour and other social justice struggles, but that also maintains an important transnational element.

The strength of such international networks is their grounding in concrete local struggles. It is nonetheless important to build beyond the local and make connections with some of the wider conditions facing migrant workers and new immigrants. Internationally, new organizations and networks such as the International Migrants Alliance have been founded to build solidarity, to share local experiences and to express the fact that the injustices faced by many migrants and immigrant workers worldwide are similar and are a result of the global displacement linked to neoliberal capitalism and its crises. In a situation in which countries like the Philippines export domestic workers around the world as a matter of state policy (Stasiulis and Bakan 2003; Rodriguez 2010), international organizing provides a means for sharing knowledge and strategies and building solidarity. However, the first step towards justice for migrant and racialized immigrant workers begins with local organizing. Carrying struggles forward requires allies such as unions and wider social movements to challenge the power of states and national and international capital.

CONCLUSION

The two cases explored in this chapter highlight some of the contradictions and dilemmas faced by migrant and immigrant workers and their allies in organizing to improve working conditions and, more fundamentally, challenge the exploitation experienced through employment in the Canadian labour market. In terms of the legal challenges to secure collective bargaining rights, it is certainly the case that legalized collective bargaining offers gains for workers employed in unionized worksites. But the process of securing this right is double-edged. Court challenges are time-consuming and resource-intensive. They are a top-down approach led by a bureaucratic organization often detached from the grassroots workers it aims to represent (see Law and Will 2012, in relation to IWC labour struggles and legal strategies). And, once the right to collectively bargaining is legally secured, it enmeshes workers in the same legalistic framework that has both sustained and contained working-class organizations in Canada since the time of the post-war compromise. Yet legal strategies and individual cases can also be a component of broader struggles to win concessions for workers if they are integrated into a political program to bring about systemic political and economic change.

Turning to the IWC, we see forms of urban labour organizing which build on traditions of community unionism, and are connected to broad domestic and international social movement and activist networks. With its emphasis on supporting workers' self-organization, direct action and building political campaigns from individual casework, the IWC arose to address unmet needs of racialized immigrant and migrant workers dealing with traditional labour unions. Today, with the growth of temporary foreign labour programs in Canada of concern to a range of forces concerned with social justice, many labour unions, facing both internal pressures from their own members and external pressures from initiatives like the IWC, are becoming more responsive to the demands for justice and dignity from migrant and racialized immigrant workers, regardless of their immigration status. Therefore, it is important not to view the IWC as a replacement for, or in competition with, labour unions. While there are sometimes unresolved tensions between the two forms of labour organization, it would seem that increased collaboration and mutual support will be an important component in future workers' struggles in Canada.

Notes

1.   The SAWP operates in British Columbia, Alberta, Saskatchewan, Manitoba, Ontario, Quebec, New Brunswick, Nova Scotia and Prince Edward Island.
2.   New program conditions were introduced in April 2011, including a two-year prohibition for employers found to be in violation of the conditions of employment contracts.
3.   Other court challenges backed by the Ontario Federation of Labour and the UFCW have sought to have agricultural workers included under occupational health and safety legislation and have challenged the federal government deductions for EI while not allowing migrant agricultural workers to receive benefits (UFCW 2011b).
4.   *Ontario (Attorney General) v. Fraser*, 2011 SCC 20. Decision Summary by Cavalluzzo Hayes Shilton McIntyre & Cornish LLP.
5.   This ongoing legal challenge revolves around a provision in Québec's Labour Code (Article 21.5) that prohibits farm workers from collective bargaining unless there are at least "three ordinary and continuous employees." The TUAC [UFCW] challenged this as discriminatory to seasonal agricultural workers. This complaint was upheld by the Québec Labour Board but has been appealed by the Québec Attorney General and the farmers' lobby group FERME.

13. LABOUR, COURTS AND THE EROSION OF WORKERS' RIGHTS IN CANADA

Charles W. Smith

Canada's contemporary labour relations regime, commonly referred to as industrial pluralism, is the product of the mass labour unrest during and immediately following the Second World War. The system that eventually took shape in the post-war period created what critical scholars call a "zone of legal toleration," which institutionalized rights for unions to organize, bargain collectively and strike under stringent conditions (Tucker 1991: 17–8; Palmer 2003: 485). Although the system legitimized unions in some workplaces, it also placed "boundaries of constraint" on workers' capacities to challenge capital and governments through non-legal actions of civil disobedience. Oddly, most unions accepted these restrictions on their collective freedoms by demanding that the institutions of industrial pluralism remain free from "judicialization."[1]

Organized labour's antagonism towards "courtroom atmospheres and lawyers" is grounded in a long history of judicial hostility towards workers' collective action (Fudge and Tucker 2001). Judicial support for the individual rights of capital was reinforced in the 1960s and early 1970s, as rank-and-file worker militancy was routinely stifled by court-imposed injunctions (Crispo and Arthurs 1968; Jamieson 1968; Palmer 1992, 2009; Sangster 2004). Similar antagonism was demonstrated in 1987 when the Supreme Court of Canada (SCC) pronounced in the "Labour Trilogy" (*Reference Re Public Service Employee Relations Act*, 1987; *P.S.A.C. v. Canada*, 1987; *R.W.D.S.U. v. Saskatchewan*, 1987) that there was no constitutional right to bargain collectively or strike. For unions, the Labour Trilogy was further evidence that "the courts have seldom been the worker's friend" (*Toronto Star* April 10, 1987: A4).

Within this context, the SCC's 2007 ruling in the BC Health Services case that the Canadian Charter of Rights and Freedoms protects a procedural right to bargain collectively was unexpected (*Health Services and Support-Facilities Subsector Bargaining Ass'n v. British Columbia*, 2007). Canadian Labour Congress (CLC) president Ken Georgetti praised the SCC's recognition that "workers' freedom of association includes the right to bargain a collective agreement that cannot be ripped apart at the government's convenience" (*National Post* June 9, 2007: A8).

Numerous scholars and labour leaders echoed Georgetti's comments (Adams 2008, 2009; Bilson 2009; Saskatchewan Federation of Labour 2009), while others condemned the decision for its narrowness (Langille 2009), as a flagrant misreading of labour history (Tucker 2008), and, more generally, for further "legalizing" labour politics (Bartkiw 2009; Savage 2009). Given these diverging opinions, how should we interpret the SCC's newfound sympathy for labour rights?

In answering this question, it is important to recognize that courts do not make decisions in a vacuum nor do they maintain a separation from society's ideological conflicts (Hutchinson and Monahan 1984: 206). Judicial interpretation of the law is determined through a historical process that is reinforced by constitutional authority of the state and material conditions associated within different economic systems. In this way, the "cobweb-like confinements" of the law act as real barriers to furthering the interests of subordinate groups within different phases of capitalism (Palmer 2003: 474). Yet, within specific historical moments, laws can be stretched or broken in a manner that is "simultaneously influenced by law and pushing law's developments in new directions" (Palmer 2003: 468). In other words, the law and its interpretation is an important terrain of social struggle.

Within the post-war economic model, industrial legality worked to stabilize the labour process in particular sectors of the economy: manufacturing, transportation, shipping, natural resources and, after 1967, the public sector (Albo 1990; Jenson 1989). In this period, industrial legality provided real gains for those (mainly white male) workers able to attain unionization. Since the 1970s, however, governments have pursued neoliberal reforms limiting the rights of existing unions to bargain and strike while making it more difficult to expand in non-union sectors, mostly dominated by women and workers of colour (Gindin and Stanford 2003; Panitch and Swartz 2003; Camfield 2011). Within this political economic context, the forces of neoliberalism have pushed labour unions into a desperate holding pattern in which the Charter has emerged as a perceived last vestige of support for a system barely tolerated by governments and capital. Labour's current reliance on the Charter, then, should be understood in two ways: first, as a defensive strategy to protect fragments of industrial pluralism; and second, as a tool of legitimization to reinforce the status of unions in Canada.

Ultimately, however, neither strategy will radically alter the balance of class forces under neoliberalism. While court challenges may open small spaces of resistance, they also act to reinforce the boundaries of constraint within the existing regime of industrial legality. It is only when workers and their unions are able to use their collective strength through direct economic and political action — a traditional source of worker power — to challenge the manner in which the law is constructed that workers and their unions can expect truly transformative laws.

THE "BOUNDARIES OF CONSTRAINT":
LAW, COURTS AND INDUSTRIAL PLURALISM, 1945–1986

In the post-war period, government legislation legitimized the activities of labour unions by incorporating them into a legal regime that altered the coercive nature of industrial regulation. In exchange for rights to bargain collectively, unions had to take responsibility for the preservation of steady and uninterrupted flows of private sector production. As Justice Ivan Rand identified in his settlement of the 1945 Ford dispute in Windsor, Ontario, only "responsible" unions were capable of representing workers (Canada, Department of Labour 1946: 126). In order to retain benefits of legal protection, the so-called Rand Formula imposed a no-strike pledge during collective agreements in exchange for mandatory dues collection (union security) and encouraged "principled leaders" to oppose "communistic ends and methods." Under the guise of responsibility, labour leaders purged radicals while unions associated with the communist left were the targets of aggressive raids from other unions (Abella 1973; Whitaker and Marcuse 1994: 313–63).

Industrial legality also transformed the internal workings of unions. Increasingly, union leaders and staff were integrated within management structures responsible for enforcing collective agreements. Workplace discipline also tightened with the development of a formalized grievance system, which allowed unions to legally challenge management violations of collective agreements. In exchange for the grievance system, management rights' clauses in contracts gave employers the authority to control workplaces except where the contract placed particular limits on their authority. As contracts became inevitably more technical and complex, rank-and-file workers were increasingly distanced from their own representatives (Matheson 1989). Whereas past disciplinary action had sometimes led to spontaneous wildcat strikes, the new regime of industrial legality imposed strict disciplinary measures on workers who stepped outside of the contract (Palmer 1992: 284). Similar forces changed the culture of union organizing, as highly trained staff carried out campaigns and legal representatives prevailed over the more militant and the more class-oriented unionism of the 1930s and the 1940s (Wells 1995a and 1995b). According to Stephanie Ross, the acceptance of the forces of legality had ideological implications on workers because it reinforced the "legitimacy of employers' rights of ownership and interests in profitability and workers' subordinate place in the labour process and economy in general" (Ross 2005: 72–3).

In order to deal with any conflict that might arise from the system of industrial pluralism, governments developed a complex legal framework comprised of labour relations boards (LRBs), conciliation boards, grievance arbitration, laws and regulations to limit industrial conflict. When workers went on strike, they did so in a legal context that set conditions on how unions could "legitimately" withdraw their labour (Fudge and Tucker 2001: 10–5). Throughout the post-war period, the boundaries of "legitimate" strike activity were routinely altered by governments and capital to meet different political and economic demands, mostly to the detriment of workers' rights. These rules shifted workplace conflict from the picket lines (controlled by workers) to LRBs and the courts (controlled by union bureaucracy, employers, government personnel, lawyers and judges). Ultimately, unions' embrace of industrial legality integrated important sections of the working class into a system that promoted stability as a means to foster conditions for long-term capital accumulation.

While organized labour unquestionably contributed to the legalization of industrial relations throughout the post-war period, unions remained hostile to judicial involvement in labour disputes. In the 1950s, capital increased its recourse to judicial review in order to restrict laws expanding the capacity of unions to organize, bargain collectively and strike. Employers argued that the post-war regime of industrial legality had altered the balance of power too far in favour of organized labour. According the Canadian Manufacturers' Association (CMA), the post-war legislative framework

> was designed to help and protect trade unions in the days when they were small and relatively weak. Whatever basis of fact there may have been for the old-time picture of the trade union as a wholly idealistic organization of downtrodden workers… [it] has little relation to the situation today…. Today there is much more need to think in terms of protecting the interests of the public, the employers and the individual employee.[2]

The CMA further argued that the Rand Formula violated the individual rights of both business and workers.[3] In order to protect individual workers, the CMA insisted that unions be punished for any illegal act, especially illegal strikes. The CMA argued that any union action challenging the boundaries of legality demonstrated a lack of "legal and moral responsibility" that should be punished with fines, imprisonment and decertification.[4]

Capital's attachment to and use of the courts indicated to unionists that courts were the domain of employers. As Canadian director of the United Auto Workers George Burt argued, "the further we stay away from the courts the better we are in the labour relations process… [and] I think I have the backing of all of the Labour in the land… [that] unions do not want to go to court to defend [their] gains."[5] Union hostility centred on management's ability to break strikes with court-imposed injunctions. According to Judy Fudge and Eric Tucker (2001), injunctions have been used since the late nineteenth century as both coercive tools to stop union activities and ideological instruments to delegitimize workers' resistance to employer control of the workplace. Recognizing this, unions such as the United Steelworkers of America (USWA) argued throughout the 1950s and 1960s for the outright elimination of injunctions. According to the USWA, the law of injunctions reinforced the capacity of property owners to stop legitimate union activities but did nothing to block management's ability to break strikes through the "hiring of *outside* strike-breakers [because it] is the theft of a man's [*sic*] job. It should be outlawed as other forms of theft are outlawed."[6]

The union movement's hostility towards courts and judges intensified over questions of court-imposed injunctions in the 1960s and 1970s. In this period, the constraints imposed by industrial pluralism were also challenged by rank-and-file militancy directed not just at capital and courts but also at labour leaders and the union bureaucracy. Through the 1960s and 1970s, intra- and inter-union conflict intensified as young workers challenged entrenched older workers for control over their unions. Additionally, women workers confronted both well-established male unionists and powerful capitalist interests while struggling for just wages and workplaces (and societies) free of sexual discrimination (Sangster 2010). The rise in workplace conflict exposed an unprecedented level of working-class unrest, as an increasingly large percentage of all strikes were illegal (wildcat), violent and defiant of law and order (Jamieson 1968: 398–403).[7] In reflecting on this period, Bryan Palmer (2009: 221) has argued that these strikes were "often a spontaneous eruption of anger, alienation, and anxiety, ordered by workers themselves rather than challenged through conservative union leaders and the procedural morass of the legally ordered trade union settlement." In combating the entrenched personalities and institutions of post-war legality, wildcat strikers indirectly showed the limits to which the ruling classes tolerated radical dissent to the economic order within capitalist democracies (Sangster 2004).[8] The civil disobedience demonstrated by the wildcat strikers was opposed by all levels of the union bureaucracy and, most furiously, by capital and the courts.

The labour unions' opposition to judicial intervention in labour disputes continued throughout the 1970s and 1980s. By the beginning of the 1970s, there was general agreement by labour unions and their lawyers that judicial intervention in labour disputes was detrimental to industrial stability (Weiler 1971). Throughout the decade, the courts slowly began to acquiesce jurisdiction to LRBs, including on issues pertaining to strikes and lockouts (*CUPE v. New Brunswick* 1979; Weiler 1980). Paradoxically, the courts' deference to labour's historic demand to limit judicial involvement in labour disputes coincided with the long decline of the industrial relations system itself. In fact, by the middle of the 1970s, the dual pressures of high unemployment and rising prices (stagflation) weakened Canada's version of post-war Fordism. As politicians and capital blamed the high wages of unionized workers for fuelling inflation, governments increasingly responded with coercive actions to limit collective bargaining and strikes (Panitch and Swartz 2003).

The struggle between unions, business and the state increased throughout this period, as the federal government amplified its anti-inflation campaign with the introduction of the 1975 Anti-Inflation Act (wage and price controls) restricting both private and public sector bargaining. In July 1976, the federal government was given additional support by the SCC when it ruled in the *Reference Re Anti-Inflation Act* that wage and price controls were fully within Ottawa's emergency powers in the British North America Act (1976). On the surface, labour leaders objected to the anti-inflation legislation because it trampled on the traditional rights of provinces. More substantively, unions were incensed that the SCC's decision in the *Reference Re: Anti-Inflation Act* reinforced the federal government's ability to intervene in the collective bargaining process in the name of a questionable national (economic) "emergency." The SCC's legitimation of the federal government's anti-union legislation fuelled the organization of a one-day nation-wide general strike in October 1976 (Mosher 1976). For many observers, the federal (and later provincial) government's support for "free" collective bargaining was significantly eroded in 1978 with the jailing of Canadian Union of Postal Workers (CUPW) president John Claude Parrot for defying federal back-to-work legislation (Parrot 2005: 114–8). CUPW's use of civil disobedience also challenged the boundaries of responsible unionism amongst union leaders, as CLC president Dennis McDermott pressured Parrot to end the strike (Swartz and Warskett, this volume). Ultimately, Parrot's incarceration demonstrated the boundaries of the zone of legal toleration for the exercise of labour rights when they conflicted with the political or economic objectives of the country's ruling classes.

The federal Liberals' anti-inflation measures led in part to the party's electoral defeat in 1979, but the Trudeau Liberals managed to sweep back into office in 1980 promising new economic, political and legal reforms. Important components of the Liberal reform package included: a patriated constitution; enhanced protection for civil liberties; income redistribution through tax reform; and a program of economic nationalism (Panitch and Swartz 2003: 29). Although many of the economic reforms were dropped because of resistance from business, the Liberals were able to successfully patriate the constitution, which included the Charter. The Charter was especially important for Trudeau because he saw the concept of universal rights as a way to challenge Québécois nationalism (Russell 1993: 111–2; McRoberts 1997). For Trudeau, a judiciary empowered with a constitutional bill of rights would strengthen "the country's unity by basing the sovereignty of the Canadian people on a set of values common to all, and in particular on the notion of equality among all Canadians" (Trudeau 1990: 407). Of course, in Trudeau's mind these new values of sovereignty and equality were entirely abstract. At the same time his government was proclaiming the triumph of legal equality, it was also implementing the so-called "6 and 5" program, which capped public sector wage bargaining and removed the right of public workers to strike (rights that actually addressed class inequality). In essence, Trudeau's Charter served a contradictory double purpose: limiting several collective rights while unifying Canadians around an abstract notion of individual legal rights within a new, more aggressive form of capitalism (Fudge 1988: 77–8).

Given Trudeau's hostility to certain forms of collective rights, labour unions were understandably divided on the Charter. On the one hand, the transfer of political power to unelected judges to interpret the Charter represented a serious challenge to workers' collective rights enshrined in post-war legislation. For instance, would judges sympathize with the position that the Rand Formula violated individual rights? On the other hand, the English Canadian labour movement was closely aligned with the federal New Democratic Party (NDP), which strongly supported Trudeau's Charter project (Mandel 1994: 258–63). Some in the NDP were convinced that the Charter could act as a tool to challenge governments and employers. Further complexity was added by the fact that the Québec labour movement was universally opposed to the Charter because, it argued, it undermined the cultural, linguistic and political status of Québec. Given this political quandary, the CLC avoided participating in any of the meetings that led to the creation of the Charter (Savage 2007). Although labour remained on the sidelines, the final version of the Charter included constitutional protection for rights to association. For many union activists, it was an open-ended question as to whether judges — long critiqued for their hostility towards workers' collective rights — would interpret this right broadly to include rights to bargain collectively and strike. With this question in mind, many unions aggressively went to court to enshrine collective bargaining in the Constitution.

CHARTER CHALLENGES, 1986–1999

In the first era of Charter challenges, the courts confirmed the worst suspicions of Charter skeptics. In five cases, the Supreme Court ruled that the Charter's right to association did not include protection of secondary picketing (*Retail, Wholesale and Department Store Union, Loc. 580 v. Dolphin Delivery Ltd.*, 1986); the right to strike (*Reference Re Public Service Employee Relations Act*, 1987; *P.S.A.C. v. Canada*, 1987; *Retail, Wholesale and Department Store Union v. Saskatchewan*, 1987); or the right to bargain collectively (*Professional Institute of the Public Service of Canada v. Northwest Territories [Commissioner]*, 1990). In these cases, the SCC took the puzzling view that rights to association were individual rather than collective in nature. Relying on this narrow interpretation of individual rights in a capitalist society, the SCC insisted that the freedom to associate only protected an individual's ability to join together in a common cause rather than the actual activities of those associations (Fudge 1988). Using this reasoning, the court argued that labour unions had no special status as a group or an association and were in fact no different than any other social, political or religious organization.

Ignoring the decade-long legislative attack on Canadian workers' rights and freedoms, in the Labour Trilogy cases the SCC relied on purely abstract reasons to suggest that modern labour law rested on a compromise "between organized labour — a very powerful socio-economic force — on the one hand, and the employers of labour — an equally powerful socio-economic force — on the other" (*Reference Re Public Service Employee Relations Act*, 1987: para. 182). The Court went on to argue that "the balance between the two forces is delicate and the public-at-large depends for its security and welfare upon the maintenance of that balance" (*Reference Re Public Service Employee Relations Act*, 1987: para. 182). Notwithstanding the fact that workers and employers rarely meet as equals, underlying the SCC's argument was the notion that labour freedoms are "modern legislative" rights and not fundamental rights deserving constitutional protection. Unwilling to upset what it perceived as a balance between equally competing groups, the SCC deferred to the legislature on the best way to address the "great changes — economic, social, and industrial — [that] are afoot" in Canada and throughout the world (*Reference Re Public Service Employee Relations Act*, 1987: para. 182). Implicit within this rationale was the Court's concern that workers' rights could not be used as a wedge to challenge the power that capital maintained to shape the "great changes… afoot" throughout the country.

The SCC's hostility to constitutionalizing the zone of legal toleration in the industrial relations regime further motivated anti-union crusaders to contest union rights in the courts. In *Lavigne v. Ontario Public Service Employees Union* (1991), a disgruntled union member named Francis "Merv" Lavigne took the Ontario Public Service Employees Union to court, arguing that the compulsory dues component in his collective agreement (the Rand Formula) violated his individual right *not* to associate with the union. Lavigne also suggested that his union's support for political, economic and social causes not directly related to collective bargaining — including support for the NDP and disarmament campaigns — violated his individual right to expression. As Lavigne's struggle was directed against an essential pillar of post-war industrial pluralism, he was supported and financed by the right-wing National Citizens Coalition (NCC).

Notwithstanding the NCC's financial support, Lavigne was unsuccessful at the Supreme Court. In the case, the SCC took the position that the Charter did include a right not to associate. Yet, the justices also recognized that the Rand Formula

> is simply to promote industrial peace through the encouragement of collective bargaining. It does not purport to align those subject to its operation with the union or any of its activities, since it specifically provides for dissent by stipulating that no member of the bargaining unit is required to become a member of the union. (*Lavigne v. Ontario Public Service Employees Union*, 1991)

Implicit in this reasoning was that the boundaries of constraint imposed by the Rand Formula benefited labour and capital equally, and therefore had to be weighed against the individual's right not to associate. In recognizing the importance of the Rand Formula, the Lavigne decision was, at best, a pyrrhic victory for labour because judicial acceptance of labour rights was weighed against the question of industrial stability, a situation that primarily benefits capital. Viewed from this perspective, labour leaders were correct to "breathe a collective sigh of relief" while recognizing that judges offered little to advance the cause of workers' rights (Savage 2007: 191).

Given the SCC's tepid response to reading union freedoms into the Charter, labour leaders recognized greater potential for progressive social change through their traditional support for the NDP. Yet, by the middle of the decade, NDP provincial governments demonstrated that they were equally willing to engage in hard bargaining while eliminating the right of workers to strike. This transition within the NDP was most prominent in the Ontario government of Bob Rae, but extended to Saskatchewan, British Columbia and later, Manitoba (Evans, this volume). Similar attitudes towards labour were apparent in the Parti Québécois governments of Jacques Parizeau, Lucien Bouchard and Bernard Landry and, perhaps less surprisingly, in the federal Liberal government of Jean Chrétien. Throughout the 1990s, liberal and social democratic governments across Canada adopted what Greg Albo has termed the "competitive austerity" approach to managing the economy (Albo 1994; Graefe, this volume). The competitive austerity model relied on a series of neoliberal policy programs that reinforced the primacy of private sector-led economic growth and competitiveness at the expense of public programs and services through lower-tax zones, privatization of important public services, new technology development through public subsidies and the creation of a flexible and less rigid labour market while also promoting worker retraining. Combined with governments' heavy-handed use of back-to-work legislation and hostile judges, competitive austerity regimes contributed to lowering union density rates and declining strike numbers throughout the country (Briskin 2007). As the decade wore on, labour unions were increasingly left to fend for themselves.

ONGOING JUDICIAL STRUGGLES, 1999–2011

By the end of the 1990s, labour unions were squarely on the defensive. Not a single Canadian government was promising, let alone implementing, new pro-union reforms in the realm of industrial relations. Faced with the impasse in legislative improvements to labour rights, some unions once again looked to the Charter as a defensive tool to protect past gains.

Between 1999 and 2002, the Supreme Court ruled in four cases that opened a small space for labour unions to challenge anti-union employers. In *United Food and Commercial Workers v. Local 1518 v. Kmart Canada Ltd.* (1999), the SCC ruled that a union had freedom of expression rights to distribute information outside businesses not directly involved in an ongoing strike. In *Retail, Wholesale Department Store Union 'Local 558' v. Pepsi-Cola Canada Beverages (West) Ltd.* (2002), the SCC took an additional step on the right to strike, overturning decades-old common law rules outlawing secondary picketing. In an Ontario dispute, the SCC ruled that the exclusion of farm workers from the province's labour relations regime violated their freedom of association rights, but still maintained that there was no constitutional right to bargain (*Dunmore v. Ontario (Attorney General)* [2001]). In the same period, the SCC upheld Québec's long-standing mandatory unionization system in the construction industry but was highly critical of the "ideological conformity" that compulsory union membership played in shaping an individual's behaviour (*R. v. Advance Cutting & Coring Ltd.* [2001]).

Although these four cases demonstrated a shifting judicial mindset with regard to freedom of association, the court continued to maintain a general hesitation towards extending full human rights protection to workers or unions. In *Newfoundland (Treasury Board) v. N.A.P.E.* (2004), for instance, the SCC took the position that a fiscal "crisis" was enough of an emergency to allow a government to unilaterally withdraw pay equity commitments to women workers.

In the Dunmore case, the United Food and Commercial Workers (UFCW) asked the court to rule on the Ontario Conservative government's decision in 1995 to discard NDP legislation that had extended collective bargaining and union organizing rights to farm workers (Choudry and Thomas, this volume). In siding with the UFCW, the Court connected union rights to the relative strength of particular groups of workers and their employers in the labour market. For the majority of the SCC, it was the relative weakness of agricultural workers' ability to form unions that triggered a positive state obligation to include them in a collective bargaining regime. Here the SCC argued that "the evidence is that the ability of agricultural workers to associate is only as great as their access to legal protection, and such a protection exists neither in statutory nor constitutional form" (*Dunmore v. Ontario [Attorney General]* [2001]: para. 5). By contrast, in areas where workers were collectively stronger — as was the case when an RCMP officer challenged federal legislation restricting unionization — the court was less supportive (*Delisle v. Canada [Deputy Attorney General]* [1999]). In other words, there was no general right to collective bargaining per se and workers' rights would always be balanced against their general occupational status (*Dunmore v. Ontario [Attorney General]* [2001]: para. 42).

Although the SCC was adamant in the Dunmore decision that there was no constitutional right to collective bargaining, the case certainly elevated the hopes of some union leaders that governments "just can't run roughshod over workers' rights" (MacCharles 2001). It was therefore not surprising that public sector unions quickly turned to the courts to challenge a unilateral decision by the BC Liberal government to remove collective bargaining rights from health-care workers in 2002. When the case finally made its way to the SCC in 2007, the Court went a step further than in the Dunmore case and ruled that the Charter "protects the capacity of members of labour unions to engage, in association, in collective bargaining on fundamental workplace issues" (*BC Health Services 2007*: para. 19). In coming to this conclusion, the Court took the unexpected action of overturning the Labour Trilogy, stating that collective bargaining is integral to peaceful relations in the workplace and should thus be protected by the Charter.

The Court's conclusion in *BC Health Services* rested on its understanding of evolving "Charter values" that promote human dignity, liberty and autonomy (*BC Health Services* [2007]: para. 82–4). In language that would certainly legitimize any union struggle for basic rights, the Court stated that the right to

> bargain collectively with an employer enhances the human dignity, liberty and autonomy of workers by giving them the opportunity to influence the establishment of workplace rules and thereby gain some control over a major aspect of their lives, namely their work. (*BC Health Services* [2007]: para. 82)

In coming to this conclusion, the Court borrowed language from the Royal Commission Inquiry into Labour Disputes (the Woods Commission), stating that collective bargaining imposed legal responsibilities on its participants and therefore deserved some form of government support. Generally, workers accepted industrial democracy but in so doing also had to consent to "the rule of law in the workplace" (*BC Health Services* [2007]: para. 85). Within this context, the Court recognized that collective bargaining is a limited right:

> The Charter protects the capacity of members of labour unions to engage, in association, in collective bargaining on fundamental workplace issues. This protection does not cover all aspects of "collective bargaining," as that term is understood in the statutory labour relations regimes that are in place across the country. Nor does it ensure a particular outcome in a labour dispute, or guarantee access to any particular statutory regime. What is protected is simply the right of employees to associate *in a process of collective action to achieve workplace goals*. (*BC Health Services* [2007]: para. 9, emphasis added)

By recognizing the corresponding rights and duties inherent in Canada's regime of industrial pluralism, the Court struck down three sections in BC's Health and Social Services Delivery Improvement Act (2002).

Commentary on the judicial intervention in labour disputes post-*BC Health Services* has been mixed. On the one hand, some have praised judicial enlightenment for extending support for a regime under constant assault from governments and employers (Adams 2008). Unions have also internalized the idea of "labour rights as human rights" in order to legitimize their activities because "the Supreme Court of Canada has ruled that workers' ability to join unions, to collective bargain, and to express themselves as trade unionists and citizens" (Saskatchewan Federation of Labour 2010: 10). To be sure, this commentary recognizes that *BC Health Services* was a dramatic step forward for the SCC. Having overturned decades of precedent, the Court went a step further to find a procedural right to bargain collectively.

On the other hand, there is little evidence that the Supreme Court justices view Charter rights as a countervailing power designed to offset the power of capital or of government-imposed restructuring in the workplace. In fact, in two recent decisions, the Court has affirmed the limited nature of *BC Health Services*. In 2009, the SCC ruled against the UFCW's decade-long attempt to unionize a Walmart in Québec (*Plourde v. Walmart Canada Corp.* [2009]). In attempting to utilize the Charter to stop an aggressive anti-union action by the world's largest private sector employer, the Court reprimanded the UFCW because the union's faith in labour rights in the Charter

> extends the reasoning in *Health Services* well beyond its natural limits. In that case the state was not only the legislator but the employer. Here the employer is a private corporation…. Care must be taken not only to avoid upsetting the balance the legislature has struck in the Code taken as a whole, but not to hand to one side (labour) a lopsided advantage because employees bargain through their union (and can thereby invoke

freedom of association) whereas employers, for the most part, bargain individually. (*Plourde v. Wal-Mart Canada Corp.* [2009]: para. 5–6)

In this case, the Court affirmed that it would not interpret Charter rights to advance the cause of labour unions as a challenge to private sector employers.[9] In fact, the SCC fell back on a traditional interpretation of individual rights in a capitalist society, placing the individual rights of corporations above the collective rights of workers and their unions.

The SCC's unwillingness to expand labour rights in a manner that threatened the balance of power in the worker-employer relationship was also demonstrated in *Ontario (Attorney General) v. Fraser* (2011). In this case, the SCC was asked to rule on the constitutionality of Ontario's Agricultural Employees Protection Act (AEPA) (2002), which was the Ontario Conservative government's legislative response to the Dunmore decision. The AEPA established an institutional structure that allowed agricultural workers to join an employee association and make representations to their employer. Unlike the Ontario Labour Relations Act, however, the AEPA did not require farm employers to negotiate with a certified union nor did it allow farm workers to strike. By the Conservative government's own admission, the AEPA was designed "to ensure that the freedom of association is meaningful" but that the legislation was "not intended to extend collective bargaining to agricultural workers" (*Ontario [Attorney General] v. Fraser* [2009]: para. 105–6). In the post-*BC Health Services* world, the UFCW argued that this type of association was anything but meaningful since no collective agreements had been signed in the Ontario farm industry since the AEPA was introduced and thus violated the Charter.

In siding with the government, the majority of SCC justices[10] clarified that *BC Health Services* only required "the parties to meet and engage in meaningful dialogue" and thus "protects the right to a general process of collective bargaining" (*Ontario [Attorney General] v. Fraser* [2009]: para. 41). The Court came to this conclusion despite the fact that the AEPA did not legally require the employer to recognize the union nor to do anything more than "to listen to or read employee representations — to assure that the employer will in fact consider the employee representation" (*Ontario [Attorney General] v. Fraser* [2009]: para. 103). In other words, the Court suggested that the mere act of "listening to" a group of workers was meaningful enough to pass the *BC Health Services* threshold despite the fact that the UFCW had been unable to sign a single collective agreement in the farm sector. The SCC's refusal to recognize the power imbalance between farm workers and their employers reinforced the notion that labour rights in the Charter would not fundamentally challenge employer power.

CONCLUSION

Canada's union movement has a long history of resisting the economic and political power of employers. The current regime of industrial pluralism is a product of the labour movement's long history of class struggle against the worst excesses of nineteenth- and twentieth-century capitalism. In fact, industrial pluralism's zone of legal toleration exists only because workers were willing to break exploitative laws through civil disobedience, sit-down strikes and mass protest. The preservation of these capacities had little to do with success in court. On the contrary, courts often used injunctions to limit the ability of unions to challenge employer power. This class tension led to a long history of labour hostility to judicial intervention in labour disputes.

Once labour won the legal right to bargain collectively, however, the regime of industrial pluralism constructed boundaries of constraint that weakened labour's capacity to resist government and employer power when the material forces underpinning that system were altered. Initially, some labour unions went to court to enshrine union rights in the newly minted Charter. More recently, unions have gone back to court simply to protect past gains and legitimize their own activities in the face of continued government and employer challenges. Although courts were initially unwilling to extend constitutional freedoms to unions, this seemed to change with the SCC's decision in *BC Health Services*. Yet, the decisions in *Plourde* and *Fraser* should act as warnings for all unions seeking to advance or alter Canada's system of labour relations. At best, court decisions have been mixed, and labour's legal strategies have served as defensive efforts to preserve a small component of the post-war labour regime. To be sure, these decisions have opened small spaces of resistance, giving labour tools to extend spaces of legitimation. Yet, in contemplating future litigation, it is useful to remember that judicial interpretation of existing laws have limitations as well as opportunities. As former CAW president Basil "Buzz" Hargrove (2009b: 44) has argued,

> expansive legal protection of fundamental labour rights… will not be extended until workers recognize their shared experiences and the strength of their collective voice. It is only when workers use the power of their numbers to demand a fundamental shift in the political and economic structures which determine the quality of their work lives that societal institutions, including the courts, will be forced to take notice.

Notes

1. Archives of Ontario (hereafter AO), RG 49-138, Proceedings of the Select Committee on Labour Relations (hereafter PSCLR), Box C 90, "Testimony of the Ontario Federation of Labour," October 1, 1957: 4807–8.
2. AO, RG 49-138, PSCLR, Box C 90, Submission of the Ontario Division of the Canadian Manufacturers' Association, October 29, 1957: 4.
3. AO, RG 49-138, PSCLR, Box C 92, Testimony of the Canadian Manufacturers' Association (Ontario Division), October 29 & 30, 1957: 2142.
4. AO, RG 49-138, PSCLR, Box C 90, Testimony of the Canadian Manufacturers' Association (Ontario Division), October 29 & 30, 1957: 2174, 2192–6.
5. AO, RG 49-138, PSCLR, Box C90, Testimony of the UAW (International Union, United Automobile, Aircraft, and Agricultural Implement Workers of America [UAW-CLC],

October 15, 1957: 2748.

6. AO, RG 49-138 Box C 92, United Steelworkers of America, Picketing, Strikes, Injunctions: Supplemental Brief to the Select Committee on Labor Relations, November 26, 1957.

7. According to Jamieson, 149 (21 percent) of the total 501 strikes in 1965 were wildcats. In 1966, 210 (33 percent) of 617 total strikes were wildcats.

8. See labour's comments before the Royal Commission Inquiry into Labour Disputes (the Rand Commission) in 1967 and 1968 (Ontario 1968). Before this commission, labour unions decried the pro-employer biases of judges in the labour relations process. When strikes occurred, unions had "an added adversary, [because] the company has been joined in their contest by the courts [and then] it's a 'what is the law for a poor man [*sic*]' sort of thing." AO, RG 18-152, Proceedings of the Royal Commission Inquiry Into Labour Disputes, Box 3 B227098, Testimony of the Toronto and District Labour Council, 19 January 1967: 644.

9. This point was clarified in *Attorney General (Ontario) v. Fraser* (2011), SCC 20, para. 73.

10. *Fraser* was a split decision. Eight justices voted to uphold the AEPA while one (Justice Abella) argued that the AEPA was unconstitutional. Of the nine justices hearing the appeal, seven voted to uphold *BC Health Services*, while two (Justice Rothstein and Justice Deschamps) argued that *BC Health Services* should be overturned.

REFERENCES

Abella, I. 1973. *Nationalism, Communism and Canadian Labour: The CIO, the Communist Party and the Canadian Congress of Labour, 1935–1956*. Toronto: University of Toronto Press.

ACORN Canada. n.d. "ACORN Canada." At <acorncanada.org>.

_____. 2010. "Making History." At <acorncanada.org/new-westminster-living-wage/192-making-history>.

ACORN USA. 2010. "Vindication Doesn't Pay the Bills." March 21. At <acorn.org/node/693>.

Acuff, S. 2000. "The Battle in Seattle and Where We Go From Here." *New Labor Forum* 6 (Spring/Summer): 30–4.

Adams, R. 2009. "Prospects for Labour's Right to Bargain Collectively After B.C. Health Services." *University of New Brunswick Law Journal* 59: 85–94.

_____. 2008. "From Statutory Right to Human Right: The Evolution and Current Status of Collective Bargaining." *Just Labour: A Canadian Journal of Work and Society* 12 (Spring): 48–67.

Ad Hoc Coalition for Women's Equality and Human Rights. 2011. "About Us." At <womensequality.ca/aboutus.html>.

Adkin, L. 1998. *The Politics of Sustainable Development: Citizens, Unions and the Corporations*. Montreal: Black Rose Books.

Alberta Federation of Labour. 2011. "Alberta women falling behind, say union leaders: Labour calls for government action to end gender inequality." Press Release, March 16. At <afl.org/index.php/Press-Release/alberta-women-falling-behind-say-union-leaders-labour-calls-for-government-action-to-end-gender-inequality.html>.

Albo, G. 2011. "NDP Campaign Platform Analysis." *GlobalNews.ca*, April 11. At <globalnews.ca/campaign+platform+analysis/4591525/story.html>.

_____. 2009. "The Crisis of Neoliberalism and the Impasse of the Union Movement." *Development Dialogue* (January): 119–31.

_____. 2002. "Neoliberalism, the State and the Left: A Canadian perspective." *Monthly Review* 54: 46–55.

_____. 1994. "'Competitive Austerity' and the Impasse of Capitalist Employment Policy." In R. Miliband and L. Panitch (eds.), *Socialist Register 1994: Between Globalism and Nationalism*. London: Merlin: 144–70.

_____. 1990. "The New Realism and Canadian Workers." In A. Gagnon and J. Bickerton (eds.), *Canadian Politics: An Introduction to the Discipline*. Toronto: Broadview Press: 471–504.

Albo, G., S. Gindin and L. Panitch. 2010. *In and Out of Crisis: The Global Financial Meltdown and Left Alternatives*. Oakland: PM Press.

Allen, V. 1966. *Militant Trade Unionism: An Analysis of Industrial Action in an Inflationary Situation*. London: Merlin.

Alper, D. 1977. "The Effects of Coalition Government on Party Structure: The Case of the Conservative Party in BC." *BC Studies* 33 (Spring): 40–9.

Anderson, J. 1972. "Nonpartisan Urban Politics in Canadian Cities." In J. Masson and J. Anderson (eds.), *Emerging Party Politics in Urban Canada*. Toronto: McClelland and Stewart.

Anderson, P. 2000. "Renewals." *New Left Review* II, 1 (January-February): 5–24.

_____. 1977. "The Limits and Possibilities of Trade Union Action." In T. Clarke and L. Clements (eds.), *Trade Unions under Capitalism*. London: Fontana Collins: 333–50.

Anderson, R. 1999. *Economic Development Among the Aboriginal Peoples in Canada*. North York: Captus Press.

Annian, H. 2006. *The Silent Spikes: Chinese Laborers and the Construction of North American Railroads*.

Beijing: China Intercontinental Press.

Annis, R. 2009. "Internal Revolt Shakes B.C. NDP, Labour Movement." *Socialist Voice*, December 17. At <socialistvoice.ca/?p=1408>.

Archer, K. and A. Whitehorn. 1993. *Canadian Trade Unions and the New Democratic Party.* Kingston: Queen's University Industrial Relations Centre.

Armstrong, P. 1996. "The Feminization of the Labour Force: Harmonizing Down in a Global Economy." In I. Bakker (ed.), *Rethinking Restructuring: Gender and Change in Canada.* Toronto: University of Toronto Press: 29–54.

Armstrong, P., and H. Armstrong. 1990. "Lessons from Pay Equity." *Studies in Political Economy* 32 (Summer): 29–54.

Ashbolt, A. 2008. "The American New Left and Community Unions." *Illawarra Unity — Journal of the Illawarra Branch of the Australian Society for the Study of Labour History* 8, 1: 37–42.

Assembly of First Nations. 1999. "Resolution No. 13: Labour Relations." Ottawa: Confederacy of Nations. At <64.26.129.156/article.asp?id=907>.

Avakumovic, I. 1978. *Socialism in Canada: A Study of the CCF-NDP in Federal and Provincial Politics.* Toronto: McClelland and Stewart.

Babcock, R.1974. *Gompers in Canada: A Study in American Continentalism Before the First World War.* Toronto: University of Toronto Press.

Bakan, A., and A. Kobayashi. 2007. "Affirmative Action and Employment Equity: Policy, Ideology and Backlash in Canadian Context." *Studies in Political Economy* 79 (Spring): 145–66.

Bakker, I. 1996. "Introduction: The Gendered Foundations of Restructuring in Canada." In I. Bakker (ed.), *Rethinking Restructuring: Gender and Change in Canada.* Toronto: University of Toronto Press: 3–28.

Banks, A. 1992. "The Power and Promise of Community Unionism." *Labor Research Review* 18: 16–31.

Barber, J. 1999. "The Ontario Election: Toronto's Strategic Voting Sends a Message." *Globe and Mail,* June 4.

Bartkiw, T. 2009. "Proceed with Caution, or Stop Wherever Possible? Ongoing Paradoxes in Legalized Labour Politics." *Canadian Labour and Employment Law Journal* 15, 1: 77–100.

Bashevkin, S. 1996. "Losing Common Ground: Feminists, Conservatives and Public Policy in Canada during the Mulroney Years." *Canadian Journal of Political Science* 29, 2: 211–42.

Basok, T. 2007. *Canada's Temporary Migration Program: A Model Despite Flaws.* Washington: Migration Policy Institute.

Battiste, M. (ed.). 2000. *Reclaiming Indigenous Voice and Vision.* Vancouver: UBC Press.

Belanger, Y. 2006. *Gambling with the Future: The Evolution of Aboriginal Gaming in Canada.* Saskatoon: Purich Publishing.

Benford, R., and D. Snow. 2000. "Framing Processes and Social Movements." *Annual Review of Sociology* 26: 611–639.

Bennett, D. 2011. *Northern Exposures: a Canadian Perspective on Occupational Health and Environment.* Amityville NY: Baywood Publishing.

_____. 2007. "Labour and the Environment at the Canadian Labour Congress - The Story of the Convergence." *Just Labour: A Canadian Journal of Work and Society* 10 (Spring): 1–7.

Bentham, K. 2007. "Labour's Collective Bargaining Record on Women's and Family Issues." In G. Hunt and D. Rayside (eds.), *Equity, Diversity and Canadian Labour.* Toronto: University of Toronto Press.

Berman, M. 1983. *All That is Solid Melts Into Air: The Experience of Modernity.* London: Verso.

Bernard, E. 1991. "Canada's New Democratic Party at Thirty." *Socialist Review* 21, 3/4 (July-December): 133–53.

Bezanson, K. 2006. *Gender, the State and Social Reproduction.* Toronto: University of Toronto

Press.

Bickerton, G., and C. Stearns. 2002. "The Struggle Continues in Winnipeg: The Workers Organizing and Resource Centre." *Just Labour: A Canadian Journal of Work and Society* 1 (Winter): 50–7.

Bilson, B. 2009. "Enter Stage Right: Players and Roles in a Post-B.C. Health Services World." *University of New Brunswick Law Journal* 59: 67–84.

Biolsi, T. 2005. "Imagined Geographies: Sovereignty, Indigenous Space, and American Indian Struggle." *American Ethnologist* 32, 3: 239–59.

Black, E., and J. Silver. 2008. *Building a Better World: An Introduction to Trade Unionism in Canada.* 2nd ed. Halifax: Fernwood.

Black, S. 2005. "Community Unionism: A Strategy for Organizing in the New Economy." *New Labor Forum* 14, 3: 24–32.

Blackett, A., and C. Sheppard. 2003. "Collective Bargaining and Equality: Making Connections." *International Labour Review* 142, 4: 473–511.

Blais, A., R. Nadeau, E. Gidengil and N. Nevitte. 2001. "Measuring Strategic Voting in Multiparty Plurality Elections." *Electoral Studies* 20: 343–52.

Blakeney, Allan. 2008. *An Honourable Calling: A Political Memoir.* Toronto: University of Toronto Press.

Bleyer, P. 2001. "Cross-movement coalitions and political agency: the popular sector and the Pro-Canada/Action Canada Network." PhD Thesis. London School of Economics and Political Science.

Blight, P. 1981. *Report on Proportional Representation.* BC NDP Provincial Council Committee.

Blomley, N. 1996. "Shut the Province Down: First Nations Blockades in British Columbia, 1984–1995." *BC Studies* 111: 5–35.

Boismenu, G., P. Dufour and D. Saint-Martin. 2004. *Ambitions libérales et écueils politiques.* Montreal: Athéna Éditions.

Borrows, J. 2005. *Crown and Aboriginal Occupations of Land: A History & Comparison.* Commissioned Report for the Ipperwash Inquiry. At <http://www.attorneygeneral.jus. gov.on.ca/inquiries/ipperwash/policy_part/research/pdf/History_of_Occupations_ Borrows.pdf>.

Brenner, N., and N. Theodore (eds). 2002. *Spaces of Neoliberalism: Urban Restructuring in North America and Western Europe.* Malden, MA: Wiley-Blackwell.

Briggs, A. 2007. "The Welfare State in Historical Perspective." In C. Pierson and F.G. Castles (eds.), *The Welfare State Reader.* 2nd ed. Malden, MA: Polity Press.

Briskin, L. 2007. "From Person-Days Lost to Labour Militancy: A New Look at the Canadian Work Stoppage Data." *Relations Industrielles/Industrial Relations* 62, 1: 31–65.

_____. 2006a. "Equity Bargaining, Bargaining Equity." Working Paper. Toronto: Centre for Research on Work and Society. At <yorku.ca/lbriskin/pdf/bargainingpaperFI-NAL3secure.pdf>.

_____. 2006b. "Victimisation and Agency: The Social Construction of Union Women's Leadership." *Industrial Relations Journal* 37, 4: 359–78.

Briskin, L., and P. McDermott. 1993. *Women Challenging Unions: Feminism, Democracy and Militancy.* Toronto: University of Toronto Press.

Briskin L., and L. Yanz (eds.). 1983. *Union Sisters: Women in the Labour Movement.* Toronto: Women's Educational Press.

British Columbia, Ministry of Finance and Corporate Relations. 1998. *Budget '98 Speech.* At <http://www.fin.gov.bc.ca/archive/budget98/bgt_cnts.htm>.

_____. 1996. *Budget '96 Budget Speech.* At <www.fin.gov.bc.ca/archive/budget96/speech. htm>.

Brodie, J. 2008. "We Are All Equal Now: Contemporary Gender Politics in Canada." *Feminist Theory* 9, 2: 145–64.

Brodie, J., and J. Jenson. 1988. *Crisis, Challenge and Change: Party and Class in Canada Revisited*. Ottawa: Carleton University Press.

Burrows, M. 1998. "Allied Forces: Unions and Environmentalists Can Work Together for Jobs and Ecological Sustainability." *Alternatives Journal* 24, 4 (Fall): 18–23.

Burton, R. 1999. "Basic rights denied with self-government." *Saskatoon StarPhoenix*, June 15.

Bush, M. 1995. "Zindabad! B.C. Farmworkers' Fight for Rights." At <vcn.bc.ca/cfu/about.htm>.

Butovsky, J., and M. Smith. 2007 "Beyond Social Unionism: Farm Workers in Ontario and Some Lessons from Labour History." *Labour/Le Travail* 59 (Spring): 69–97.

Calugay, J., M. Henaway and E. Shragge. 2011. "Working Through the Loopholes Undermining Workplace Gains, One Temp Worker at a Time." *Canadian Dimension* 45 (November/December): 2.

Camfield, D. 2011. *Canadian Labour in Crisis: Reinventing the Workers' Movement*. Halifax: Fernwood.

_____. 2007. "Renewal in Canadian Public Sector Unions: Neoliberalism and Union Praxis." *Relations Industrielles/Industrial Relations* 62, 2: 282–304.

_____. 2006. "Neoliberalism and Working-Class Resistance in British Columbia: The Hospital Union Employees' Struggle 2002–2004." *Labour/Le Travail* 57 (Spring): 9–42.

Canada. 2006. Canadian Parliamentary Debates. *Hansard*. November 10.

Canada. Department of Labour. 1975. *Labour Organization in Canada*. Ottawa: Department of Labour.

_____. 1946. "Award on Issue of Union Security in Ford Dispute." *Labour Gazette* (January): 123–31.

Canada Without Poverty — Canada Sans Pauvreté. n.d. "About." At < http://www.cwp-csp.ca/about-us/>.

Canadian Auto Workers. n.d. "Unemployment Insurance and Labour Market Deregulation." At <caw.ca/en/about-the-caw-policies-and-papers-unemployment-insurance-and-labour-market-deregulation.htm>.

_____. 2011. "50 Priority Ridings which will Determine the Outcome of this Election." At <caw.ca/en/10124.htm>.

_____. 2008. "40 'Slim Win' Ridings which will Determine the Outcome of this Election." At <caw.ca/en/4149.htm>.

_____. 2007. "Aboriginal and Workers of Colour." At <caw.ca/en/3416.htm>.

_____. 2006a. "Put the Tories on a Short Leash." *Context*, January 25. At <caw.ca/en/4580.htm>.

_____. 2006b. "NEB Encourages Withdrawal of Support for NDP." *Contact*, March 24. At <caw.ca/en/3773.htm>.

_____. 2006c. "Movement and Party." *Facts from the Fringe*, January 30. At <caw.ca/en/4762.htm>

_____. 2006d. "Nova Scotia NDP Recognizes Labour Independence." *Contact*, May 12. At <caw.ca/en/3780.htm>.

_____. 2005a. "CAW Delegates Vote in Favour of Federal Election Strategy." *Contact*, December 9. At <caw.ca/en/3862.htm>.

_____. 2005b. "CAW Council Election Strategy Recommendation." *Contact*, December 9. At <caw.ca/en/4578.htm>.

_____. 2003. "NDP, CAW and Environmental Groups Unveil Green Car Strategy." *Contact*, July 20. At <caw.ca/en/3979.htm>.

_____. 2002. "Task Force on Working Class Politics in the 21st Century." Toronto: CAW.

_____. 2001. "CAW Ends Financial Support for OCAP." *Contact*, July 29. At <caw.ca/en/4209.htm>.

_____. 1999. "Elections and Political Action." *Contact*, June 13. At <caw.ca/en/4295.htm>.

_____. 1998. "CAW Activists Discuss Strategy To Defeat Harris." *Contact*, November 15. At <caw.ca/en/4358.htm>.

Canadian Bar Association. 2006. "Low Skilled Worker Pilot Project." Ottawa: CBA.

Canadian Labour Congress. n.d. "The Union Advantage." At <http://www.canadianlabour.ca/about-clc/union-advantage>.

_____. 2008. "Women in the Workforce: Still A Long Way from Equality." Ottawa: CLC. At <canadianlabour.ca/sites/default/files/pdfs/womensequalityreportEn.pdf>.

_____. 1999. "CLC Policy on Just Transition for Workers During Environmental Change." At <action.web.ca/home/clcenvir/attach/justtrans.pdf>.

Canadian Labour Congress/Vector Research. 2003. *Canadians Talk About Unions*. Ottawa: CLC/Vector Research.

Canadian Union of Public Employees. 2010. "CUPE Partners with the Métis Nation to Celebrate Back to Batoche." July 7. At <cupe.ca/aboriginal/partners-mtis-nation-celebrate-batoche>.

_____. 2007. "Healthy, Clean & Green: a Worker's Action Guide to a Greener Workplace." At <cupe.ca/updir/Green_booklet.pdf >.

_____. 2003. "Highlights of *CUPE et al. v Attorney-General (Ont) et al.* Settlement." At <cupe.ca/updir/shortsummaryjune12_03.pdf>.

Carr, B. 1999. "Globalization from Below: Labour Internationalism Under NAFTA." *International Social Science Journal* 51, 159: 49–59.

Carroll, W. 2005. "Introduction: Social Democracy in Neoliberal Times." In W. Carroll and R. Ratner (eds.), *Challenges and Perils: Social Democracy in Neoliberal Times*. Halifax. Fernwood Publishing: 7–24.

Carroll, W., and R. Ratner. 2007. "Ambivalent Allies: Social Democratic Regimes and Social Movements." *BC Studies* 154 (Summer): 41–66.

_____(eds.). 2005. *Challenges and Perils: Social Democracy in Neoliberal Times*. Halifax: Fernwood Publishing.

Castles, S. 2004. "The Factors that Make and Unmake Migration Policies." *International Migration Review* 28, 3: 852–84.

CBC News Online. 2006. "Playing the endorsement game." *CBC.ca*. At <cbc.ca/canadavotes2006/analysiscommentary/endorsement.html>.

Charest, J. 2004. "Labour Market Transformations and Labour Law: The Québec Labour Movement in Search of Renewed Growth." In A-G. Gagnon (ed.), *Québec: State and Society*. 3rd ed. Peterborough: Broadview: 271–86.

Charest, R. 2009. "Le mouvement syndical québécois à la croisée des chemins: se battre ou subsister?" *Nouveaux Cahiers du Socialisme* 2 (Fall): 175–83.

Chorney, H., and P. Hansen. 1985. "Neo-conservatism, social democracy and 'Province-building': The experience of Manitoba." *Review of Canadian Sociology and Anthropology* 22, 1: 1–29.

Choudry, A., J. Hanley, S. Jordan, E. Shragge and M. Stiegman. 2009. *Fightback: Workplace Justice for Immigrants*. Halifax: Fernwood Publishing.

Chronicle Herald. 2009. "NDP Platform: Cautious Change." May 16. At <thechronicleherald.ca/print_article.html?story=1122234>.

Citizenship and Immigration Canada. 2010. "Facts and Figures: Immigration Overview — Permanent and Temporary Residents." Ottawa: Research and Evaluation Branch, CIC. At <www.cic.gc.ca/english/pdf/research-stats/facts2010.pdf>.

_____. 2005. *The Monitor*. Summer. Ottawa: CIC.

Clark, D., and R. Warskett. 2010. "Labour fragmentation and New Forms of Organizing and Bargaining in the Service Sector." In N. Pupo and M. Thomas (eds.), *Interrogating the New Economy: Restructuring Work in the 21st Century*. Toronto: University of Toronto Press: 235–56.

REFERENCES

Clarke, J. 2011. "Raise the Rates." *Canadian Dimension* 45, 3: 20.

_____. 2009. "Going for Broke: OCAP and the Economic Crisis." *Upping the Anti: A Journal of Theory and Action* 8: 95–107.

_____. 2002. "Fight to Win." *Labour/Le Travail* 50 (Fall): 383–90.

Clawson, D. 2003. *The Next Upsurge: Labor and the New Social Movements.* Ithaca, N.Y.: Cornell University Press.

Cohen, M. 1994. "British Columbia: Playing Safe is a Dangerous Game." *Studies in Political Economy* 43 (Spring): 149–59.

Cohen, S. 2006. *Ramparts of Resistance: Why Workers Lost Their Power and How to Get it Back.* London: Pluto.

Commons, J. 1921. *Industrial Government.* New York: Macmillan.

Communications, Energy and Paperworkers Union of Canada. 2000. "Just Transition to a Sustainable Economy in Energy." At <oldsite.cep.ca/policies/policy_915_e.pdf>.

Conway, J. 2009. "Wall Declares War on Organized Labour in Saskatchewan." *The Bullet* 239. At <socialistproject.ca/bullet/239.php>.

Corporation des Enseignants du Québec. 1973. *Le Nouveau-Québec, ou comment des colonisés traitent leur colonie.* (Mémoire adressé au ministre de l'Education et à l'assemblée nationale du Québec).

Coulter, K. 2011. "Unionizing Retail: Lessons From Young Women's Grassroots Organizing in the Greater Toronto Area in the 1990s." *Labour/Le Travail* 67 (Spring): 77–93.

_____. 2009. "Women, Poverty Policy and the Production of Neoliberal Politics in Ontario, Canada." *Journal of Women, Politics and Policy* 30: 23–45.

Coward, B., and S. Garrod. 1975. "Special Supplement: Northwest Development Conference." *Western Voice* 4, 11: 7–10.

Cranford, C., M. Gellatly, D. Ladd and L. Vosko. 2006. "Community Unionism and Labour Movement Renewal: Organizing for Fair Employment." In C. Schenk and P. Kumar (eds.), *Paths to Union Renewal: Canadian Experiences.* Peterborough, ON: Broadview Press: 237–50.

Cranford, C., T. Das Gupta, D. Ladd and L. Vosko. 2005. "Thinking Through Community Unionism." In L. Vosko (ed.), *Precarious Employment: Understanding Labour Market Insecurity.* Montreal: McGill-Queen's University Press: 353–78.

Cranford, C., and D. Ladd. 2003. "Community Unionism: Organising for Fair Employment in Toronto." *Just Labour: A Canadian Journal of Work and Society* 3: 46–59.

Creese, G. 1999. *Contracting Masculinity: Gender, Class and Race in a White-collar Union, 1944–1994.* Don Mills, ON: Oxford University Press.

Crispo, J., and H. Arthurs. 1968. "Industrial Unrest in Canada: A Diagnosis of Recent Experience." *Relations Industrielles/Industrial Relations* 23, 2: 237–64.

Decima Research. 2006. "Strategic Voting in the 2006 General Election." Unpublished report.

DeFillipis J., R. Fisher and E. Shragge. 2010. *Contesting Community: The Limits and Potential of Local Organizing.* London: Rutgers University Press.

_____. 2006. "Neither Romance Nor Regulation: Re-evaluating Community." *International Journal of Urban and Regional Research* 30, 3: 673–89.

Delgado, G. 1986. *Organizing the Movement: The Roots and Growth of ACORN.* Philadelphia: Temple University Press.

Department of Finance Canada. 2008. "Table 15: Gross and Net Debt." Fiscal Reference Tables, September. At <fin.gc.ca/frt-trf/2008/frt08_3-eng.asp>.

Deverell, J. 1987. "Unions fear Charter ruling will restrict right to strike." *The Toronto Star*, April 10.

Dobbin, M. 2010. "Asbestos: Quebec Labour's Shame." *The Tyee*, June 28. At <thetyee.ca/Opinion/2010/06/28/QuebecLaboursShame/>.

Dominick, B. 1999. "Reinventing Antipoverty: The Ontario Coalition Against Poverty Employs Fresh, Winning Tactics." *ZNet*, January 1. At <zcommunications.org/reinventing-antipoverty-by-brian-dominick>.

Doody, B., and H. Milner. 2004. "Twenty Years After René Lévesque Failed to Change the Electoral Systems, Quebec May be Ready to Act." In H. Milner (ed.), *Steps Toward Making Every Vote Count*. Peterborough: Broadview: 267–80.

Dreiling, M., and I. Robinson. 1998. "Union Responses To NAFTA in the U.S. And Canada: Explaining Intra- and International Variation." *Mobilization: An International Journal* 3, 2: 163–84.

Drucker, P. 1958. *The Native Brotherhoods: Modern Intertribal Organizations of the Northwest Coast*. Washington: U.S. Government Printing Office.

Dufour, P. 2009. From Protest to Partisan Politics: When and How Collective Actors Cross the Line: Sociological Perspective on Québec Solidaire." *Canadian Journal of Sociology* 34, 1: 55–81.

Dumenil, G., and D. Levy. 2005. "The Neoliberal (Counter) Revolution." In A. Saad-Filho and D. Johnson (eds.), *Neoliberalism: A Critical Reader*. London: Pluto Press.

Dunk, T. 1994. *It's a Working Man's Town: Male Working-class Culture*. Montreal: McGill-Queen's University Press.

Elections Canada. 2008. "Third Party Election Advertising Reports for the 40th General Election." At <elections.ca/fin/thi/advert/tp40/tp-0011.pdf>.

Engelen, E. 2003. "How to Combine Openness and Protection? Citizenship, Migration, and Welfare Regimes." *Politics and Society* 31, 4: 503–36.

Evans, B., and G. Albo. 2007. "Limited Horizons: Assessing Ontario's Election." *Relay: A Socialist Project Review* 20 (November/December): 4–7.

Facal, J. 2003. "Le Parti québécois fera-t-il le choix de l'examen de consicence sincère ou celui de l'orthodoxie intransigeante et nostalgique?" *La Presse*, September 17. At <archives.vigile.net/ds-actu/docs3a/03-9-17-1.html#17lpjf>.

Fairbrother, M. 2003. "The Freedom of the State?: Recent NDP Governments and a Reply to the Globalization Sceptics." *The Canadian Review of Sociology and Anthropology* 40, 3 (August): 311–29.

Fantasia, R. 1988. *Cultures of Solidarity: Consciousness, Action, and Contemporary American Workers*. Berkeley: University of California Press.

Fantasia, R., and K. Voss. 2004. *Hard Work: Remaking the American Labor Movement*. Berkeley: University of California Press.

Fédération des Travailleurs et Travailleuses du Québec. 2006. *Participer aux organismes de développement de l'emploi*. Montreal: Service de la recherche de la FTQ. At <ftq.qc.ca/librairies/sfv/telecharger.php?fichier=3481&menu=14&sousmenu=53>.

Federici, S. 2004. *Caliban and the Witch: Women, the Body and Primitive Accumulation*. Brooklyn, NY: Autonomedia.

Feltes, N. 2001. "The New Prince in a New Principality: OCAP and the Toronto Poor." *Labour/Le Travail* 48 (Fall): 125–55.

Fine, J. 2005. "Community Unions and the Revival of the American Labor Movement." *Politics and Society* 33, 1: 153–99.

_____. 2003a. "Community Unions in Baltimore and Long Island: Beyond the Politics of Particularlism." PhD dissertation. Massachusetts Institute of Technology.

_____. 2003b. "Non-union, Low-wage Workers are Finding a Voice as Immigrant Workers Centers Grow." *Labor Notes*, August 1. At <labornotes.org/print/node/735>.

Finer, H. 1924. *The Case Against PR*. London: Fabian Society.

Finkel, A. 2006. *Social Policy and Practice in Canada: A History*. Waterloo: Wilfrid Laurier Press.

Fisher, R. (ed.). 2009. *The People Shall Rule: ACORN, Community Organizing, and the Struggle for Economic Justice*. Nashville: Vanderbilt University Press.

Flanders, A. 1970. *Management and Unions.* London: Faber.

Fletcher Jr., B., and R. Hurd. 1998. "Beyond the Organizing Model: The Transformation Process in Local Unions." In K. Bronfenbrenner, S. Friedman, R. Hurd, R. Oswald and R. Seeber (eds.), *Organizing to Win.* Ithaca, NY: Cornell University Press: 37–53.

Flynn, D. 2009. "Canada Seen Worst of G8 Not Curbing Climate Change." *Reuters. com,* July 1. At <reuters.com/article/2009/07/01/us-g8-climate-wwf-idUS-TRE5603M420090701>.

Fodor, M. 2009. "The Dexter NDP: Old Wine, New Bottle?" *Relay: A Socialist Project Review* 28 (October-December): 6–9.

Foot, R. 2009. "N.S.'s NDP Premier exhorts convention to escape shackles of past." *CanWest News Service,* August 15.

Forrest, A. 2009. "Bargaining for Economic Equality: A Path to Union Renewal, Then and Now." In J. Foley and P. Baker (eds.), *Unions, Equity, and the Path to Union Renewal.* Vancouver: UBC Press: 98–118.

Foster, J.B. 2002. *Ecology Against Capitalism.* New York: Monthly Review Press.

Freeman, J. 2000. *Working Class New York.* New York: The New Press.

Fudge, J. 1988. "Labour, the New Constitution and Old Style Liberalism." *Queen's Law Journal* 13: 61–111.

Fudge, J., and E. Tucker. 2004. *Labour Before the Law: The Regulation of Workers' Collective Action in Canada, 1900–1948.* Republished ed. Toronto: University of Toronto Press.

_____. 2001. *Labour Before the Law: The Regulation of Workers' Collective Action in Canada 1900–1948.* Oxford: Oxford University Press.

Gall, G. (ed.). 2009. *Union Revitalisation in Advanced Economies: Assessing the Contribution of Union Organising.* London/New York: Palgrave Macmillan.

_____. 2003. *The Meaning of Militancy?: Postal Workers and Industrial Relations.* Aldershot, UK: Ashgate.

Gamble, A., and T. Wright. 1999. *The New Social Democracy.* Oxford: Blackwell.

Garroutte, E. 2003. *Real Indians: Identity and the Survival of Native America.* Berkeley: University of California Press.

Galarneau, D. 2010. "Temporary labour in the downturn." Perspectives. Statistics Canada. At <http://www.statcan.gc.ca/pub/75-001-x/2010111/pdf/11371-eng. pdf>.November.

Geddes, J. 2011. "The NDP's Union-made Caucus." *Maclean's,* May 16. At <macleans. ca/2011/05/16/union-made>.

Gerber, L. 1991. "The United States and Canadian National Industrial Conferences of 1919: A Comparative Analysis." *Labor History* 32, 1 (Winter): 42–65.

Gibb, H. 2006. *Farmworkers from Afar: Results from an International Study of Seasonal Farmworkers from Mexico and the Caribbean Working on Ontario Farms.* Ottawa: North-South Institute.

Giddens, A. 2003. *The Progressive Manifesto: New Ideas for the Centre Left.* Cambridge: Polity Press.

_____. 1998. *The Third Way: The Renewal of Social Democracy.* Cambridge: Policy Press.

Gindin, S. 2006. "Toward A New Politics? After the CAW-NDP Divorce." *The Bullet* 27. At <http://www.socialistproject.ca/bullet/bullet027.html>.

_____. 2004. "Frozen in Neoliberalism's Headlights: Labour and the Polarization of Options." Presented at Workers and Labour Markets in the Global Economy AUTO21 Conference, Hamilton, ON, October 22–23 [revised version].

_____. 1997. "Toronto: Days of Action, Days of Hope." *Canadian Dimension* 31 (January/February): 11.

Gindin, S., and J. Stanford. 2003. "Canadian Labour and the Political Economy of Transformation." In W. Clement and L. Vosko (eds.), *Changing Canada: Political Economy as Transformation.* Montreal: McGill-Queen's University Press: 422–42.

Globe and Mail. 1992. "Saskatchewan unveils economic plan." *The Globe and Mail,* November

4: A7.

Glover, A., and K. Rose. 1999. "Overcoming the obstacles: Forging Effective Labor-community Alliances." *New Labor Forum* 5: 59–67.

Glyn, A. 2001. *Social Democracy in Neoliberal Times*. Oxford and New York: Oxford University Press.

Godlewska, C., and J. Webber. 2007. "The Calder Decision, Aboriginal Title, Treaties, and the Nisga'a." In H. Foster, H. Raven and J. Webber (eds.), *Let Right Be Done: Aboriginal Title, the Calder Case, and the Future of Indigenous Rights*. Vancouver: UBC Press: 1–33.

Goffman, E. 1974. *Frame Analysis: An Essay on the Organization of Experience*. London: Harper & Row.

Gogal, S., R. Reigert and J. Jamieson. 2005. "Aboriginal Impact and Benefit Agreements: Practical Considerations." *Alberta Law Review* 43: 129–58.

Gompers, S. 1919. *Labor and the Common Welfare*. New York: E.P. Dutton Inc.

Gonick, C. 2007. "Gary Doer's Manitoba." *Canadian Dimension* 41, 4 (July/August): 12–5, 40–1.

_____. 2003. "Manitoba: What the NDP Does When It Governs." *Canadian Dimension* 37, 2 (March/April): 5.

Good Jobs for All Coalition. n.d. "Good Jobs for All Declaration." At <goodjobsforall.ca/wp-content/gallery/resource/gj4a-declaration.pdf>.

Goode, J. 2001. "Let's Get Our Act Together: How Racial Discourses Disrupt Neighbourhood Activism." In J. Goode and J. Maskovsky (eds.), *The New Poverty Studies: The Ethnography of Power, Politics and Impoverished People in the United States*. New York: New York University Press: 364–98.

Gottlieb, R. 2001. *Environmentalism Unbound: Exploring New Pathways for Change*. Cambridge, MA: MIT Press.

Goutor, D. 2007. *Guarding the Gates: The Canadian Labour Movement and Immigration, 1872–1934*. Vancouver: UBC Press.

Graefe, P. 2011. "The Politics of Social and Economic Development in Quebec." In S. Gervais, C. Kirkey and J. Rudy (eds.), *Quebec Questions: Quebec Studies for the Twenty-First Century*. New York: Oxford University Press.

_____. 2007. "State Restructuring and the Failure of Competitive Nationalism: Trying Times for Quebec Labour." In M. Murphy (ed.), *Quebec and Canada in the New Century: New Dynamics, New Opportunities*. Kingston: Institute of Intergovernmental Relations.

Grant, K. 2010. "This is why I'm voting for Rob Ford." *The Globe and Mail*, September 3. At <theglobeandmail.com/news/national/toronto/this-is-why-im-voting-for-rob-ford/article1695994/>.

Gray, L.S. 1993. "The Route to the Top: Female Union Leaders and Union Policy." In D. S. Cobble (ed.), *Women and Unions: Forming a Partnership*. Ithaca, NY: ILR Press: 378–93.

Greene, J. 2005. "'Whatever it Takes:' Poor People's Organizing, OCAP, and Social Struggle." *Studies in Political Economy* 75 (Spring): 5–28.

Greenpeace International and European Renewable Energy Council. 2009. *Working for the Climate — Renewable Energy and the Green Job [R]evolution*. Sydney: Greenpeace International.

Groff, R. 1997. "Class Politics by any Other Name: Organizing the Unemployed." *Studies in Political Economy* 54 (Fall): 91–117.

Guard, J. 2004. "Authenticity on the Line: Women Workers, Native "Scabs," and the Multi-ethnic Politics of Identity in a Left-led Strike in Cold War Canada." *Journal of Women's History* 15, 4: 117–40.

Gunningham, N., R. Kagan and D. Thornton. 2004. "Social License and Environmental Protection: Why Businesses go Beyond Compliance." *Law and Social Inquiry* 29, 2: 307–41.

Güntzel, R. 2000. "Rapprocher les lieux de pouvoir: The Quebec Labour Movement and Quebec Sovereigntism, 1960–2000." *Labour/Le Travail* 46 (Fall): 369–95.

Haddow, R., and T. Klassen. 2005. *Partisanship, Globalization and Canadian Labour Market Policy*. Toronto: University of Toronto Press.

Haiven, J. 2007. "Union Responses to Pay Equity: A Cautionary Tale." In G. Hunt and D. Rayside (eds.), *Equity, Diversity and Canadian Labour*. Toronto: University of Toronto Press: 75–100.

Haiven, L. 2009. *The Sky is Falling. The Sky is Falling. Or is it?: The NDP Government's Independent Review of Finances an exercise to Kill Expectations*. Nova Scotia: Canadian Centre for Policy Alternatives.

Hale, G. 1997. "Changing Patters of Party Support in Ontario." In S. Noel (ed.), *Revolution at Queen's Park: Essays on Governing Ontario*. Toronto: James Lorimer & Co.: 107–24.

Harden-Donahue, A., and A. Peart. 2009. "Green, Decent and Public." The Council of Canadians/Canadian Labour Congress, December. At <canadians.org/energy/documents/climatejustice/green-decent-public.pdf>.

Harder, L. 2003. *State of Struggle: Feminism and Politics in Alberta*. Edmonton: University of Alberta Press.

Hargrove, B. 2009a. *Laying it on the Line: Driving a Hard Bargain in Challenging Times*. Toronto: Harper Collins.

_____. 2009b. "Striking a Collective Bargain: The Supreme Court Decision in B.C. Health Services." *University of New Brunswick Law Journal* 59: 41–7.

Hart, J. 1992. *Proportional Representation: Critics of the British Electoral System*. Oxford: Clarendon Press.

Harter, J-H. 2004. "Environmental Justice for Whom? Class, New Social Movements, and the Environment: A Case Study of Greenpeace Canada, 1971–2000." *Labour/Le Travail* 54 (Fall): 83–119.

Hartviksen, W. 2001. "Making Politics Matter: The Shining Light of PR, the Rocky Road of Election Finance Reform, and the Disconnect Between Activists and Politics." *Straight Goods* 4 (June).

Harvey, D. 1998. "The Geography of Class Power." In L. Panitch and C. Leys (eds.), *The Socialist Register 1998: The Communist Manifesto Now*. London: Merlin: 49–74.

_____. 1995. "Militant Particularism and Global Ambition: The Conceptual Politics of Place, Space, and Environment in the Work of Raymond Williams." *Social Text* 42 (Spring): 69–98.

Henaway, M. 2012. "Immigrant Worker Organizing in a Time of Crisis: Adapting to the New Realities of Class and Resistance." In A. Choudry, J. Hanley and E. Shragge (eds.), *Organize!: Building from the Local for Global Justice*. Oakland, CA.: PM Press.

Henderson, J. 2006. *First Nations Jurisprudence and Aboriginal Rights:Defining the Just Society*. Saskatoon: Native Law Centre.

Hennessy, T., and A. Yalnizyan. 2009. "Canada's 'He-cession:' Men Bearing the Brunt of Rising Unemployment." *Behind the Numbers* 10, 4: 1–3.

Heron, C. 1996. *The Canadian Labour Movement: A Short History*. 2nd ed. Toronto: Lorimer.

_____. 1984. "Labourism and the Canadian Working Class." *Labour/Le Travail* 13 (Spring): 45–76.

Hesketh, B. 1987. "The Abolition of Preferential Voting in Alberta." *Prairie Forum* 12, 1 (Spring): 123–44.

Hitch, M., and C. Fidler. 2007. "Impact and Benefit Agreements: A Contentious Issue for Environmental and Aboriginal Justice." *Environments* 35, 2: 45–69.

Hoag, C., and G. Hallet, Jr. 1926. *Proportional Representation*. New York: Macmillan.

Hollifield, J. 2004. "The Emerging Migration State." *International Migration Review* 28, 3: 885–912.

Hopkins, J. 1920. *The Canadian Annual Review 1919*. Toronto: Canadian Annual Review Ltd.

Horowitz, G. 1968. *Canadian Labour in Politics*. Toronto: University of Toronto Press.

Howlett, M., and K. Brownsey. 1992. "Public Sector Politics in a Rentier Resource Economy." In *The Provincial State: Politics in Canada's Provinces and Territories*. Toronto: Copp Clark Pitman.

Hoxie, R. 1920. *Trade Unionism in the United States*. New York: D. Appleton and Co.

_____. 1914. "Trade Unionism in the United States." *Journal of Political Economy* 22, 3: 201–17.

Hrynyshyn, D., and S. Ross. 2011. "Canadian Autoworkers, the Climate Crisis, and the Contradictions of Social Unionism." *Labor Studies Journal* 36, 1: 5–36.

Human Resources and Skills Development Canada. 2011. "Work — Unemployment Rate." At <hrsdc.gc.ca/.3ndic.1t.4r@-eng.jsp?iid=16>.

_____. 2010. *Union Membership in Canada — 2009*. Revised January 15, 2010. Ottawa: HRSDC.

_____. 2007. *Pilot Project for Occupations Requiring Lower Levels of Formal training (NOC C and D): Changes to the Pilot Project as of February 23, 2007*. Ottawa: HRSDC.

Hunt, G., and J. Eaton. 2007. "We Are Family: Labour Responds to Gay, Lesbian, Bisexual and Transgender Workers." In G. Hunt and D. Rayside (eds.), *Equity, Diversity and Canadian Labour*. Toronto: University of Toronto Press: 130–55.

Hunt, G., and D. Rayside. (eds.) 2007. *Equity, Diversity and Canadian Labour*. Toronto: University of Toronto Press.

Hutchinson, A., and P. Monahan. 1984. "Law, Politics and the Critical Legal Scholars: The Unfolding Drama of American Legal Thought." *Stanford Law Review* 36, 199–245.

Hyman, R. 2002. "The Future of Unions." *Just Labour: A Canadian Journal of Work and Society* 1: 7–15.

_____. 1975. *Industrial Relations: A Marxist Introduction*. London: Macmillan.

_____. 1971. *Marxism and the Sociology of Trade Unionism*. London: Pluto.

Institute on Governance. 1998. "The Exercise of Power Round Table, Parliament, Politics and Citizens: A Conversation with Bob Rae." At <iog.ca/sites/iog/files/xrt6.pdf>.

Isitt, B. 2009. "Elusive Unity: The Canadian Labor Party in British Columbia, 1924–1928." *BC Studies* 163 (Fall): 33–64.

Isitt, B., and M. Moroz. 2007. "The Hospital Employees' Union Strike and the Privatization of Medicare in British Columbia, Canada." *International Labor and Working-Class History* 71: 91–111.

Ivison, J. 2010. "Taking the socialist out of the NDP." *National Post*, October 7. At <fullcomment.nationalpost.com/2010/10/07/john-ivison-taking-the-socialist-out-of-the-ndp/>.

Jacoby, S. 1991. "American Exceptionalism Revisited: The Importance of Management." In S. Jacoby (ed.), *Masters to Managers: Historical and Comparative Perspectives on American Employers*. New York: Columbia University Press: 173–200.

Jamieson, S. 1973. *Industrial Relations in Canada*. Toronto: Macmillan

_____. 1968. "Times of Trouble: Labour Unrest and Industrial Conflict in Canada, 1900–66." *Canadian Industrial Relations: Report on the Task Force on Labour Relations*. The Woods Commission. Ottawa: Crown Copyrights.

Jansen, H., and L. Young. 2009. "Solidarity Forever? The NDP, Organized Labour, and the Changing Face of Party Finance in Canada." *Canadian Journal of Political Science* 42, 3 (September): 657–78.

Janson, F. 1928. "Minority Governments in Sweden." *American Political Science Review* 22, 2 (May): 407–13.

Jenson, J. 2009. "Rolling Out or Backtracking on Quebec's Child Care System: Ideology Matters." In M. Cohen and J. Pulkingham (eds.), *Public Policy for Women: The State, Income Security and Labour Market Issues*. Toronto: University of Toronto Press: 50–70.

_____. 1989. "'Different' but not 'exceptional': Canada's Permeable Fordism." *Canadian Review of Sociology and Anthropology* 26, 1: 69–94.

Kaminski, M., and E. Yakura. 2006. "Women's Union Leadership: Closing the Gender Gap." *WorkingUSA* 11 (December): 459–75.

Kazis, R., and R. Grossman. 1991. *Fear At Work: Job Blackmail, Labor and the Environment*. Gabriola Island, BC: New Society Publishers.

Kealey, G. 1995. *Workers and Canadian History*. Montreal: McGill-Queen's University Press.

_____. 1994. "1919: The Canadian Labour Revolt." In D. Bercuson and D. Bright (eds.), *Canadian Labour History, Selected Readings*. Toronto: Copp Clark Longman: 193–222.

_____. 1976. "'The Honest Workingman' and Workers' Control: The Experience of Toronto Skilled Workers, 1860–1892." *Labour /Le Travailleur* 1: 32–68.

Keefer, T. 2010. "Contradictions of Canadian Colonialism: Non-Native Responses to the Six Nations Reclamation at Caledonia." In L. Davis (ed.), *Alliances: Re/Envisioning Indigenous-non-Indigenous Relationships*. Toronto: University of Toronto Press: 77–90.

Keil, R. 1994. "Green Work Alliances: The Political Economy of Social Ecology." *Studies in Political Economy* 44 (Summer): 7–38.

Kelly, J. 1996. *Rethinking Industrial Relations: Mobilization, Collectivism and Long Waves*. London: Routledge.

King, M. 2009. "Laid-off employees take action." *Montreal Gazette*, November 26: B1.

Kingfisher, C. 2002. "Neoliberalism I: Discourses of Personhood and Welfare Reform." In C. Kingfisher (ed.), *Western Welfare in Decline: Globalization and Women's Poverty*. Philadelphia: University of Pennsylvania Press: 13–31.

Kitschelt, H. 1994. *The Transformation of European Social Democracy*. Cambridge, UK: Cambridge University Press.

Knight, R. 1978. *Indians at Work: An Informal History of Native Indian Labour in British Columbia, 1858–1930*. Vancouver: New Star Books.

Kumar, P., and G. Murray. 2006. "Innovation in Canadian Unions: Patterns, Causes and Consequences." In P. Kumar and C. Schenk (eds.), *Paths to Union Renewal: Canadian Experiences*. Peterborough, ON: Broadview Press: 79–102.

Kumar, P., and C. Schenk (eds.). 2006. *Paths to Union Renewal: Canadian Experiences*. Peterborough, ON: Broadview Press.

Kuokkanen, R. 2007. *Reshaping the University: Responsibility, Indigenous Epistemes and the Logic of the Gift*. Vancouver: UBC Press.

Kusch, L. 2009. "NDP leadership race: The policy debate." *Winnipeg Free Press*, October 17.

"La création du SPQ libre ne laisse personne indifférent." 2004. *L'aut journal* 229 (May). At <archives.lautjournal.info/autjourarchives.asp?article=1948&noj=229>.

Labour Environmental Alliance Society. n.d. "LEAS History." At <leas.ca/LEAS-History.htm>.

LaFleche, G. 2011. "Tories, NDP gain local union endorsements." *St. Catharines Standard*, April 11. At <stcatharinesstandard.ca/ArticleDisplay.aspx?e=3066611>.

Laforest, R. 2007. "The Politics of State/Civil Society Relations in Québec." In M. Murphy (ed.), *Québec and Canada in the New Century: New Dynamics, New Opportunities*. Kingston: Institute of Intergovernmental Relations: 177–98.

Langille, B. 2009. "The Freedom of Association Mess: How We Got into It and How We Can Get out of It." *McGill Law Journal* 54: 177–212.

Latendresse, A. 2009. "Montréal en quête d'une légitimité." *À babord!* (October/November). At <ababord.org/spip.php?article948>.

Latham, M. 2001. "The Third Way: An Outline." In A. Giddens (ed.), *The Global Third Way Debate*. Cambridge: Polity Press.

Law, A., and J. Will. 2012. "Some Comments on Law and Organizing." In A. Choudry, J. Hanley and E. Shragge (eds.), *Organize!: Building from the Local for Global Justice*. Oakland,

CA.: PM Press.

Laxer, J. 1984. *Rethinking the Economy: The Laxer Report on Canadian Economic Problems and Policies.* Toronto: NC Press.

Leah, R. 1999. "Do You Call Me "Sister"? Women of Colour and the Canadian Labour Movement." In D. Enakshi and A. Robertson (eds.) *Scratching the Surface: Canadian Anti-Racists Feminist Thought.* Toronto: Women's Press: 97–126.

Lemieux, A. 2009. "North of Poverty: Community-Labor Organizing and Living Wage Campaigns in Canada." *Social Policy* 39, 2 (Summer): 34–6.

Lester, R. 1958. *As Unions Mature: An Analysis of the Evolution on American Unionism.* Princeton, NJ: Princeton University Press.

Lett, D. 1998. "NDP redraws image for voters." *Winnipeg Free Press*, December 16.

Lett, D. 1997. "Doer closes in on the do-it stage." *Winnipeg Free Press*, November 16.

Leyton-Brown, K. The Labour-Management Dispute (Temporary Provisions) Act, The Encyclopedia Of Saskatchewan. At <esask.uregina.ca/entry/legislation_in_saskatchewan.html>.

Lightbody, J. 1978. "Electoral Reform in Local Government." *Canadian Journal of Political Science* 11, 2 (June): 307–32.

Lipsig-Mummé, C. 2003. "Forms of Solidarity: Trade Unions." At <actu.asn.au/organising/news/1053579943_13456.html>.

_____. 1991. "Future Conditional: Wars of Position in the Quebec Labour Movement." *Studies in Political Economy* 36 (Fall): 73–107.

Lisée, J-F. 2007. *Nous.* Montréal: Boréal.

Little, M. 2007. "Militant Mothers Fight Poverty: The Just Society Movement, 1968–1971." *Labour/Le Travail* 59 (Spring): 179–97.

_____. 2001. "A Litmus Test for Democracy: The Impact of Ontario Welfare Changes on Single Mothers." *Studies in Political Economy* 66 (Autumn): 9–36.

_____. 1998. *'No Car, No Radio, No Liquor Permit:' The Moral Regulation of Single Mothers in Ontario, 1920–1997.* Toronto: Oxford University Press.

Lorence, J. 1996. *Organizing the Unemployed: Community and Union Activists in the Industrial Heartland.* Albany: State University of New York Press.

Luxton, M. 2001. "Feminism as a Class Act: Working-class Feminism and the Women's Movement in Canada." *Labour/Le Travail* 48 (Fall): 63–88.

MacCharles, T. 2001. "Ontario farm labour law struck down." *The Toronto Star*, December 21.

MacDowell, L.S. 1978. "The Formation of the Canadian Industrial Relations System During World War Two." *Labour/Le Travailleur* 3: 175–96.

Mackenzie, H., and J. Stanford. 2008. "A Living Wage for Toronto." At <policyalternatives.ca/sites/default/files/uploads/publications/Ontario_Office_Pubs/2008/A_Living_Wage_for_Toronto_Summary.pdf>.

MacKinnon, S., and E. Black. 2008. *Manitoba Budget 2008: Make Poverty Reduction a Priority.* Manitoba: Canadian Centre for Policy Alternatives.

Manchee, J. 2006. "Unions and the United Way: From Charity to Change." *Our Times* (April/May): 27–35.

Mandel, D. 2010. "Fighting Austerity? The Public Sector and the Common Front in Quebec." *The Bullet* 396. At <socialistproject.ca/bullet/396.php>.

Mandel, M. 1994. *The Charter of Rights and the Legalization of Politics in Canada.* Toronto: Thompson.

Mandryk, M. 2009. "Playing the right (and left) cards." *Leader Post*, April 15.

Marcus, A. 2005. "The Culture of Poverty Revisited: Bringing Back the Working Class." *Anthropologica* 47, 1: 35–52.

Maroney, H. 1983. "Feminism at Work." *New Left Review* I, 141 (September-October): 51–71

REFERENCES

Marshall, H., J. Stuart and T. Jaunzens. 2010. "Community Organizing Goes Green." *Social Policy* 39, 4 (Winter): 8–10.

Martinello, F. 2000. "Mr. Harris, Mr. Rae and Union Activity in Ontario." *Canadian Public Policy/Analyse de Politiques* 26, 1: 17–33.

Marx, K. 1990. *Capital: Volume 1*. London: Penguin Books.

Masson, J. 1985. *Alberta's Local Governments and Their Politics*. Edmonton: Pica Press.

Matheson, D. 1989. "The Canadian Working Class and Industrial Legality." MA thesis: Queen's University.

Mathew, B. 2005. *Taxi! Cabs and Capitalism in New York City*. New York: New Press.

Mayer, B. 2009. *Blue-Green Coalitions: Fighting for Safe Workplaces and Healthy Communities*. Ithaca, NY: ILR Press.

Mayson, M. 1999. "Ontario Works and Single Mothers: Redefining 'Deservedness' and the Social Contract." *Journal of Canadian Studies* 34: 89–109.

McBride, J., and I. Greenwood. (eds.). 2009. *Community Unionism: A Comparative Analysis of Concepts and Contexts*. London: Palgrave Macmillan.

McBride, S. 2001. *Paradigm Shift: Globalization and the Canadian State*. Halifax: Fernwood Books.

_____. 1995. "The Continuing Crisis of Social Democracy: Ontario's Social Contract in Perspective." *Studies in Political Economy* 50 (Summer): 65–93.

McCue, H. 1994. "The modern age, 1945–1980." In E. Rogers and D. Smith (eds.), *Aboriginal Ontario: Historical Perspectives on the First Nations*. Toronto: Dundurn Press: 377–417.

McDonald, R. 2006. "Sir Charles Hibbert Tupper and the Political Culture of British Columbia, 1903–1924." *BC Studies* 149 (Spring): 63–88.

McInnis, P.S. 2002. *Harnessing Labour Confrontation: Shaping the Postwar Settlement in Canada, 1943–1950*. Toronto: University of Toronto Press.

McKenzie, R., and A. Silver. 1968. *Angels in Marble: Working Class Conservatives in Urban England*. Chicago: University of Chicago Press.

McRoberts, K. 1997. *Misconceiving Canada: The Struggle for National Unity*. Toronto: Oxford University Press.

_____. 1988. *Québec: Social Change and Political Crisis*. 3rd ed. Toronto: McClelland & Stewart.

McRoberts, K., and D. Postgate. 1980. *Québec: Social Change and Political Crisis*. Revised ed. Toronto: McClelland & Stewart.

Mehra, N. 2006 "A Community Coalition in Defense of Public Medicare." In C. Schenk and P. Kumar (eds.), *Paths to Union Renewal: Canadian Experiences*. Peterborough, ON: Broadview Press: 261–76.

Menzies, C. 2010. "Indigenous Nations and Marxism: Notes on an Ambivalent Relationship." *New Proposals: Journal of Marxism and Interdisciplinary Inquiry* 3, 3: 5–6.

Milkman, R., and K. Voss. 2004. "Introduction." In R. Milkman and K. Voss (eds.), *Rebuilding Labor: Organizing and Organizers in the New Union Movement*. Ithaca, NY: Cornell University Press: 1–16.

Mills, A. 2006. "Layton energizes supporters." *Toronto Star*, January 15.

Mills, C.W. 1960. "Letter to the New Left." *New Left Review* I, 5: 18–23.

_____. 1948. *The New Men of Power: America's Labor Leaders*. Chicago: University of Illinois Press.

Mills, S. 2011. "Aboriginal Employment and Labour Unions in Northern Resource Development: A Case Study of Voisey's Bay Nickel Mine Development." Report prepared for Nunatsiavut Government. Nain, NL.

Mills, S., and L. Clarke. 2009. "'We Will Go Side-by-side With You': Labour union engagement with Aboriginal peoples in Canada." *Geoforum* 40, 6: 991–1001.

Mills, S., and T. McCreary. 2006. "Culture and power in the workplace: Aboriginal women's perspectives on practices to increase Aboriginal inclusion in forest processing mills." *Journal of Aboriginal Economic Development* 5, 1: 40–50.

Mitchell, J. 1960. "The Mohawks In High Steel." In E. Wilson (ed.), *Apologies to the Iroquois*. New York: American Book-Stratford Press: 3–38.

Moody, Kim. 2007. *U.S. Labor in Trouble and Transition*. New York: Verso.

_____. 1997. "Towards an International Social-Movement Unionism." *New Left Review* I, 225 (September–October): 52–72.

_____. 1988. *An Injury to All: The Decline of American Unionism*. New York: Verso.

Morris, P., and G. Fondahl. 2002. "Negotiating the Production of Space in Tl'azt'en Territory, Northern British Columbia." *The Canadian Geographer* 46, 2: 108–25.

Morton, D. 1977. *NDP: Social Democracy in Canada*. Toronto: A.M. Hakkert.

Moschonas, G. 2002. *In the Name of Social Democracy: The Great Transformation, 1945 to the Present*. London: Verso.

Mosher, P. 1976. "Wage, price scheme ruled constitutional." *The Globe and Mail*, July 13.

Motta, S., and D. Bailey. 2007. "Neither pragmatic adaptation nor misguided accommodation: Modernisation as domination in the Chilean and British Left." *Capital and Class* 92:107–36.

Munro, M. 1997. "'Days of Action' and Strategic Choices for the Left in Canada." *Studies in Political Economy* 53 (Summer): 125–40.

Muste, A. 1948. "Army and Town Meeting." In E. Wight Bakke and C. Kerr (eds.), *Unions, Management and the Public*. New York: Harcourt Brace and Co.: 136–38.

National Mobilization Against Sweat Shops. 2011. "Workers' Centers & the New Labor Movement." At <http://www.nmass.org/nmass/articles/workers%20centers.htm>.

Naylor, J. 1991. *The New Democracy, Challenging the Social Order in Industrial Ontario, 1914–1925*. Toronto: University of Toronto Press.

Ness, I. 2003. "Unions and American Workers: Whither the Labor Movement?" In J.C. Berg (ed.), *Teamsters and Turtles? U.S. Progressive Political Movements in the 21st Century*. Oxford, UK: Rowman & Littlefield: 53–82.

Netherton, A. 1992. "The Shifting Points of Politics: A Neo-institutional Analysis." In K. Brownsey and M. Howlett (eds.), *The Provincial State: Politics in Canada's Provinces and Territories*. Mississauga: Copp Clark Pitman.

New Democratic Party. 2011. *Giving your family a break*. Ottawa: NDP.

_____. 2004. *Jack Layton and the NDP: New Energy: A Positive Choice*. Ottawa: NDP.

_____. 1997. *A Framework for Canada's Future: Alexa McDonough and Canada's NDP*. Ottawa: NDP.

New York Times. 1922. "Gompers Defends Political Program." May 5.

Newfeld, A., and A. Parnaby. 2000. *The IWA in Canada: The Life and Times an Industrial Union*. Vancouver: IWA Canada/New Star Books.

Newhouse, D. 1993. "Modern Aboriginal Economies: Capitalism with an Aboriginal Face." In *Sharing the Harvest: The Road to Self-Reliance*. Report of the National Round Table on Aboriginal Economic Development and Resources (RCAP). Ottawa: Canada Communication Group.

Nissen, B. 2004. "The Effectiveness and Limits of Labor-Community Coalitions: Evidence from south Florida." *Labor Studies Journal* 29, 1: 67–89.

_____. 2003. "Alternative Strategic Directions for the U.S. Labor Movement: Recent Scholarship." *Labor Studies Journal* 28, 1: 133–55.

_____. 1995. *Fighting for Jobs: Case Studies of Labor-Community Coalitions Confronting Plant Closings*. Albany, NY: State University of New York Press.

Noël, A. 2007. "La dénationalisation." *Policy Options* (December): 108.

_____. 2004. "Commentary: A Focus on Income Support: Implementing Quebec's Law Against Poverty and Social Exclusion." Ottawa: Canadian Policy Research Networks. At <http://www.cprn.org/documents/29659_en.pdf>.

Norcross, E. 1984. "Mary Ellen Smith: The Right Woman in the Right Place at the Right Time." In B. Lantham and R. Pazdro (eds.), *Not Just Pin Money*. Victoria: Camosun

College: 357–64.

Northwest Study Conference. 1975. *Resolutions Passed By Workshops at Northwest Study Conference 75*. Terrace: NSC.

Nova Scotia NDP. 2009. *Better Deal 2009: The NDP plan to make life better for today's families*.

Nugent, J. 2011. "Changing the Climate: Ecoliberalism, Green New Dealism, and the Struggle over Green Jobs in Canada." *Labor Studies Journal* 36, 1: 58–82.

Obach, B. 2004. "New Labour: Slowing the Treadmill of Production?" *Organization and Environment* 17, 3: 337–54.

_____. 2002. "Labor-Environmental Relations: An Analysis of the Relationship between Labor Unions and Environmentalists." *Social Science Quarterly* 83, 1: 82–100.

Oliver, M., and C. Taylor. 1991. "Québec." In L. Heaps (ed.), *Our Canada*. Toronto: James Lorimer: 141–49.

O'Connor, J. 1964. "Towards a Theory of Community Unions I." *Studies on the Left* (Spring).

O'Neil, P. 2007. "Collective bargaining protected by charter; supreme court rules." *National Post*, June 9.

Ontario. 1968. *Report of the Royal Commission Inquiry Into Labour Disputes*. Toronto: Queen's Printer.

Ontario, Legislative Assembly. 1990. *Hansard*, November 20. At <http://www.ontla.on.ca/web/house-proceedings/house_detail.do?Date=1990-11-20&Parl=35&Sess=1&locale=en>.

Ontario, Ministry of Finance. 1991. *1991 Ontario Budget*. Toronto: Queen's Printer.

Ontario Coalition Against Poverty. n.d. "A Short History of OCAP." At <ocap.ca/files/history of ocap.pdf>.

_____. 2007. "In Support of the Mohawks of Tyendinaga." At <ocap.ca/files/fsb-rgb-final.pdf>.

Ontario New Democratic Party. 2002. *Proportional Representation Task Force Submissions Index*.

Ontario Public Service Employees Union. 1999. "Our Strategy in the Spotlight." At <opseu.org/leah/presidentmay.htm>.

Organization for Economic Cooperation and Development. 2008. *International Migration Outlook*. Paris: OECD.

Orliffe, H. 1938. "Proportional Representation." *Canadian Forum* 22, 205 (February): 388–90.

Palmer, B. 2009. *Canada's 1960s: The Ironies of Identity in a Rebellious Era*. Toronto: University of Toronto Press.

_____. 2003. "What's Law Got to Do with It? Historical Considerations on Class Struggle, Boundaries of Constraint, and Capitalist Authority." *Osgoode Hall Law Journal* 41: 465–90.

_____. 1992. *Working-Class Experience: Rethinking the History of Canadian Labour, 1800–1991*. Toronto: McClelland & Stewart.

_____. 1987. *Solidarity: The Rise and Fall of an Opposition in British Columbia*. Vancouver: New Star.

_____. 1983. *Working-Class Experience: The Rise and Reconstitution of Canadian Labour, 1800–1980*. Toronto: Butterworth.

Panitch, L. 1977. "The Role and Nature of the Canadian State." In L. Panitch (ed.), *The Canadian State: Political Economy and Political Power*. Toronto: University of Toronto Press, 3–27.

Panitch, L., and C. Leys. 1997. *The End of Parliamentary Socialism: From New Left to New Labour*. London and New York: Verso.

Panitch, L., and D. Swartz. 2003. *From Consent to Coercion: The Assault on Trade Union Freedoms*. Toronto: Garamond Press.

Parker, M., and M. Gruelle. 1999. *Democracy is Power: Rebuilding Unions from the Bottom Up*. Detroit: Labor Notes.

Parnaby, A. 2008. *Citizen Docker: Making a New Deal on the Vancouver Waterfront, 1919–1939*. Toronto: University of Toronto Press.

_____. 2006. "The Best Men That Ever Worked the Lumber: Aboriginal Longshoremen on Burrard Inlet, BC 1863–1939." *Canadian Historical Review* 87, 1: 53–78.

Parrot, J. 2005. *My Union, My Life: Jean-Claude Parrot and the Canadian Union of Postal Workers*. Halifax: Fernwood.

_____. 1983. "Jean-Claude Parrot: An Interview." *Studies in Political Economy* 11: 49–70.

Parti Québécois. 1994. *Québec in a New World*. Toronto: Lorimer.

Payton, L. 2011. "Layton vows not to meddle in Bank of Canada rates." *CBC News*, April 29. At <cbc.ca/news/politics/canadavotes2011/story/2011/04/29/cv-election-layton-rates.html>.

Penades, A. 2008. "Choosing Rules for Government: The Institutional Preferences of Early Socialist Parties." In J. Maravall and I. Sanchez-Cuenca (eds.), *Controlling Governments: Voters, Institutions, and Accountability*. Cambridge: Cambridge University Press: 202–46.

Penner, N. 1977. *The Canadian Left: A Critical Analysis*. Toronto: Prentice-Hall.

Phillips, H. 1976. "Challenges to the Voting System in Canada, 1874–1974." Ph.D. dissertation. University of Western Ontario.

Phillips, L. 1997. "The Rise of Balanced Budget Laws in Canada: Legislating Fiscal (Ir) responsibility." *Osgoode Hall Law Journal* 34, 4: 682–740.

Phillips, P. 1998. "Whither Saskatchewan? A Look at Economic Policies 1975–2000." *Canadian Business Economics* 6, 4: 36–49.

Phillips, S. 2010. *Women's Equality a Long Way Off in Alberta*. Edmonton: Parkland Institute.

Pilon, D. 2010a. "Democracy, BC Style." In M. Howlett, D. Pilon and T. Summerville (eds.), *British Columbia Politics and Government*. Toronto: Emond Montgomery: 87–108.

_____. 2010b. "The 2005 and 2009 Referenda on Voting System Change in British Columbia." *Canadian Political Science Review* 4, 2–3 (June–September): 73–89.

_____. 2009. "Investigating Media as a Deliberative Space: Newspaper Opinions about Voting Systems in the Ontario Provincial Referendum." *Canadian Political Science Review* 3, 3 (September): 1–23.

_____. 2007. *The Politics of Voting*. Toronto: Emond Montgomery.

_____. 2006. "Explaining Voting System Reform in Canada, 1873–1960." *Journal of Canadian Studies* 40, 3 (Fall): 135–61.

_____. 2004. "The Uncertain Path of Democratic Renewal in Ontario." In H. Milner (ed.), *Steps Toward Making Every Vote Count*. Peterborough: Broadview.

_____. 2001. *Canada's Democratic Deficit: Is Proportional Representation the Answer?* Toronto: CSJ Foundation for Research and Education.

Pilon, D., S. Ross and L. Savage. 2011. "Solidarity Revisited: Organized Labour and the New Democratic Party." *Canadian Political Science Review* 5, 1: 20–37.

Piotte, J-M. 2001. "Un microcosme du Québec." In Y. Bélanger, R. Comeau and C. Métivier (eds.), *La FTQ, ses syndicats et la société québécoise*. Montreal: Comeau & Nadeau, 167–85.

Piven, F. 2008. "Globalization and Labour Power." Unpublished manuscript.

_____. (ed.). 1992. *Labor Parties in Postindustrial Societies*. New York: Oxford University Press.

Piven, F., and R. Cloward. 1979. *Poor People's Movements: Why They Succeed, How They Fail*. New York: Vintage Books.

Porritt, J. 1984. *Seeing Green*. Oxford: Blackwell.

Porritt, J., and D. Winner. 1988. *The Coming of the Greens*. London: Fontana.

Porter, A. 2003. *Gendered States: Women, Unemployment Insurance and the Political Economy of the Welfare State in Canada, 1945–1997*. Toronto: University of Toronto Press.

Preibisch, K. 2010. "Pick-your-own labor: Migrant Workers and Flexibility in Canadian Agriculture." *International Migration Review* 44, 2: 404–41.

Preibisch, K., and L. Binford. 2007 "Interrogating Racialized Global Labour Supply: An

Exploration of the Racial/National Replacement of Foreign Agricultural Workers in Canada." *Canadian Review of Sociology and Anthropology* 44, 1: 5–36.

Prince Rupert Daily News. 1975. "Northwest Study Session Unites Natives, Unions." *Daily News,* May 26.

Przeworski, A. 1985. *Capitalism and Social Democracy.* Cambridge: Cambridge University Press.

Przeworski, A., and J. Sprague. 1986. *Paper Stones: A History of Electoral Socialism.* Chicago: University of Chicago Press.

Public Service Alliance of Canada. 2011. "The End of Pay Equity for Women in the Federal Public Service: A Critical Analysis of the Public Sector Equitable Compensation Act." At <psac-afpc.com/issues/equite-salariale/history-e.shtml>.

_____. 2007. "Letter to members of the Public Service Alliance recommending MMP."

Pugh, M. 2002. "The Rise of Labour and the Political Culture of Conservatism, 1890–1945." *History* 87, 288 (October): 514–37.

_____. 1978. *Electoral Reform in War and Peace 1906–18.* London: Routledge and Kegan Paul.

Puxley, C. 2009. "Selinger to lead Manitoba; NDP delegates choose former finance minister to succeed popular Gary Doer as premier." *Toronto Star,* October 18.

Rand, I. 1958. "Rand Formula." *Canadian Law Reports,* 2150. Ottawa: Canada.

Rankin, P., and J. Vickers. 1998. "Locating Women's Politics." In C. Andrew and M. Tremblay (eds.), *Women and Political Representation in Canada.* Ottawa: University of Ottawa Press: 341–68.

Rathke, W. (n.d.) "Chief Organizer Blog." At <chieforganizer.org>.

_____. *CitizenWealth: Winning the Campaign to Save Working Families.* San Francisco: Berrett-Koehler Publishers, Inc.

Rayside, D. 2007. "Equity, Diversity and Canadian Labour: A Comparative Perspective." In G. Hunt and D. Rayside (eds.), *Equity, Diversity and Canadian Labour.* Toronto: University of Toronto Press: 208–43.

Rebick, J. 2005. *Ten Thousand Roses: The Making of a Feminist Revolution.* Toronto: Penguin.

Reed, A. 2000. *Class Notes: Posing as Politics and Other Thoughts on the American Scene.* New York: The New Press.

Reed, L. 1966. *The Labor Philosophy of Samuel Gompers.* Port Washington, NY: Kennikat.

Renner, M., S. Sweeney, J. Kubit and L. Mastny. 2008. *Green Jobs: Working for People and the Environment.* Washington DC: Worldwatch Institute.

Reshef, Y., and S. Rastin. 2003. *Unions in the Time of Revolution: Government Restructuring in Alberta and Ontario.* Toronto: University of Toronto Press.

Reynolds, D. (ed.). 2004. *Partnering for Change: Unions and Community Groups Build Coalitions for Economic Justice.* Armonk, NY: M.E. Sharpe.

Richards, J., R. Cairns and L. Pratt. 1991. *Social Democracy Without Illusions: Renewal of the Canadian Left.* Toronto: McClelland & Stewart.

Rivers, N., and M. Jaccard. 2009. "Talking Without Walking: Canada's Ineffective Climate Effort." In B. Eberlein and G. B. Doern (eds.), *Governing the Energy Challenge: Canada and Germany in a Multi-Level Regional and Global Context.* Toronto: University of Toronto Press: 285–313.

Robin, M. 1968. *Radical Politics and Canadian Labour.* Kingston: Industrial Relations Centre, Queen's University.

Robinson, I. 2000. "Neoliberal Restructuring and U.S. Unions: Towards Social Movement Unionism?" *Critical Sociology* 26, 1&2: 109–38.

Rodriguez, R. 2010. "On the Question of Expertise: A Critical Reflection on 'Civil Society' Processes." In A. Choudry and D. Kapoor (eds.), *Learning From the Ground Up: Global Perspectives on Social Movements and Knowledge Production.* New York: Palgrave Macmillan: 53–68.

Rokkan, S. 1970. *Citizens, Elections, Parties: Approaches to the Comparative Study of Processes of*

Development. New York: David McKay Company.

Roman, B. 2010. "But is it organizing?" *Talking Union*, December 15. At <http://talkingunion.wordpress.com/2010/12/15/but-is-it-organizing/>.

Rose, J. 1983. "Some Notes on the Building Trades-Canadian Labour Congress Dispute." *Industrial Relations* 22, 1: 87–93.

Ross, G., and J. Jenson. 1986. "Post-War Class Struggle and the Crisis of Left Politics." In R. Miliband, M. Liebman, J. Saville and L. Panitch (eds.), *Socialist Register 1985/86: Social Democracy and After*. London: Merlin: 23–49.

Ross, S. 2011. "Social Unionism in Hard Times: Union-Community Coalition Politics in the CAW Windsor's *Manufacturing Matters* Campaign." *Labour/Le Travail* 68 (Fall).

_____. 2008. "Social Unionism and Membership Participation: What Role for Union Democracy?" *Studies in Political Economy* 81 (Spring): 129–57.

_____. 2007. "Varieties of Social Unionism: Towards a Framework for Comparison." *Just Labour: A Canadian Journal of Work and Society* 11: 16–34.

_____. 2005. "The Making of CUPE: Structure, Democracy and Class Formation." Ph.D. dissertation. York University.

Rouillard, J. 2011. "Le rendez-vous manqué du syndicalisme québécois avec un parti des travailleurs (1966–1973)." *Bulletin d'histoire politique* 19, 2: 161–82.

_____. 2008. *L'expérience syndicale au Québec*. Montreal: VLB éditeur.

Royal Commission on Industrial Relations. 1919. "Report of Commission appointed under Order-in-Council (P.C. 670) to enquire into Industrial Relations in Canada together with a Minority Report and Supplementary Report." *Labour Gazette*.

Russell, F. 2010. "Harper's defence of women rings hollow." *Winnipeg Free Press*, February 20.

Russell, P. 1993. *Constitutional Odyssey: Can the Canadians Become a Sovereign People?* Toronto: University of Toronto Press.

Saberi, P., and S. Kipfer. 2010 "Rob Ford in Toronto: Why the Ascendancy of Hard-Right Populism in the 2010 Mayoral Election?" *New Socialist*, November 24. At <newsocialist.org/index.php?option=com_content&view=article&id=314:rob-ford-in-toronto-why-the-ascendancy-of-hard-right-populism-in-the-2010-mayoral-election&catid=51:analysis&Itemid=98>.

Sadler, D. 2004. "Trade Unions, Coalitions and Communities: Australia's Construction, Forestry, Mining and Energy Union and the International Stakeholder Campaign Against Rio Tinto." *Geoforum* 35: 35–46.

Sandoval, C. 2000. *Methodology of the Oppressed*. Minneapolis: University of Minnesota Press.

Sangster, J. 2010. *Transforming Labour: Women and Work in Postwar Canada*. Toronto: University of Toronto Press.

_____. 2004. "We No Longer Respect the Law": The Tilco Strike, Labour Injunctions, and the State." *Labour/Le Travail* 53 (Spring): 47–87.

Saskatchewan Federation of Labour. 2010. *Labour Rights, Human Rights: What's Happening in Saskatchewan*. Regina: SFL.

_____. 2009. *Our Rights are Essential: Labour Rights are Human Rights*. Regina: SFL.

Satzewich, V. 1991. *Racism and the Incorporation of Foreign Labour: Farm Labour Migration to Canada Since 1945*. London and New York: Routledge.

Savage, L. 2010. "Contemporary Party-Union Relations in Canada." *Labor Studies Journal* 35, 1: 8–26.

_____. 2009. "Workers' Rights as Human Rights: Organized Labour and Rights Discourse in Canada." *Labor Studies Journal* 34, 1: 8–20.

_____. 2008a. "From Centralization to Sovereignty-association: The Canadian Labour Congress and the Constitutional Question." *Review of Constitutional Studies* 13, 2: 149–77.

_____. 2008b. "Quebec Labour and the Referendums." *Canadian Journal of Political Science* 41, 4: 861–87.

_____. 2007. "Organized Labour and the Canadian Charter of Rights and Freedoms." *The Supreme Court Law Review* 36: 175–99.

Savage, L., and D. Soron. 2011. "Organized Labor, Nuclear Power, and Environmental Justice: a comparative analysis of the Canadian and U.S. labor movements." *Labor Studies Journal* 36, 1: 37–57.

Schenk, C. 2003. "Social Movement Unionism: Beyond the Organizing Model." In P. Fairbrother and C. Yates (eds.), *Trade Unions in Renewal: A Comparative Study*. London: Continuum: 244–62.

Schenk, C., and E. Bernard. 1992. "Social Unionism: Labor as a Political Force." *Social Policy* 23 (July): 38–46.

Schmidt, S. 2000. "Class clown." *This Magazine* 33, 4 (January / February).

Schwartz, K. 2009. "The Successful Campaign for a $10 Minimum Wage." *Labour/Le Travail* 64 (Fall): 155–57.

Seidle, F. 2007. "Provincial Electoral Systems in Question: Changing Views of Party Representation and Governance." In A. Gagnon and B. Tanguay (eds.), *Canadian Parties in Transition*. 3rd ed. Peterborough: Broadview: 303–34.

_____. 1996. "The Canadian Electoral System and Proposals for Reform." In B. Tanguay and A. Gagnon (eds.), *Canadian Parties in Transition*. 2nd ed. Toronto: Nelson.

Service Employees International Union Local 2. 2011. "Strategic Voting — Deny a Tory Majority." At <seiulocal2.org/admin/Assets/AssetContent/e19ab3d8-f189-4718-834b-8301df63f21a/546bfa9e-94e2-495f-9d30-54cc81f55e47/1df65238-10b5-4c86-b394-45be575f451e/1/STRATEGIC_VOTING.pdf>.

Shantz, J. 2009. "The Limits of Social Unionism in Canada." *WorkingUSA* 12, 1: 113–29.

_____. 2002. "Fighting to Win: The Ontario Coalition Against Poverty." *Capital & Class* 78: 1–8.

Sharma, N. 2006. *Home Economics: Nationalism and the Making of 'Migrant Workers' in Canada*. Toronto: University of Toronto Press.

Shields, J., and B.M. Evans. 1998. *Shrinking the State: Globalization and Public Administration "Reform"*. Halifax: Fernwood.

Sierra Club. 2009. "Should the Sierra Club Be Befriending Unions?" At <sierraclub.typepad.com/mrgreen/2009/06/should-the-sierra-club-be-befriending-unions.html>.

Sigurdson, R. 1997. "The British Columbia New Democratic Party: Does It Make a Difference?" In R.K. Carty (ed.), *Politics, Policy and Government in British Columbia*. Vancouver: UBC Press.

Silverman, V. 2006. "Green Unions in a Grey World: Labour Environmentalism and International Relations." *Organization and Environment* 19, 2: 191–213.

Skidelsky, R. 2009. *Keynes: The Return of the Master*. London: Allen Lane.

Slattery, B. 2006. "The Metamorphosis of Aboriginal Title." *Canadian Bar Review* 85: 255–86.

Smith, B. 2011. "Sierra Club Stands With Workers." March 7. At <sierraclub.typepad.com/scrapbook/2011/03/the-sierra-club-stands-with-workers.html>.

Smith, C. 2010. "A sleeper issue in the NDP leadership race." *Georgia Straight*, December 7. At <straight.com/article-363301/vancouver/sleeper-issue-bc-ndp-leadership-race-gordon-campbells-tax-cuts>.

Snow, D., and R. Benford. 1988. "Ideology, Frame Resonance, and Participant Mobilization." *International Social Movement Research* 1: 197–217.

Special Project Collective Labour Agreement between Voisey's Bay Employers Association Inc. and Resource Development Trades Council of Newfoundland and Labrador for The Construction Phase of the Voisey's Bay Mine/Mill Development. 2002. St. John's, NL and Labrador.

Standing, G. 2011. *The Precariat: The New Dangerous Class*. London: Bloomsbury Academic.

Stanford, J. 2001. "Social Democratic Policy and Economic Reality: The Canadian

Experience." In P. Arestis and M. Sawyer (eds.), *The Economics of the Third Way: Experiences from Around the World.* Cheltenham: Edward Elgar: 79–105.

Stasiulis, D. and A. Bakan. 2003. *Negotiating Citizenship: Migrant Women in Canada and the Global System.* Toronto: University of Toronto Press.

Statistics Canada. 2011. "Women in Canada: A Gender-based Statistical Report." At <statcan.gc.ca/pub/89-503-x/89-503-x2010001-eng.htm>.

_____. 2010a. "Employment Services." Service Bulletin, March. At <http://www.statcan.gc.ca/pub/63-252-x/63-252-x2010001-eng.pdf>.

_____. 2010b. "Unionization 2010." *Perspectives on Labour and Income* (October). At <http://www.statcan.gc.ca/pub/75-001-x/2010110/pdf/11358-eng.pdf>.

_____. 2009. "Minimum Wage." *Perspectives on Labour and Income* (March). At <statcan.gc.ca/pub/75-001-x/topics-sujets/pdf/topics-sujets/minimumwage-salaireminimum-2009-eng.pdf>.

Steel City Solidarity. 2011. "Stop wage theft." April 8. At <hamiltonworkersunited.com>.

Steele, A. 2010. "The Tax-and-cut NDP." *The Globe and Mail,* April 7. At <theglobeandmail.com/news/politics/second-reading/andrew-steele/the-tax-and-cut-ndp/article1526543/>.

_____. 2009. "Lessons from Nova Scotia." *The Globe and Mail,* June 10. At <globeandmail.com/blogs/andrew-steele/lessons-from-nova-scotia/article176683/>.

Steering Committee Northwest Study Session. 1975. *Northwest Study Conference '75.* Invitation. April 1.

Stevens, C. 2009. *Green Jobs and Women Workers: Employment, Equity, Equality.* At <sustainlabour.org/IMG/pdf/women.en.pdf>.

Stewart, P., J. McBride, I. Greenwood, J. Stirling, J. Holgate, C. Stephenson and D. Wray. 2009. "Introduction." In J. McBride and I. Greenwood (eds.), *Community Unionism: A Comparative Analysis of Concepts and Contexts.* New York: Palgrave Macmillan.

Storey, R. 2004. "From the Environment to the Workplace… and Back Again? Occupational Health and Safety Activism in Ontario, 1970s — 2000+." *Canadian Review of Sociology/Revue canadienne de sociologie* 41, 4: 419–47.

Suen, R. 2000. "You Sure Know How to Pick 'Em: Human Rights and Migrant Farm Workers in Canada." *Georgetown Immigration Law Journal* 15, 1: 199–227.

Sugiman, P. 1994a. "Unionism and Feminism in the Canadian Auto Workers Union, 1961–1992." In L. Briskin and P. McDermott (eds.), *Women Challenging Unions: Feminism, Democracy and Militancy.* Toronto: University of Toronto Press: 172–190.

_____. 1994b. *Labour's Dilemma: The Gender Politics of Auto Workers in Canada, 1937–79.* Toronto: University of Toronto Press.

Sufrin, E. 1982. *The Eaton Drive: The Campaign to Organize Canada's Largest Department Store, 1948–1952.* Toronto: Fitzhenry & Whiteside.

Supreme Court of Canada. 2011. *Ontario (Attorney General) v. Fraser.* (2011) SCC 20.

_____. 2009. *Plourde v. Walmart Canada Corp.* (2009) 3 SCR 465.

_____. 2007. *Health Services and Support-Facilities Subsector Bargaining Ass'n v. British Columbia.* (2007) 2 SCR 391.

_____. 2004. *Newfoundland (Treasury Board) v. N.A. P.E.* (2004) 3 SCR 381.

_____. 2002. *Retail, Wholesale Department Store Union Local 558 v. Pepsi-Cola Canada Beverages (West) Ltd.* (2002) 1 SCR 156.

_____. 2001a. *Dunmore v. Ontario (Attorney General)* (2001) 3 SCR 1016.

_____. 2001b. *R. v. Advance Cutting & Coring Ltd.* (2001) 3 SCR 209.

_____. 1999a. *Delisle v. Canada (Deputy Attorney General,* (1999) 2 SCR 989.

_____. 1999b. *United Food and Commercial Workers v. Local 1518 v. Kmart Canada Ltd.* (1999) 2 SCR 1083.

_____. 1991. *Lavigne v. Ontario Public Service Employees Union* (1991) 2 SCR 211.

_____. 1990. *Professional Institute of the Public Service of Canada v. Northwest Territories (Commissioner)* (1990) 2 SCR 367.

_____. 1987a. *Retail, Wholesale and Department Store Union v. Saskatchewan* (1987) 1 SCR 460.

_____. 1987b. *P.S.A.C. v. Canada* (1987) 1 SCR 424.

_____. 1987c. *Reference Re Public Service Employee Relations Act* (1987) 1 SCR 313.

_____. 1986. *Retail, Wholesale and Department Store Union, Local 580 v. Dolphin Delivery Ltd.* (1986) 2 SCR 573.

_____. 1979. *Canadian Union of Public Employees v. New Brunswick Liquor Corp.* (1979) 2 SCR 227.

_____. 1976. *Reference Re Anti Inflation Reference* (1976) 2 SCR 373.

Swanson, J. 2001. *Poor Bashing: The Politics of Exclusion*. Toronto: Between the Lines.

Swartz, D. 1992. "United We Fall: Solidarity v. Democracy in Canadian Unions." *Our Times* 11, 4/5 (September): 37–41.

Tait, V. 2007. "Expanding Labor's Vision: The Challenges of Workfare and Welfare Organizing." In D. Cobble (ed.), *The Sex of Class: Women Transforming American Labor*. Ithaca: ILR Press.

_____. 2005. *Poor Workers' Unions: Rebuilding Labor From Below*. Cambridge: South End Press.

Tanguay, A. 2009. "Transforming Representative Democracy: Taming the 'Democratic Deficit.'" In J. Bickerton and A. Gagnon (eds.), *Canadian Politics*. 5th ed. Toronto: University of Toronto Press: 221–48.

_____. 2002. "Parties, Organized Interests, and Electoral Democracy: The 1999 Ontario Provincial Election." In W. Cross (ed.), *Political Parties, Representation, and Electoral Democracy in Canada*. Don Mills: Oxford University Press: 145–60.

Tarrow, S. 1998. *Power in Movement: Social Movements and Contentious Politics*. Cambridge: Cambridge University Press.

Tattersall, A. 2010. *Power in Coalition: Strategies for Strong Unions and Social Change*. Ithaca, NY: Cornell University Press.

_____. 2005. "There is Power in Coalition: A Framework for Assessing How and When Union-Community Coalitions are Effective and Enhance Union Power." *Labour and Industry* 16, 3: 97–112.

Taylor, J. 1999. *Union Learning: Canadian Labour Education in the 20th Century*. Toronto: Thompson.

Teeple, G. 2000. *Globalization and the Decline of Social Reform: Into the Twenty-First Century*. Aurora, ON: Garamond Press.

Tennant, P. 1990. *Aboriginal Peoples and Politics: The Indian Land Question in British Columbia, 1849–1989*. Vancouver: UBC Press.

Terrace Herald. 1975. "Conference on Northwest Development and Land Claims." March 12.

Therborn, G. 1983. "Why Some Classes are More Successful Than Others." *New Left Review* I, 138 (March-April): 37–55.

Thobani, S. 2007. *Exalted Subjects: Studies in the Making of Race and Nation in Canada*. Toronto: University of Toronto Press.

Thomas, M. 2010. "Labour Migration and Temporary Work: Canada's Foreign Worker Programs in the 'New Economy.'" In N. Pupo and M. Thomas (eds.), *Interrogating the New Economy: Restructuring Work in the 21ˢᵗ Century*. Toronto: University of Toronto Press: 149–72.

Tilly, C. 1978. *From Mobilization to Revolution*. London: Longman Higher Education.

Tourand, K. 2004. "Embracing Aboriginal Values and Traditions in a Unionized Environment." *Journal of Aboriginal Economic Development* 4, 1: 14–21.

Townson, M. 2009. *Women's Poverty and the Recession*. Ottawa: Canadian Centre for Policy Alternatives.

Trudeau, P. 1990. "The Values of a Just Society." In T. Axworthy and P. Trudeau (eds.), *Towards a Just Society: The Trudeau Years*. Toronto: Penguin: 357–85.

Tucker, E. 2008. "The Constitutional Right to Bargain Collectively: The Ironies of Labour History in the Supreme Court of Canada." *Labour/Le Travail* 61 (Spring): 151–80.

_____. 1991. "'That Indefinite Area of Toleration': Criminal Conspiracy and Trade Unions in Ontario, 1837–77." *Labour/Le Travail* 27 (Spring): 15–54.

Tufts, S. 2007. "Emerging Labour Strategies in Toronto's Hotel Sector: Toward a Spatial Circuit of Union Renewal." *Environment and Planning A* 39: 2383–2404.

_____. 1998. "Community Unionism in Canada and Labor's (Re)organization of Space." *Antipode* 30, 3: 227–50.

Underhill, F. 1935. "Our Fantastic Electoral System." *Canadian Forum* 15 (November): 32–4.

United Food and Commercial Workers Canada. 2011a. "Organizing Victory for Québec Retail Workers." At <ufcw.ca/index.php?option=com_content&view=article&id =2326%3Aorganizing-victory-for-quebec-retail-workers&catid=6%3Adirections-newsletter&Itemid=6&lang=en>.

_____. 2011b. *The Status of Migrant Farmworkers in Canada, 2010–11*. Toronto: UFCW Canada.

_____. 2010a. "Farmworkers' quest for human rights arrives at the Supreme Court." News Release. December 16.

_____. 2010b. "UFCW Canada union victory for Quebec farm workers." News Release. April 20.

_____. 2010c. "Springhill Farms UFCW Canada Local 832 members ratify new agreement." News Release. February 8.

_____. 2009a. "Season of justice for Ontario farm workers must be now." News Release. January 12.

_____. 2009b. "UFCW Canada Local 832 negotiates landmark protections for migrant worker union members." News Release. January 7.

_____. 2008. "Ratification of UFCW Canada first-contract at Manitoba farm historic breakthrough for migrant workers." News Release. June 23.

_____. 2007. *The Status of Migrant Farmworkers in Canada, 2006–07*. Toronto: UFCW Canada.

_____. 2006. "Agricultural workers' right to unionize likely grounds for appeal." News Release, January 12.

_____. 2004. "Ag workers take Ontario government to court." News Release, April 2.

_____. 2003. Agricultural workers closer to unionization with UFCW Canada. News Release. September 2.

United Steelworkers. 2008. "News Conference to Launch Association to Protect Home Workers." News Release. June 5. At <http://www.usw.ca/union/partners/ news?id=0010>.

_____. 2006. *Securing Our Children's World: Our Union and the Environment*. Pittsburgh, PA: USW International Executive Board Environmental Task Force. At <usw.ca/community/ environmental/issues?id=0002>.

Upchurch, M., G. Taylor and A. Mathers. 2009. *The Crisis of Social Democratic Trade Unionism in Western Europe: The Search For Alternatives*. Surrey, UK: Ashgate.

Usher, P. 2003. "Environment, Race and Nation Reconsidered: Reflections on Aboriginal Land Claims in Canada." *The Canadian Geographer* 47, 4: 365–82.

Valiani, S. 2007a. *Briefing Note — The Temporary Foreign Worker Program and its Intersection with Canadian Immigration Policy*. Ottawa: CLC.

_____. 2007b. *Labour and Migration Update: Policy and Research News — June 2007*. Ottawa: CLC.

Verney, D. 1957. *Parliamentary Reform in Sweden, 1866–1921*. Oxford: Clarendon Press.

Vosko, L. (ed.). 2006. *Precarious Employment: Understanding Labour Market Insecurity in Canada*. Montreal: McGill-Queen's University Press.

_____. 1995. "Recreating Dependency: Women and UI Reform." In D. Drache and A. Rabikin (eds.), *Warm Heart, Cold Country*. Toronto: Caledon Press: 213–31.

Waiser, Bill. 2003. *All Hell Can't Stop Us: The On-To-Ottawa Trek and Regina Riot*. Markham,

REFERENCES

ON: Fitzhenry & Whiteside.

Walby, S. 2009. "Gender and the Financial Crisis." Paper prepared for UNESCO Project on Gender and the Financial Crisis.

Walchuk, B. 2010. "Changing Union-Party Relations in Canada: The Rise of the Working Families Coalition." *Labor Studies Journal* 35, 1: 27–50.

Walia, H. 2010. "Transient Servitude: Migrant Labour in Canada and the Apartheid of Citizenship." *Race and Class* 52, 1: 71–84.

Walkom, T. 2011. "But what does Layton's NDP stand for?" *Toronto Star*, May 12. At <thestar.com/news/canada/politics/article/989721--walkom-but-what-does-layton-s-ndp-stand-for>.

_____. 2010. "The Art of Reverse Class Resentment." *Toronto Star*, February 27. At <thestar.com/news/insight/article/771726--walkom-the-art-of-reverse-class-resentment>.

_____. 1994. *Rae Days: The Rise and Follies of the NDP*. Toronto: Key Porter

Wallace, R., M. Struthers and R. Bauman. 2010. "Winning Fishing Rights: The Successes and Challenges of Building Grassroots Relations Between the Chippewas of Nawash and their Allies." In L. Davis (ed.), *Alliances: Re/Envisioning Indigenous-non-Indigenous Relationships*. Toronto: University of Toronto Press: 91–113.

Wallis, M. and S. Kwok (eds.). 2008. *Daily Struggles: The Deepening Racialization and Feminization of Poverty in Canada.* Toronto: Canadian Scholars' Press Inc.

Warnock, J. 2004. *Saskatchewan: The Roots of Discontent and Protest*. Montreal: Black Rose Books.

Warskett, R. 2007. "Remaking the Canadian Labour Movement: Transformed Work and Transformed Labour Strategies." In V. Shalla and W. Clement (eds.), *Work in Tumultuous Times: Critical Perspectives*. Montreal: McGill-Queen's University Press: 380–400.

_____. 2001. "Feminism's Challenge to Unions in the North: Possibilities and Contradictions." In L. Panitch, C. Leys, G. Albo and D. Coates (eds.), *Socialist Register 2001: Working Classes, Global Realities.* London: Merlin: 329–42.

_____. 1992. "Defining Who We Are: Solidarity Through Diversity in the Ontario Labour Movement." In C. Leys and M. Mendell (eds). *Culture and Social Change*. Montreal: Black Rose Books: 109–27.

_____. 1990. "Wage Solidarity and Equal Value: Or Gender and Class in the Structuring of Workplace Hierarchies." *Studies in Political Economy* 32 (Summer): 55–83.

_____. 1988. "Bank Worker Unionization and the Law." *Studies in Political Economy* 25 (Spring): 41–74.

Webb, C. 2009. "An Inconvenient Party: The Manitoba NDP, Neoliberalism and Poverty." *Canadian Dimension* 22 (November). At <canadiandimension.com/blog/2590/>.

Weiler, P. 1980. *Reconcilable Differences: New Directions in Canadian Labour Law*. Toronto: Carswell.

_____. 1971. "The 'Slippery Slope' of Judicial Intervention: The Supreme Court and Canadian Labour Relations, 1950–1970." *Osgoode Hall Law Journal* 9, 1: 1–80.

Weir, F. 2004. *Saskatchewan at a Crossroads: Fiscal Policy and Social Democratic Politics*. Saskatoon: Canadian Centre for Policy Alternatives — Saskatchewan.

Wells, D. 1995a. "The Impact of the Postwar Compromise on Canadian Unionism: The Formation of an Auto Worker Local in the 1950s." *Labour/Le Travail* 36 (Fall): 147–73.

_____. 1995b. "Origins of Canada's Wagner Model of Industrial Relations: The United Auto Workers in Canada and the Suppression of 'Rank and File' Unionism, 1936–1953." *Canadian Journal of Sociology* 20, 2: 193–225.

Wesley, J. 2006. "The Collective Center: Social Democracy and Red Tory Politics in Manitoba." Unpublished paper presented at the Annual meeting of the Canadian Political Science Association, York University, Toronto, Ontario, June 2.

Western Voice. 1975. "Worker-Native unity advances." June 11: 1.

Wheeler, H. 2002. *The Future of the American Labor Movement*. Cambridge: Cambridge University Press.

Whitaker, R. and G. Marcuse. 1994. *Cold War Canada: The Making of a National Insecurity State, 1945–1957*. Toronto: University of Toronto Press.

White, Julie. 1993. *Sisters and Solidarity: Women and Unions in Canada*. Toronto: Thompson Educational Publishing.

_____. 1990. *Mail and Female: Women and the Canadian Union of Postal Workers*. Toronto: Thompson Educational Publishing.

Whitehorn, A. 2006. "The NDP and the Enigma of Strategic Voting." In J. Pammett and C. Dornan (eds.), *The Canadian Federal Election of 2006*. Toronto: Dundurn Press: 93–121.

_____. 1992. *Canadian Socialism: Essays on the CCF-NDP*. Toronto: Oxford University Press.

Williams, R. 1989. *Resources of Hope*. London: Verso.

Wilson, S. 2008. *Research is Ceremony: Indigenous Research Methods*. Halifax: Fernwood.

Winson, A. and B. Leach. 2002. *Contingent Work, Disrupted Lives: Labour and Community in the New Rural Economy*. Toronto: University of Toronto Press.

Wood, E. 1988. *The Retreat from Class: A New "True" Socialism*. London: Verso.

Woodsworth, J. 1948. "Grace before Meat." In *Following the Gleam: Selections from the Writings of J. S. Woodsworth*. Ottawa: CCF Publications.

_____. 1926. *Following the Gleam: A Modern Pilgrim's Progress — To Date*. Ottawa: J.S Woodsworth.

World Economic Forum. 2010. *The Global Gender Gap Report*. Geneva: World Economic Forum.

Wright, M. 2008. "Building the Great Lucrative Fishing Industry: Aboriginal Gillnet Fishers and Protests over Salmon Fishery Regulations for the Nass and Skeena Rivers, 1950s–1960s." *Labour/Le Travail* 61 (Spring): 99–130.

Yates, Charlotte. 2007. "Missed Opportunities and Forgotten Futures: Why Union Renewal in Canada has Stalled." In C. Phelan (ed.), *Trade Union Revitalisation: Trends & Prospects in 34 Countries*. Oxford: Peter Lang: 57–74.

_____. 2006. "Challenging Misconceptions about Organizing Women into Unions." *Gender, Work and Organization* 13, 6 (November): 565–84.

_____. 2004. "Rebuilding The Labour Movement By Organizing The Unorganized: Strategic Considerations." *Studies in Political Economy* 74 (Autumn): 171–79.

_____. 2000. "Staying the Decline in Union Membership: Union Organizing in Ontario, 1985–1999". *Relations Industrielles/Industrial Relations* 55, 4: 640–74.

Yeates, N. 2001. "Planning and Budgeting in Saskatchewan." In L. Bernier and E. Potter (eds.), *Business Planning in Canadian Public Administration*. Toronto: IPAC: 55–68.

Young, I. 1990. *Justice and the Politics of Difference*. New Haven, CT: Yale University Press.

Young, W. 1976–77. "Ideology, Personality and the Origin of the CCF in British Columbia." *BC Studies* 32 (Winter): 139–62.

Zuberi, D. 2007. "Organizing for Better Working Conditions and Wages: The UNITE-HERE! Hotel Workers Rising Campaign." *Just Labour: A Canadian Journal of Work and Society* 10: 60–73.

ACKNOWLEDGEMENTS

Contributors to this volume met on April 15–16, 2011, at York University in Toronto to workshop their chapters, engage with each other, take stock of the labour movement's political experiences and capacities, and consider the strategic lessons to be drawn. We are grateful that such a talented group of researchers agreed to take part in this book. We also are grateful to the Social Sciences and Humanities Research Council of Canada for financially supporting our workshop, thus allowing a primarily new generation of scholars to take up important questions about the past, present and future of Canada's labour movement. Thanks must also be extended to the Brock University Centre for Labour Studies, the Brock University Jobs and Justice Research Unit, the Offices of the Dean and Associate Dean Research of the Faculty of Liberal Arts and Professional Studies at York University and the York University Centre for Research on Work and Society for additional financial support.

We owe a debt of gratitude to Hans Rollman for his excellent help in transcribing the proceedings of the workshop, which proved invaluable to the contributors when revising their chapters, and for providing editorial support in preparing the manuscript.

We would also like to acknowledge the support of Fernwood Publishing, including Errol Sharpe, Brenda Conroy, Candida Hadley, Nancy Malek, Beverley Rach, and Mary Beth Tucker, and the editorial collective of Fernwood's Labour in Canada Series. The comments of John Peters, Peter Graefe, Benjamin Isitt, Dennis Pilon, Marjorie Cohen and the anonymous reviewers were much appreciated, as were the discussions we had with Charles Smith, Sarah Declerck and Tanya Ferguson.

A special thank you is reserved for Derek and Mike for their support and patience while we talked about the book day and night and engaged in several marathon editing sessions. Finally, we thank our students, colleagues, friends and allies in the labour movement who have contributed to our ideas and insights over the years.

CONTRIBUTORS

Simon Black is a PhD candida⸱ ⸱in the Department of Political Science at York University in Tor⸱ ⸱to ⸱⸱t⸱⸱

**Aziz Cho⸱ !⸱ ⸱ ⸱ ⸱ ⸱ ⸱ ⸱d Studies in Education at McGill ⸱ ⸱⸱⸱⸱⸱⸱⸱ ⸱⸱ ⸱⸱ ⸱⸱ al, ⸱⸱⸱⸱⸱⸱.

Amanda Coles teaches in the Centre for Labour Studies at Brock University in St. Catharines, Ontario.

Kendra Coulter teaches in the Department of Sociology, Anthropology and Criminology and the Labour Studies Program at the University of Windsor in Windsor, Ontario.

Bryan Evans teaches in the Department of Politics and Public Administration at Ryerson University in Toronto, Ontario.

Peter Graefe teaches in the Department of Political Science at McMaster University in Hamilton, Ontario.

Tyler McCreary is a PhD candidate in the Department of Geography at York University in Toronto, Ontario.

Suzanne Mills teaches in the School of Labour Studies at McMaster University in Hamilton, Ontario.

Dennis Pilon teaches in the Department of Political Science at York University in Toronto, Ontario.

Stephanie Ross is co-director of the Centre for Research on Work and Society and teaches in the Work and Labour Studies Program at York University in Toronto, Ontario.

Larry Savage teaches in the Centre for Labour Studies and the Department of Political Science at Brock University in St. Catharines, Ontario.

Charles Smith teaches in the Department of Political Studies at St. Thomas More College at the University of Saskatchewan in Saskatoon, Saskatchewan.

Dennis Soron teaches in the Department of Sociology at Brock University in St. Catharines, Ontario.

Donald Swartz is retired from teaching at the School of Public Policy and Administration at Carleton University in Ottawa, Ontario, and is the editor of *Studies in Political Economy*.

Mark Thomas is co-director of the Centre for Research on Work and Society and teaches in the Department of Sociology at York University in Toronto, Ontario.

Rosemary Warskett teaches in the Department of Law at Carleton University in Ottawa, Ontario.

Charlotte Yates is dean of Social Sciences and teaches in the School of Labour and Studies and the Department of Political Science at McMaster University in Hamilton, Ontario.